POEMS

POEMS

BY JOHN DONNE

With an Introduction by Elizabeth Howard

The Christian Heritage Series
Published by Canon Press
P.O. Box 8729, Moscow, Idaho 83843
800.488.2034 | www.canonpress.com

John Donne, *Poems*

First published in 1633.

Cover design by James Engerbretson
Cover illustration by Forrest Dickison
Interior design by Valerie Anne Bost and James Engerbretson

Printed in the United States of America.

Library of Congress Cataloging-in-Publication Data forthcoming

Donne, John, 1572-1631, author. | Howard, Elizabeth, 1987- writer of introduction.
Poems / by John Donne ; with an introduction by Elizabeth Howard.
Moscow, Idaho : Canon Press, [2021] | Series: The Christian heritage series
LCCN 2021014181 | ISBN 9781954887084 (paperback)
Subjects: LCGFT: Poetry.
Classification: LCC PR2246 2021 | DDC 821/.3—dc23
LC record available at https://lccn.loc.gov/2021014181

21 22 23 24 25 26 10 9 8 7 6 5 4 3 2 1

CONTENTS

TURN THE SOUL AROUND

by Elizabeth Howard

Introduction

"Let man's soul be a sphere." To the modern ear, the opening line of John Donne's poem "Good Friday, 1613, Riding Westward" (p.156) sounds like a petition. It is, however, first and foremost, a proposition, like the beginning of a Euclidian proof. If in geometry class we write, "Let there be a triangle, ΑΒΓ," Donne proposes in the same way, "Let there be a sphere, a soul sphere." Or, as we might say today, "Let's imagine, for sake of argument, that man's soul were a sphere." What would follow? For Donne, a whole host of possibilities, including the kind of essential movement that the soul would take on: a turning. Donne connects the natural movement of the sphere to the theological movement of the soul; rotations and orbits map onto the activity of repentance, imaginatively expanding the connotations of *tshv*, the Hebrew word for "repentance," which literally means "to turn around." In the end, of course, the proposition that opens the poem grounds the poem's major petition: the propositional statement "Let man's soul be a sphere" transforms into the heart's (and poem's) earnest prayer, "Yes, Lord! Let my soul be a sphere! Let it turn towards you!"

The pairing of the orbiting sphere and the reformation of the soul is the argumentative crux of "Good Friday, 1613." The pairing also illustrates one of the signature rhetorical tropes of the English metaphysical poets: the conceit, in which the tethering of two unlikely things by their seemingly accidental qualities makes for a surprising and probing comparison. Donne's holy week meditation on Christ's death on the cross provokes him to investigate how to turn his soul from business (traveling westward) back to Calvary (the poem's east), and his investigation opens up many new lines of inquiry, including planetary motion and its linguistic connection to wandering, stellar movement, navigation, compasses, and the soul's progress towards God. One of Donne's few dated poems, "Good Friday, 1613" describes both the discrete experience of a personal Good Friday's reflection in his life and the shared struggle of all Christians as it asks how we participate in the miracle of turning our soul in a God-ward direction.

The Poet's Life

Some, like Donne's early biographer Izaak Walton, describe the personal trajectory of Donne's life as more-or-less of an arc from the wanton hedonism of youth to a mature, sincere love for God with age—a movement from the passionate poet to the pastoral priest. The arrangement of the second edition of Donne's *Poems* in 1635 mimics this biographical progression with Donne's "Songs and Poems" gathered at the beginning before the "Holy Sonnets." I'd like to think that the rough-and-tumble organization of the 1633 edition is more historically descriptive, if we want to use the ordering of Donne's poems to map his biography. Walton's elegant narrative arc is overly simplistic, particularly because scholars have dated examples of devotional poetry incredibly early in his life and some of his more erotic poetry rather late in his career. Nonetheless, scholars agree that the general trajectory of Donne's spiritual life moves towards public piety as he becomes the dean of St. Paul's (old) cathedral and towards private intimacy with God, particularly in wrestling through crushing losses.[1] Donne grieved two babies buried at birth, and three more who died as children. He then lost his wife five days after the stillborn birth of their youngest.

Donne's youth is often characterized by its impulsivity and wantonness. It is no secret he spent much of his early income on women and travel. As a young man, aspiring to political notoriety, Donne managed to lose his cherished public post and future prospects when he fell in love with Ann Moore, his employer's wife's niece. Donne married Ann secretly in 1601, earning himself time in jail when he broke the news to her father, until their marriage could be validated as legitimate. The newly wedded Donnes were, as John Donne wrote, financially "undone" by the ostracism of his father-in-law and a marriage "irremediably donne." Such professional loss, however, was not Donne's first.

Born into a Catholic family in 1572 (his mother was the great-niece of Sir Thomas More), Donne left Cambridge without a degree in 1589 because as a practicing Catholic he would not take Elizabeth I's Oath of Supremacy. Later, after he had converted to Anglicanism, Donne did receive an honorary divinity doctorate 1615 from Cambridge at King James I's demanding, and Donne took Holy Orders.[2] Although Donne initially resisted a post in the church, preferring a political position in court, he stewarded his deanship faithfully as a preacher and shepherd. In 1621 Donne became the dean of St. Paul's in London. Just before he died in 1631, Donne preached the sermon "Death's Duell" at Whitehall, a sermon interpreted by many to be Donne's valedictory preaching of his own funeral sermon on Christ's conquest of death.

1. Barbara Lewalski, *Protestant Poetics and the Seventeenth-Century Religious Lyric* (Princeton, N.J: Princeton University Press, 2016), 253.

2. See Cambridge University's record of Donne's matriculation and honorary degree: venn.lib.cam.ac.uk/cgi-bin/search-2018.pl?sur=&suro=w&fir=&firo=c&cit=&cito=c&c=all&z=all&tex=DN615J&sye=&eye=&col=all&maxcount=50.

Donne in Print: 1633

In 1633, two years after Donne's death, the English literary market witnessed the posthumous publication of not one but *two* collections of poetry—both by Anglican ministers who would, in time, be principally remembered for their poetry: *The Temple* by George Herbert and Donne's *Poems by J.D. With Elegies on the Author's Death.*[3] Remembered jointly as metaphysical poets whose protestant poetics distinguished them as poets of the word, Donne and Herbert's poetic and theological legacies were brought closer through the event of their overlapping publication.

What you hold in your hands here is a modernized reproduction of the first print edition of Donne's poems in 1633. The purpose of this present edition is two-fold: to make Donne accessible (in the sense of understandable to the modern reader)—and to offer you a particular historical reading experience of Donne, complete with its early modern idiosyncrasies of arrangement. Rather than publishing the *complete* works of John Donne (as other excellent editions have), we offer here a modern edition of the first published collection of Donne's poetry from 1633.

We have chosen the first edition of Donne's *Poems* (1633) to introduce you to the ranging, piercing poetry of John Donne, and also to provoke you to think about a publication year as a literary event. Consider reading this edition of Donne paired with Herbert's *The Temple* (1633) as an extended, poetic publication event: *Anno Domini, 1633*, if you will.

Manuscript & Print

As opposed to his sermons, which were preached publicly and were more widely printed,[4] Donne circulated a good deal of his poetry in

3. In 1633, the second edition of Donne's Juvenilia (London: Henry Seyle, 1633) was also published.

4. Piers Brown, "Donne's Text and Materials," in *John Donne in Context*, ed. Michael Schoenfeldt (Cambridge, CUP: 2019), 21. The National Endowment for the Humanities did a project in 2014 to construct what it might have been like to hear Donne preach in St. Paul's without amplified sound.

manuscript to patrons and colleagues. Part of Donne's choice was motivated by early modern professional dispositions against the "stigma of print,"[5] particularly given Donne's public-facing vocation as a statesman and a clergyman. A second factor in Donne's decision to circulate his poetry by manuscript was his poetry's "intimacy and exclusivity"—a feel more suited to manuscript with its pen and ink, the binding of small groupings of poems, and direct circulation among friends.[6] The private circulation of Donne's poems, most of which have not survived in Donne's handwriting, also means that many poems have accumulated numerous variants, which often change or expand the meaning of a particular line or phrase.[7] Even the early printed collections of Donne's poetry accreted handwritten additions or indexes on the blank, bound pages. The Mapletoft volume, for example, sports an impressive 80 pages of manuscript added to a first edition copy of *Poems* (1633).[8]

Since copying and private circulation are a part of the early modern experience of reading poetry, I'd strongly encourage you to take up your pen as you read *Poems* (1633), adding a "voice" in the margins both for yourself and for those to whom you will lend this copy. Write out striking quotations and additional poems in the blank spaces. Consider copying out a favorite poem from Herbert's *The Temple* inside the front and back cover of this edition of Donne and add Donne poems inside the covers of Herbert's collection. Join together the manuscript and print legacies of Donne, making *Poems* (1633) your own partial palimpsest.

---

5. See J. W. Saunders, "The Stigma of Print: A Note on the Social Bases of Tudor Poetry," *Essays in Criticism* 1.2 (1951), 139–64.

6. Brown, "Donne's Text and Materials," 19-20.

7. A.J. Smith suggests that "in general a student often needs to have in front of him all the readings of a line which the early versions offer" in *The Complete English Poems*, ed. A.J. Smith (London: Penguin Classics, 1977), 13. Today the *Donne Variorum* works on relating manuscript variants to each other.

8. "STC 7045," United States Air Force Academy, http://drc.usask.ca/projects/jon/donne/view.php?table=manuscript&id=15.

Donne's Little Worlds

The mental labors of reading poetry, metaphysical or otherwise, are different than the labors of reading an essay or sermon. The arguments of the poem rarely follow linearly from premises to conclusion. Rather, poems tend to rely on poetic form to frame the argument, so that, if Donne writes a sonnet, we should expect that he will pivot his argument sharply in his final two lines, inverting the case he had taken pains to build in the first twelve lines. Across two hundred poems, Donne writes in 11 poetic genres,[9] including 21 religious sonnets and three hymns.[10] Furthermore, like a short story, each poem offers its own little world that the reader must enter and navigate.

In a collection of poetry like Donne's, groups of poems are often arranged in clusters or series that interact with one another; the poems together are moving in some direction.[11] For example, earthly love can become a means of cultivating divine love, an argumentative trajectory scholars call "Augustinian" after St. Augustine's insistence that rightly-ordered earthly loves can lead one to God.[12] Donne does this both within poems and across poems. Other times, Donne showcases his ability to craft poems in a variety of genres. We call this sequential performance of poetic skill "Virgilian" since Virgil's poetry began with his pastorals, followed by a tour of genres: georgics, elegiacs, and then his epic *The Aeneid*.

---

9. Patrick Cheney, "Donne's Literary Career," in *John Donne in Context*, 9.

10. Achsah Guibbory, "John Donne," in *The Cambridge Companion to English Poetry, Donne to Marvell*, ed. Thomas N. Corns (Cambridge: CUP, 1993), 124.

11. Cheney, "Donne's Literary Career," 11.

12. Loving the beloved "in God" includes moving from the deep love of another creature towards gratitude to God and to worship, as well as recognizing the good that we love in another creature finds its source not ultimately in the creature but in God Himself. Loving the beloved in God also means rejecting the temptation to make the beloved an idol that competes with God. While the idea of loving the beloved in God pervades his work, Augustine specifically describes this disposition in *Confessions* IV.12.18, and also in *On Christian Doctrine* I.27.28.

Some of Donne's poems move in an Augustinian direction; others demonstrate a virtuosic Virgilian range; sometimes they do both concurrently; other times they do neither. It is impossible to give a simple, totalizing description of the structures, trajectory, and content of Donne's canon. One of the principal labors, therefore, of reading a collection of his poetry is the need to engage the individual poems while simultaneously tracing episodic organization(s) across the collection. The activity is not unlike enjoying any singular dish for its own merits in a multi-course dinner while also noting the ways each plays with the other flavors, pairs with the wine, responds to greens from the first course, and anticipates the dessert. In the collection of poetry and the banquet, any labor of attention serves only to heighten the senses for the *increase* of pleasure.

Just as Donne's poems engage one another in their arrangement, they also often respond to specific poems or conventions outside of Donne's canon. A poem like Donne's "The Bait" (p. 170) replies to the mock courtship poems of his peers like Marlowe and Raleigh, and Donne's "Woman's Constancy" (p. 177) and its emphasis on the *imperfect* lover serves as a counterargument aimed at past laureates (like Petrarch).[13] Donne's poems "writt[en] in response"[14] to others make it hard on a reader to understand the aims of his rejoinders without always knowing the context. In this volume you have only one half of the "correspondence," as it were; you hear only the "reply." Unfortunately, it is beyond the scope of this reader's edition to trace each debate, but if you are interested in editions that frame each of Donne's poems within their respective debates, I'd recommend investing in an edition of Donne like the *Oxford World Classic* with its capacious notes on each poem, or investing in an early modern anthology that

13. Donne "suggests the beloved as a human being rather than as an impossible distant goddess-figure of the Petrarchan sort." Alexander Witherspoon, ed., *Seventeenth-Century Prose and Poetry* (New York: Harcourt College Pub, 1983), 712.

14. Cheney, "Donne's Literary Career," 10.

arranges authors next to one another like Alexander Witherspoon's *Seventeenth-Century Prose and Poetry* (1983) which arranges authors by genre.

Where to Start

For this particular collection, I'll provide three roadmaps for reading: three terrains, if you will. First, you can, of course, read this collection cover to cover, allowing the bewildering range of little worlds to give you a bit of whiplash. The disorientation is the primary drawback. The advantage to reading Donne this way, however, is that you get a fully immersive experience in Donne's exploration of reality with all of its contradictions and the various "voices" that Donne adopts in his poems as he bounces back and forth between sacred poems and secular ones. Donne famously takes on a variety of personae in his poems, include two that Donne himself names: in a letter to Sir Robert Ker, Donne distinguishes poems by "Jack Donne" versus "Dr. Donne."[15] A comparison might be made to Donne's contemporary Shakespeare and the constellation of characters populating Shakespeare's dramas. In Donne's poetic universe, the "characters" are not so clearly delineated nor so clearly related to one another, but as Achsah Guibbory describes, there is certainly a cast: including Donne's "libertine rake," the faithful "lover," the "cynic," and the "despairing sinner."[16]

If, however, you want to augment your understanding of Donne with a charted route and are interested in pairing Donne's *Poems* (1633) with Herbert's *The Temple* (1633),[17] I'd recommend skipping past the *Metempsychosis* at first, reading the Holy Sonnets (pp. 23 –33) since they set Donne most directly in dialogue with Herbert. The comical epigrams which follow (pp. 35–37) are a nice palate cleanser

15. See Cheney, "Donne's Literary Career," 5; Guibbory, "John Donne," 123; and Brown, "Donne's Texts and Materials," 23.

16. Guibbory, "John Donne," 123.

17. The Temple, *Christian Heritage Series* (Moscow, ID: Canon Press, 2020).

after the density of the Holy Sonnets.[18] I'd recommend reading a smattering of Donne's songs and sonnets until you feel the need for a shift in genre. Then read the elegies *about* Donne at the collection's end (pp. 325–349) as a comparative exercise that will help you hear how Donne's poetic voice sounds different from that of his contemporaries. Now that you have built some endurance for Donne's seemingly erratic comparisons and the syntactic gymnastics of early modern poetry, challenge yourself by reading the run of long Donne poems from page 209 to page 247 before returning to conclude with the *Metempsychosis* and its combined philosophical and poetic experiments.

The third and final way to read Donne is to cultivate the early modern habit of indexing and to read by theme. If, for example, one wanted to read on the theme of constancy and inconstancy—a theme to which Donne returned repeatedly— I would recommend a grouping of "The Good-morrow" (p. 175), "Song" (p. 176), "Woman's Constancy" (p. 177), "The Indifferent" (p. 179), "Love's Deity" (p. 251), and "Love's Diet" (p. 252). For Donne on death, I'd recommend the combative and ever popular "Holy Sonnet 6" also known by its first line "Death, be not proud" (p. 29), and the soul jangled by the death of his wife in "A Nocturn upon St. Lucy's Day" (p. 168). In the appendix we have included a seventeenth-century reader-made index from a copy of Donne's *Poems* (1633) that organizes the poems topically. The trick of the reader-made index, however, is that it only allows for thematic reading a *second* time—as an act of re-reading. The first reading, one busy with notation and categorization, enables a second reading to be a thematic reading.

18. Another order of reading would be to follow the 1635 edition's ordering. The 1635 edition begins with Donne's songs and sonnets, which you can find in roughly the same order starting with "The Good-morrow," on p. 175. In the 1633 edition, the set of songs and sonnets is interrupted in the middle by the republication of two of Donne's long poems or *Anniversaries: An Anatomy of the World* and *Of the Progress of the Soul.*

Synthesis and Serendipity

Whichever way you read Donne's *Poems* (1633), the largest challenge within each poem will be the exhausting, exhilarating labor of following an argument whose dominant mode of organization is contrariness and apparent coincidence in the rhetorical devices of the paradox, the pun, the irony, and the conceit with its "farfetched comparisons."[19] While all this pairing can feel frivolous for treatments of grief, redemption, and love, Donne's project is a deeply synthetic one; the comparisons and juxtapositions are rarely frivolous. Donne operates out of and repeatedly underscores a worldview in which every last diverse piece of the universe holds together in Christ, and therefore, seemingly siloed objects, emotions, and experiences are not, in reality, divorced from one another. On the contrary, Donne draws them towards each other, making one part of reality serve as an illuminating commentary on another part. Sometimes he brings God's word to bear directly on his world, sometimes his world on his world, sometimes his world on his word.

The result: we as readers get to enjoy an experience akin to serendipity—the gift of an unlooked-for connection that answers questions we didn't know we had. The delight that we experience in solving the "puzzle" draws us, more often than not, in the direction of moral formation, in the way Sir Philip Sidney describes in his "Defense of Poesy" (1595). The pleasure of poetry is often its principal power in turning us around and moving us towards the good and the beautiful, and in them, towards God himself.

~Elizabeth Howard

19. Witherspoon, *Seventeenth-Century Prose and Poetry*, 712.

INFINITATI SACRUM
16 AUGUSTI, 1601

METEMPSYCHOSIS
POEMA SATYRICON

Epistle

Others at the porches and entries of their buildings set their arms; I my picture; if any colors can deliver a mind so plain and flat and through-light as mine. Naturally at a new author I doubt, and stick, and do not say quickly, good. I censure much and tax; and this liberty costs me more than others. Yet I would not be so rebellious against myself, as not to do it, since I love it; nor so unjust to others, to do it *sine talione.* As long as I give them as good hold upon me, they must pardon me my bitings. I forbid no reprehender but him, that like the Trent Council, forbids not books, but authors, damning whatever such a name hath or shall write. None write so ill, that he gives not something exemplary to follow, or fly. Now when I begin this book, I have no purpose to come into any man's debt; how my stock will hold out, I know not; perchance waste, perchance increase in use. If I do borrow any thing of antiquity, besides that I make account that I pay it to posterity, with as much, and as good, you shall still find me to acknowledge it, and to thank not him only, that hath digged out treasure for me, but that hath lighted me a candle to the place. All which I will bid you remember (for I will have no such readers, as I can teach) is, that the Pythagorean doctrine doth not only carry one soul from man to man, or man to beast, but indifferently to plants also: and therefore you must not grudge to find the same soul in an emperor, in a post-horse, and in a macaron; since no unreadiness in the soul, but an indisposition in the organs works this. And therefore, though this soul could not move when it was a melon, yet it may remember and can now tell me at what lascivious banquet it was served. And though it could not speak, when it was a spider, yet it can remember, and now tell me, who used it for poison to attain dignity. However the bodies have dulled her other faculties, her memory hath ever been her own; which makes me so seriously deliver you by her relation all her passages from her first making, when she was that apple which Eve eat, to this time when she is she, whose life you shall find in the end of this book.

THE PROGRESS OF THE SOUL

First Song

I.

I sing the progress of a deathless soul,
Whom Fate, which God made, but doth not control,
Placed in most shapes; all times before the law
Yoked us, and when and since in this I sing;
And the great world to his aged evening,
From infant morn through manly noon I draw;
What the gold Chaldee, or silver Persian saw,
Greek brass, or Roman iron, is in this one;
A work to outwear Seth's pillars, brick and stone,
And (holy writ excepted) made to yield to none.

II.

Thee, eye of Heaven, this great soul envies not;
By thy male force is all we have begot.
In the first east thou now begin'st to shine,
Suck'st early balm, and island spices there;

And wilt anon in thy loose-reined career
At Tagus, Po, Seine, Thames, and Danaw dine,
And see at night thy western land of mine;
Yet hast thou not more nations seen than she,
That before thee one day began to be;
And, thy frail light being quenched shall long, long outlive thee.

III.

Nor, holy Janus, in whose sovereign boat
The church and all the monarchies did float;
That swimming college and free hospital
Of all mankind, that cage and vivary
Of fowls and beasts, in whose womb Destiny
Us and our latest nephews did install;
(From thence are all derived, that fill this All)
Didst thou in that great stewardship embark
So divers shapes into that floating park,
As have been moved and informed by this heavenly spark.

IV.

Great Destiny, the commissary of God,
That hast marked out a path and period
For everything; who, where we offspring took,
Our ways and ends seest at one instant; thou
Knot of all causes; thou, whose changeless brow
Ne'er smiles nor frowns, O vouchsafe thou to look,
And show my story in thy eternal book.
That (if my prayer be fit) I may understand
So much myself as to know with what hand
How scant or liberal this my life's race is spanned.

V.

To my six lusters, almost now outwore,
Except thy book owe me so many more;
Except my legend be free from the lets
Of steep ambition, sleepy poverty,
Spirit-quenching sickness, dull captivity,
Distracting business, and from beauty's nets,
And all that calls from this and the other's whets;
O! let me not launch out, but let me save
The expense of brain and spirit; that my grave
His right and due, a whole unwasted man, may have.

VI.

But if my days be long, and good enough,
In vain this sea shall enlarge, or enrough
Itself; for I will through the wave and foam,
And hold in sad lone ways a lively sprite,
Make my dark heavy poem light and light.
For, though through many straits and lands I roam,
I launch at paradise, and I sail towards home:
The course, I there began, shall here be stayed;
Sails hoisted there, struck here; and anchors laid
In Thames, which were at Tigris and Euphrates weighed.

VII.

For the great soul, which here amongst us now
Doth dwell, and moves that hand, and tongue, and brow,
Which, as the moon the sea, moves us; to hear
Whose story with long patience you will long;
(For 'tis the crown, and last strain of my song)
This soul, to whom Luther and Mahomet were
Prisons of flesh; this soul, which oft did tear,

And mend the wracks of the Empire, and late Rome,
And lived when every great change did come,
Had first in Paradise a low but fatal room.

VIII.

Yet no low room, nor than the greatest less,
If (as devout and sharp men fitly guess)
That cross, our joy and grief, (where nails did tie)
That all, which always was all, everywhere,
Which could not sin, and yet all sins did bear,
Which could not die, yet could not choose but die,
Stood in the self-same room in Calvary,
Where first grew the forbidden learned tree;
For on that tree hung in security
This soul, made by the Maker's will from pulling free.

IX.

Prince of the orchard, fair as dawning morn,
Fenced with the law, and ripe as soon as born,
That apple grew, which this soul did enlive;
Till the then-climbing serpent, that now creeps
For that offence, for which all mankind weeps,
Took it, and to her, whom the first man did wive
(Whom, and her race, only forbiddings drive)
He gave it, she to her husband; both did eat:
So perished the eaters and the meat;
And we (for treason taints the blood) thence die and sweat.

X.

Man all at once was there by woman slain;
And one by one we are here slain o'er again
By them. The mother poisoned the well-head,

The daughters here corrupt us rivulets;
No smallness 'scapes, no greatness breaks their nets:
She thrust us out, and by them we are led
Astray, from turning to whence we are fled.
Were prisoners judges, 't would seem rigorous;
She sinned, we bear; part of our pain is thus
To love them, whose fault to this painful love yoked us.

XI.

So fast in us doth this corruption grow,
That now we dare ask why we should be so;
Would God (disputes the curious rebel) make
A law, and would not have it kept? Or can
His creature's will cross his? Of every man,
For one, will God (and be just) vengeance take?
Who sinned? 'twas not forbidden to the snake,
Nor her, who was not then made; nor is it writ,
That Adam cropt, or knew the apple; yet
The worm, and she, and he, and we endure for it.

XII.

But snatch me, heavenly spirit, from this vain
Reckoning their vanity; less is their gain
Than hazard, still to meditate on ill,
Though with good mind; their reason's like those toys
Of glassy bubbles, which the gamesome boys
Stretch to so nice a thinness through a quill,
That they themselves break, and do themselves spill.
Arguing is heretic's game; and exercise,
As wrestlers, perfects them: not liberties
Of speech, but silence; hands, not tongues, end heresies.)

XIII.

Just in that instant, when the serpent's gripe
Broke the slight veins, and tender conduit-pipe,
Through which this soul from the tree's root did draw
Life and growth to this apple, fled away
This loose soul, old, one and another day.
As lightning, which one scarce dare say he saw,
'Tis so soon gone, (and better proof the law
Of sense, than faith requires) swiftly she flew
To a dark and foggy plot; her, her fates threw
There through the earth's pores, and in a plant housed her anew.

XIV.

The plant, thus abled, to itself did force
A place, where no place was; by nature's course
As air from water, water fleets away
From thicker bodies; by this root thronged so
His spungy confines gave him place to grow:
Just as in our streets, when the people stay
To see the prince, and so fill up the way,
That weasels scarce could pass; when she comes near,
They throng, and cleave up, and a passage clear,
As if for that time their round bodies flattened were.

XV.

His right arm he thrust out towards the east,
Westward his left; the ends did themselves digest
Into ten lesser strings, these fingers were:
And as a slumberer stretching on his bed,
This way he this, and that way scattered
His other leg, which feet with toes upbear;
Grew on his middle part, the first day, hair,

To show, that in love's business he should still
A dealer be, and be used, well or ill:
His apples kindle; his leaves force of conception kill.

XVI.

A mouth, but dumb, he hath; blind eyes, deaf ears;
And to his shoulders dangle subtle hairs;
A young Colossus there he stands upright:
And, as that ground by him were conquered,
A leafy garland wears he on his head
Enchased with little fruits, so red and bright,
That for them you would call your love's lips white;
So of a lone unhaunted place possest,
Did this soul's second inn, built by the guest,
This living buried man, this quiet mandrake, rest.

XVII.

No lustful woman came this plant to grieve,
But 'twas because there was none yet but Eve;
And she (with other purpose) killed it quite:
Her sin had now brought in infirmities,
And so her cradled child the moist red eyes
Had never shut, nor slept, since it saw light;
Poppy she knew, she knew the mandrake's might,
And tore up both, and so cooled her child's blood:
Unvirtuous weeds might long unvexed have stood;
But he's short-lived, that with his death can do most good.

XVIII.

To an unfettered soul's quick nimble haste
Are falling stars, and heart's thoughts, but slow paced:
Thinner than burnt air flies this soul, and she,

Whom four new coming, and four parting suns
Had found, and left the mandrake's tenant, runs
Thoughtless of change, when her firm destiny
Confined, and engaoled her, that seemed so free,
Into a small blue shell; the which a poor
Warm bird o'erspread, and sat still evermore,
Till her enclosed child kicked, and picked itself a door.

XIX.

Out crept a sparrow, this soul's moving inn,
On whose raw arms stiff feathers now begin,
As childrens' teeth through gums, to break with pain;
His flesh is jelly yet, and his bones threads;
All a new downy mantle overspreads.
A mouth he opes, which would as much contain
As his late house, and the first hour speaks plain,
And chirps aloud for meat. Meat fit for men
His father steals for him, and so feeds then
One, that within a month, will beat him from his hen.

XX.

In this world's youth wise nature did make haste;
Things ripened sooner, and did longer last;
Already this hot cock in bush and tree,
In field and tent o'erflutters his next hen;
He asks her not who did so taste, nor when;
Nor if his sister or his niece she be,
Nor doth she pule for his inconstancy,
If in her sight he change; nor doth refuse
The next, that calls; both liberty do use;
Where store is of both kinds, both kinds may freely choose.

XXI.

Men, till they took laws which made freedom less,
Their daughters and their sisters did ingress;
Till now, unlawful, therefore ill, 'twas not;
So jolly, that it can move this soul, is
The body; so free of his kindnesses,
That self-preserving it hath now forgot,
And slackeneth so the soul's and body's knot,
Which temperance straitens: freely on his she friends
He blood and spirit, pith and marrow spends,
Ill steward of himself, himself in three years ends.

XXII.

Else might he long have lived; man did not know
Of gummy blood, which doth in holly grow,
How to make bird-lime, nor how to deceive
With feign'd calls, his nets, or enwrapping spare,
The free inhabitants of th' pliant air.
Man to beget, and woman to conceive,
Asked not of roots, nor of cock-sparrows, leave:
Yet chooseth he, though none of these he fears,
Pleasantly three, than straitened twenty, years
To live, and to increase his race, himself outwears.

XXIII.

This coal with over-blowing quenched and dead,
The soul from her too-active organs fled
To a brook; a female fish's sandy roe
With the male's jelly newly leavened was,
For they had intertouched as they did pass,
And one of those small bodies, fitted so,
This soul informed, and abled it to row

Itself with finny oars, which she did fit;
Her scales seemed yet of parchment, and as yet
Perchance a fish, but by no name, you could call it.

XXIV.

When goodly, like a ship in her full trim,
A swan so white, that you may unto him
Compare all whiteness, but himself to none,
Glided along, and, as he glided, watched,
And with his arched neck this poor fish catched:
It moved with state, as if to look upon
Low things it scorned; and yet, before that one
Could think he sought it, he had swallowed clear
This, and much such; and, unblamed, devoured there
All, but who too swift, too great, or well armed were.

XXV.

Now swam a prison in a prison put,
And now this soul in double walls was shut;
Till, melted with the swan's digestive fire,
She left her house the fish, and vapored forth:
Fate, not affording bodies of more worth
For her as yet, bids her again retire
To another fish, to any new desire
Made a new prey: for he, that can to none
Resistance make, nor complaint, sure is gone;
Weakness invites, but silence feasts, oppression.

XXVI.

Pace with the native stream this fish doth keep,
And journeys with her towards the glassy deep,
But oft retarded; once with a hidden net,

Though with great windows, (for when need first taught
These tricks to catch food, then they were not wrought,
As now, with curious greediness, to let
None 'scape—but few, and fit for use, to get)
As in this trap a ravenous pike was ta'en,
Who, though himself distressed, would fain have slain
This wretch; so hardly are ill habits left again.

XXVII.

Here by her smallness she two deaths o'erpast;
Once innocence 'scaped, and left the oppressor fast;
The net through-swum, she keeps the liquid path,
And whether she leap up sometimes to breathe,
And suck in air, or find it underneath,
Or working-parts like mills, or limbecks hath,
To make the water thin and air-like, faith
Cares not, but safe the place she's come unto,
Where fresh with salt waves meet; and what to do
She knows not, but between both makes a board or two.

XXVIII.

So far from hiding her guests water is,
That she shows them in bigger quantities,
Than they are. Thus her, doubtful of her way,
For game, and not for hunger, a sea-pie
Spied through his traitorous spectacle from high
The silly fish, where it disputing lay,
And, to end her doubts and her, bears her away;
Exalted she is but to the exalter's good,
(As are by great ones, men which lowly stood.)
It's raised to be the raiser's instrument and food.

XXIX.

Is any kind subject to rape like fish?
Ill unto man they neither do, nor wish;
Fishers they kill not, nor with noise awake;
They do not hunt, nor strive to make a prey
Of beasts, nor their young sons to bear away;
Fowls they pursue not, nor do undertake
To spoil the nests industrious birds do make;
Yet them all these unkind kinds feed upon;
To kill them is an occupation,
And laws make fasts and lents for their destruction.

XXX.

A sudden stiff land-wind in that self hour
To seaward forced this bird, that did devour
The fish; he cares not, for with ease he flies,
Fat gluttony's best orator: at last
So long he hath flown, and hath flown so fast,
That leagues o'erpast at sea, now tired he lies,
And with his prey, that till then languished, dies;
The souls, no longer foes, two ways did err.
The fish I follow, and keep no calendar
Of the other: he lives yet in some great officer.

XXXI.

Into an embryon fish our soul is thrown,
And in due time thrown out again, and grown
To such vastness as, if unmanacled
From Greece Morea were, and that, by some
Earthquake unrooted, loose Morea swum;
Or seas from Afric's body had severed
And torn the hopeful promontory's head;

This fish would seem these, and when all hopes fail,
A great ship overset, or without sail
Hulling, might (when this was a whelp) be like this whale.

XXXII.

At every stroke his brazen fins do take,
More circles in the broken sea they make,
Than cannons' voices when the air they tear:
His ribs are pillars, and his high-arched roof
Of bark, that blunts best steel, is thunder-proof:
Swim in him swallowed dolphins without fear,
And feel no sides, as if his vast womb were
Some inland sea; and ever, as he went,
He spouted rivers up, as if he meant
To join our seas with seas above the firmament.

XXXIII.

He hunts not fish, but as an officer
Stays in his court, at his own net, and there
All suitors of all sorts themselves enthrall;
So on his back lies this whale wantoning,
And in his gulf-like throat sucks everything,
That passeth near. Fish chaseth fish, and all,
Flyer and follower, in this whirlpool fall;
O might not states of more equality
Consist? and is it of necessity
That thousand guiltless smalls, to make one great, must die?

XXXIV.

Now drinks he up seas, and he eats up flocks;
He jostles islands, and he shakes firm rocks:
Now in a roomful house this soul doth float,

And, like a prince, she sends her faculties
To all her limbs, distant as provinces.
The sun hath twenty times both crab and goat
Parched, since first launched forth this living boat;
'Tis greatest now, and to destruction
Nearest: there's no pause at perfection;
Greatness a period hath, but hath no station.

XXXV.

Two little fishes, whom he never harmed,
Nor fed on their kind, two, not thoroughly armed
With hope that they could kill him, nor could do
Good to themselves by his death (they did not eat
His flesh, nor suck those oils, which thence outstreat)
Conspired against him; and it might undo
The plot of all, that the plotters were two,
But that they fishes were, and could not speak.
How shall a tyrant wise strong projects break,
If wretches can on them the common anger wreak?

XXXVI.

The flail-finned thrasher, and steel-beaked sword-fish
Only attempt to do, what all do wish:
The thrasher backs him, and to beat begins;
The sluggard whale yields to oppression,
And, to hide himself from shame and danger, down
Begins to sink; the sword-fish upward spins,
And gores him with his beak; his staff-like fins
So well the one, his sword the other plies,
That, now a scoff and prey, this tyrant dies,
And (his own dole) feeds with himself all companies.

XXXVII.

Who will revenge his death? or who will call
Those to account, that thought and wrought his fall?
The heirs of slain kings we see are often so
Transported with the joy of what they get,
That they revenge and obsequies forget;
Nor will against such men the people go,
Because he is now dead, to whom they should show
Love in that act. Some kings by vice being grown
So needy of subjects' love, that of their own
They think they lose, if love be to the dead prince shown.

XXXVIII.

This soul, now free from prison and passion,
Hath yet a little indignation,
That so small hammers should so soon down-beat
So great a castle, and having for her house
Got the strait cloister of a wretched mouse,
(As basest men, that have not what to eat,
Nor enjoy ought, do far more hate the great,
Than they, who good reposed estates possess)
This soul, late taught that great things might by less
Be slain, to gallant mischief doth herself address.

XXXIX.

Nature's great master-piece, an elephant
(The only harmless great thing) the giant
Of beasts, who thought none had to make him wise,
But to be just and thankful, loth to offend,
(Yet nature hath given him no knees to bend)
Himself he up-props, on himself relies,
And, foe to none, suspects no enemies,

Still sleeping stood; vexed not his fantasy
Black dreams, like an unbent bow carelessly
His sinewy proboscis did remissly lie.

XL.

In which, as in a gallery, this mouse
Walked, and surveyed the rooms of this vast house;
And to the brain, the soul's bed-chamber, went,
And gnawed the life-cords there: like a whole town
Clean undermined, the slain beast tumbled down;
With him the murderer dies, whom envy sent
To kill, not 'scape (for only he, that meant
To die, did ever kill a man of better room)
And thus he made his foe his prey and tomb:
Who cares not to turn back, may any-whither come.

XLI.

Next housed this soul a wolf's yet unborn whelp,
Till the best midwife, Nature, gave it help
To issue: it could kill, as soon as go.
Abel, as white and mild as his sheep were,
(Who, in that trade, of church and kingdoms there
Was the first type) was still infested so
With this wolf, that it bred his loss and woe;
And yet his bitch, his sentinel, attends
The flock so near, so well warns and defends,
That the wolf (hopeless self) to corrupt her intends.

XLII.

He took a course, which since successfully
Great men have often taken, to espy
The counsels, or to break the plots, of foes;

To Abel's tent he stealeth in the dark,
On whose skirts the bitch slept; ere she could bark,
Attached her with strait gripes, yet he called those
Embracements of love; to love's work he goes,
Where deeds move more than words; nor doth she show,
Nor much resist, nor needs he straiten so
His prey, for were she loose, she would not bark nor go.

XLIII.

He hath engaged her; his she wholly bides:
Who not her own, none other's secrets hides.
If to the flock he come, and Abel there,
She feigns hoarse barkings, but she biteth not;
Her faith is quite, but not her love, forgot.
At last a trap, of which some everywhere
Abel had placed, ends all his loss and fear,
By the wolf's death; and now just time it was,
That a quick soul should give life to that mass
Of blood in Abel's bitch, and thither this did pass.

XLIV.

Some have their wives, their sisters some begot;
But in the lives of emperors you shall not
Read of a lust, the which may equal this:
This wolf begot himself, and finished,
What he began alive, when he was dead.
Son to himself, and father too, he is
A riding lust, for which Schoolmen would miss
A proper name. The whelp of both these lay
In Abel's tent, and with soft Moaba,
His sister, being young, it used to sport and play.

XLV.

He soon for her too harsh and churlish grew,
And Abel (the dam dead) would use this new
For the field; being of two kinds thus made,
He, as his dam, from sheep drove wolves away,
And, as his sire, he made them his own prey.
Five years he lived, and cozened with his trade,
Then, hopeless that his faults were hid, betrayed
Himself by flight, and by all followed,
From dogs a wolf, from wolves a dog, he fled;
And, like a spy to both sides false, he perished.

XLVI.

It quickened next a toyful ape, and so
Gamesome it was, that it might freely go
From tent to tent, and with the children play;
His organs now so like theirs he doth find,
That, why he cannot laugh and speak his mind,
He wonders. Much with all, most he doth stay
With Adam's fifth daughter, Siphatecia:
Doth gaze on her, and, where she passeth, pass,
Gathers her fruits, and tumbles on the grass;
And, wisest of that kind, the first true lover was.

XLVII.

He was the first, that more desired to have
One than another; first, that e'er did crave
Love by mute signs, and had no power to speak;
First, that could make love-faces, or could do
The vaulter's sombersalts, or used to woo
With hoiting gambols, his own bones to break,
To make his Mistress merry; or to wreak

Her anger on himself. Sins against kind
They eas'ly do, that can let feed their mind
With outward beauty; beauty they in boys and beasts do find.

XLVIII.

By this misled, too low things men have proved,
And too high; beasts and angels have been loved:
This ape, though else through-vain, in this was wise;
He reached at things too high, but open way
There was, and he knew not she would say nay.
His toys prevail not, likelier means he tries,
He gazeth on her face with tear-shot eyes,
And up-lifts subtly with his russet paw
Her kid-skin apron without fear or awe
Of nature; nature hath no jail, though she hath law.

XLIX.

First she was silly, and knew not what he meant:
That virtue, by his touches chaft and spent,
Succeeds an itchy warmth, that melts her quite;
She knew not first, nor cares not what he doth,
And willing half and more, more than half tooth,
She neither pulls nor pushes, but outright
Now cries, and now repents; when Thelemite,
Her brother, entered, and a great stone threw
After the Ape, who thus prevented flew.
This house thus battered down, the soul possessed anew.

L.

And whether by this change she lose or win,
She comes out next, where the Ape would have gone in.
Adam and Eve had mingled bloods, and now,

Like Chemic's equal fires, her temperate womb
Had stewed and formed it: and part did become
A spongy liver, that did richly allow,
Like a free conduit on a high hill's brow,
Life-keeping moisture unto every part;
Part hardened itself to a thicker heart,
Whose busy furnaces life's spirits do impart.

LI.

Another part became the well of sense,
The tender well-armed feeling brain, from whence
Those sinew-strings, which do our bodies tie,
Are raveled out; and, fast there by one end,
Did this soul limbs, these limbs a soul attend;
And now they joined, keeping some quality
Of every past shape; she knew treachery,
Rapine, deceit, and lust, and ills enough
To be a woman: Themech she is now,
Sister and wife to Cain, Cain, that first did plough.

LII.

Whoe'er thou be'st, that read'st this sullen writ,
Which just so much courts thee, as thou dost it,
Let me arrest thy thoughts; wonder with me
Why ploughing, building, ruling, and the rest,
Or most of those arts, whence our lives are blest,
By cursed Cain's race invented be,
And blest Seth vexed us with astronomy.
There's nothing simply good nor ill alone,
Of every quality comparison
The only measure is, and judge, opinion.

HOLY SONNETS

I. LA CORONA

Deign at my hands this crown of prayer and praise,
Weaved in my lone devout melancholy,
Thou, which of good bast, yea, art treasury,
All-changing unchanged, Ancient of days;
But do not with a vile crown of frail bays
Reward my Muse's white sincerity,
But what thy thorny crown gained, that give me
A crown of glory, which doth flower always.
The ends crown our works, but thou crown'st our ends,
For at our ends begins our endless rest;
The first last end now zealously possest,
With a strong sober thirst, my soul attends.
'Tis time that heart and voice be lifted high,
Salvation to all that will is nigh.

II. ANNUNCIATION

Salvation to all that will is nigh;
That All, which always is all everywhere,

Which cannot sin, and yet all sins must bear,
Which cannot die, yet cannot choose but die,
Lo, faithful Virgin, yields himself to lie
In prison in thy womb; and though he there
Can take no sin, nor thou give, yet he'll wear,
Taken from thence, flesh, which Death's force may try.
Ere by the spheres time was created, thou
Wast in his mind (who is thy son and brother,
Whom thou conceiv'st) conceived; yea, thou art now
Thy Maker's maker, and thy Father's mother,
Thou 'st light in dark, and shut in little room
Immensity, cloistered in thy dear womb.

III. NATIVITY

Immensity, cloistered in thy dear womb,
Now leaves his well-beloved imprisonment,
There he hath made himself to his intent
Weak enough, now into our world to come;
But oh, for thee, for him, hath the inn no room?
Yet lay him in this stall, and from the orient
Stars and wise men will travel, to prevent
The effect of Herod's jealous general doom.
Seest thou, my soul, with thy faith's eye, how he,
Which fills all place, yet none holds him, doth lie?
Was not his pity towards thee wondrous high,
That would have need to be pitied by thee?
Kiss him, and with him into Egypt go,
With his kind mother, who partakes thy woe.

IV. TEMPLE

With his kind mother, who partakes thy woe,
Joseph, turn back; see where your child doth sit
Blowing, yea, blowing out those sparks of wit,
Which himself on the Doctors did bestow;
The Word but lately could not speak, and lo
It suddenly speaks wonders: whence comes it,
That all which was, and all which should be writ,
A shallow-seeming child should deeply know?
His Godhead was not soul to his manhood,
Nor had time mellowed him to this ripeness;
But as for one which hath a long task, 'tis good
With the sun to begin his business,
He in his age's morning thus began,
By miracles exceeding power of man.

V. MIRACLES

By miracles exceeding power of man
He faith in some, envy in some begat,
For, what weak spirits admire, ambitious hate;
In both affections many to him ran,
But oh! the worst are most, they will and can,
Alas! and do, unto the immaculate,
Whose creature Fate is, now prescribe a fate,
Measuring self-life's infinity to a span,
Nay, to an inch. Lo, where condemned he
Bears his own cross with pain; yet by and by,
When it bears him, he must bear more and die.
Now thou art lifted up, draw me to thee,

And, at thy death giving such liberal dole,
Moist with one drop of thy blood my dry soul.

VI. RESURRECTION

Moist with one drop of thy blood, my dry soul
Shall (though she now be in extreme degree
Too stony-hard, and yet too fleshly) be
Freed by that drop, from being starved, hard, or foul;
And life, by this death abled, shall control
Death, whom thy death slew; nor shall to me
Fear of first or last death bring misery,
If in thy life's book my name thou enroll:
Flesh in that long sleep is not putrefied,
But made that there, of which, and for which,'twas,
Nor can by other means be glorified.
May then sin sleep, and death soon from me pass,
That, waked from both, I again risen may
Salute the last and everlasting day.

VII. ASCENSION

Salute the last and everlasting day,
Joy at the uprising of this Sun and Son,
Ye, whose just tears or tribulation
Have purely washed or burnt your drossy clay;
Behold the Highest, parting hence away,
Lightens the dark clouds, which he treads upon.
Nor doth he by ascending shew alone,
But first he, and he first, enters the way.
O strong Ram, which hast battered heaven for me,

Mild Lamb, which with thy blood hast marked the path,
Bright torch, which shin'st, that I the way may see,
Oh! with thy own blood quench thy own just wrath:
And if thy holy Spirit my Muse did raise,
Deign at my hands this crown of prayer and praise!

HOLY SONNETS

I.

As due by many titles, I resign
Myself to thee, O God. First I was made
By thee and for thee, and, when I was decayed,
Thy blood bought that the which before was thine;
I am thy son, made with thyself to shine,
Thy servant, whose pains thou hast still repaid,
Thy sheep, thine image, and, till I betrayed
Myself, a temple of thy Spirit divine.
Why doth the devil then usurp on me?
Why doth he steal, nay, ravish that's thy right?
Except thou rise, and for thine own work fight,
Oh! I shall soon despair, when I shall see
That thou lov'st mankind well, yet wilt not choose me
And Satan hates me, yet is loth to lose me.

II.

O! my black soul, now thou art summoned
By sickness, death's herald and champion,
Thou'rt like a pilgrim, which abroad hath done
Treason, and durst not turn to whence he is fled;
Or like a thief, which, till Death's doom be read,
Wisheth himself delivered from prison;
But, damned and hauled to execution,

Wisheth that still he might be imprisoned;
Yet grace, if thou repent, thou canst not lack;
But who shall give thee that grace to begin?
O, make thyself with holy mourning black,
And red with blushing, as thou art with sin;
Or wash thee in Christ's blood, which hath this might,
That, being red, it dyes red souls to white.

III.

This is my play's last scene; here heavens appoint
My pilgrimage's last mile; and my race,
Idly yet quickly run, hath this last pace,
My span's last inch, my minute's latest point;
And gluttonous death will instantly unjoint
My body and soul, and I shall sleep a space;
But my ever-waking part shall see that face,
Whose fear already shakes my every joint:
Then, as my soul to heaven, her first seat, takes flight,
And earth-born body in the earth shall dwell,
So fall my sins, that all may have their right,
To where they're bred, and would press me to hell.
Impute me righteous, thus purged of evil,
For thus I leave the world, the flesh, the devil.

IV.

At the round earth's imagined corners blow
Your trumpets, Angels, and arise, arise
From death, you numberless infinities
Of souls, and to your scattered bodies go,
All whom th' flood did, and fire shall, overthrow;
All whom war, death, age, ague's tyrannies,
Despair, law, chance hath slain; and you whose eyes

Shall behold God, and never taste death's woe;
But let them sleep, Lord, and me mourn a space;
For, if above all these my sins abound,
'Tis late to ask abundance of thy grace,
When we are there. Here on this lowly ground
Teach me how to repent; for that's as good,
As if thou 'd'st sealed my pardon with thy blood.

V.

If poisonous minerals, and if that tree,
Whose fruit threw death on else immortal us,
If lecherous goats, if serpents envious
Cannot be damned, alas! why should I be?
Why should intent or reason, born in me,
Make sins, else equal, in me more heinous?
And mercy being easy and glorious
To God, in his stern wrath why threatens he?
But who am I, that dare dispute with thee?
O God, oh! of thine only worthy blood,
And my tears, make a heavenly Lethean flood,
And drown in it my sin's black memory:
That thou remember them, some claim as debt;
I think it mercy, if thou wilt forget.

VI.

Death, be not proud, though some have called thee
Mighty and dreadful, for thou art not so;
For those, whom thou think'st thou dost overthrow,
Die not, poor Death, nor yet canst thou kill me.
From rest and sleep, which but thy pictures be,
Much pleasure, then from thee much more must flow:
And soonest our best men with thee do go,

Rest of their bones, and soul's delivery.
Thou'rt slave to Fate, Chance, kings, and desperate men,
And dost with poison, war, and sickness dwell,
And poppy or charms can make us sleep as well,
And better than thy stroke, why swell'st thou then?
One short sleep past, we wake eternally,
And Death shall be no more; Death, thou shalt die.

VII.

Spit in my face, you Jews, and pierce my side,
Buffet and scoff, scourge and crucify me:
For I have sinned and sinned; and only he,
Who could do no iniquity, hath died:
But by my death cannot be satisfied
My sins, which pass the Jews' impiety:
They killed once an inglorious man, but I
Crucify him daily, being now glorified.
O, let me then his strange love still admire:
Kings pardon, but he bore our punishment;
And Jacob came, clothed in vile harsh attire,
But to supplant, and with gainful intent;
God clothed himself in vile man's flesh, that so
He might be weak enough to suffer woe.

VIII.

Why are we by all creatures waited on?
Why do the prodigal elements supply
Life and food to me, being more pure than I,
Simpler, and further from corruption?
Why brook'st thou, ignorant horse, subjection?
Why do you, bull and boar, so sillily
Dissemble weakness, and by one man's stroke die,

Whose whole kind you might swallow and feed upon?
Weaker I am, woe's me! and worse than you;
You have not sinned, nor need be timorous;
But wonder at a greater, for to us
Created nature doth these things subdue;
But their Creator, whom sin nor nature tied,
For us, his creatures and his foes, hath died.

IX.

What if this present were the world's last night?
Mark in my heart, O Soul, where thou dost dwell,
The picture of Christ crucified, and tell
Whether his countenance can thee affright;
Tears in his eyes quench the amazing light,
Blood fills his frowns, which from his pierced head fell;
And can that tongue adjudge thee unto hell,
Which prayed forgiveness for his foes' fierce spite?
No, no; but as in my idolatry
I said to all my profane mistresses,
Beauty of pity, foulness only is
A sign of rigor; so I say to thee;
To wicked spirits are horrid shapes assigned,
This beauteous form assumes a piteous mind.

X.

Batter my heart, three-personed God, for you
As yet but knock; breathe, shine, and seek to mend;
That I may rise and stand; o'erthrow me, and bend
Your force, to break, blow, burn, and make me new.
I, like a usurped town to another due,
Labor to admit you, but oh, to no end;
Reason, your victory in me, me should defend,

But is captived, and proves weak or untrue;
Yet dearly I love you, and would be loved fain,
But am betrothed unto your enemy:
Divorce me, untie, or break that knot again,
Take me to you, imprison me, for I,
Except you 'enthrall me, never shall be free;
Nor ever chaste, except you ravish me.

XI.

Wilt thou love God, as he thee? then digest,
My Soul, this wholesome meditation,
How God the Spirit, by angels waited on
In heaven, doth make his temple in thy breast;
The Father having begot a Son most blest,
And still begetting, (for he ne'er begun)
Hath deigned to choose thee by adoption,
Coheir to his glory, and Sabbath's endless rest.
And as a robbed man, which by search doth find
His stolen stuff sold, must lose or buy it again,
The sun of glory came down, and was slain,
Us, whom he had made and Satan stole, to unbind.
'Twas much, that man was made like God before;
But, that God should be made like man, much more.

XII.

Father, part of his double interest
Unto thy kingdom thy Son gives to me;
His jointure in the knotty Trinity
He keeps, and gives to me his death's conquest.
This Lamb, whose death with life the world hath blest,
Was from the world's beginning slain; and he
Hath made two wills, which, with the legacy

Of his and thy kingdom, thy sons invest:
Yet such are these laws, that men argue yet,
Whether a man those statutes can fulfill;
None doth; but thy all-healing grace and Spirit
Revive again what law and letter kill:
Thy law's abridgment and thy last command
Is all but love; O, let this last will stand!

EPIGRAMS

Hero and Leander

Both robbed of air, we both lie in one ground,
Both whom one fire had burnt, one water drowned.

Pyramus and Thisbe

Two by themselves each other love and fear;
Slain, cruel friends, by parting, have joined here.

Niobe

By children's births and death I am become
So dry, that I am now mine own sad tomb.

A Burnt Ship

Out of a fired ship, which, by no way
But drowning, could be rescued from the flame,
Some men leaped forth, and ever as they came
Near the foe's ships, did by their shot decay;
So all were lost, which in the ship were found,
They in the sea being burnt, they in the burnt ship drowned.

Fall of a Wall

Under an undermined and shot-bruised wall
A too bold captain perished by the fall,
Whose brave misfortune happiest men envied,
That had a tower for tomb his bones to hide.

A Lame Beggar

I am unable, yonder beggar cries,
To stand or move; if he say true, he lies.

A Self-Accuser

Your Mistress, that you follow whores, still taxeth you;
'Tis strange that she should thus confess it, though 't be true.

A Licentious Person

Thy sins and hairs may no man equal call;
For as thy sins increase, thy hairs do fall.

Antiquary

If in his study he hath so much care
To hang old strange things, let his wife beware.

Disinherited

Thy father all from thee by his last will
Gave to the poor; thou hast good title still.

Phryne

Thy flattering picture, Phryne, 's like to thee
Only in this, that you both painted be.

An Obscure Writer

Philo with twelve years study hath been grieved
To be understood; when will he be believed?
Klokius so deeply hath sworn ne'er more to come
In bawdy-house, that he dares not go home.

Raderus

Why this man-gelded Martial, I muse;
Except himself alone his tricks would use,
As Katherine, for the Court's sake, put down stews.

Mercurius Gallo-Belgicus

Like Aesop's fellow slaves, O Mercury,
Which could do all things, thy faith is; and I
Like Aesop's self, which nothing; I confess,
I should have had more faith, if thou hadst less;
Thy credit lost thy credit: 'Tis sin to do,
In this case, as thou would'st be done unto,
To believe all: Change thy name; thou art like
Mercury in stealing, but liest like a Greek.
Compassion in the world again is bred:
Ralphius is sick, the broker keeps his bed.

ELEGIES

ELEGY I

Jealousy

Fond woman, which would'st have thy husband die,
And yet complain'st of his great jealousy:
If swoln with poison he lay in his last bed,
His body with a cere-cloth covered,
Drawing his breath, as thick and short as can
The nimblest crotcheting musician,
Ready with loathsome vomiting to spew
His soul out of one hell into a new,
Made deaf with his poor kindred's howling cries,
Begging with few feigned tears great legacies,
Thou would'st not weep, but jolly and frolic be,
As a slave, which to-morrow should be free;
Yet weep'st thou, when thou seest him hungerly
Swallow his own death, heart's-bane jealousy.
O give him many thanks, he's courteous,
That in suspecting kindly warneth us;
We must not, as we used, flout openly.
In scoffing riddles, his deformity,

Nor, at his board together being sat,
With words, nor touch, scarce looks, adulterate.
Nor, when he, swollen and pampered with high fare
Sits down and snorts, caged in his basket-chair,
Must we usurp his own bed any more,
Nor kiss and play in his house, as before.
Now do I see my danger; for it is
His realm, his castle, and his diocese.
But if (as envious men, which would revile
Their Prince, or coin his gold, themselves exile
Into another country and do it there)
We play in another's house, what should we fear?
There will we scorn his household policies,
His silly plots and pensionary spies;
As the inhabitants of Thames' right side
Do London's Mayor, or Germans the Pope's pride.

ELEGY II

The Anagram

Marry, and love thy Flavia, for she
Hath all things, whereby others beauteous be;
For though her eyes be small, her mouth is great;
Though theirs be ivory, yet her teeth be jet;
Though they be dim, yet she is light enough,
And though her harsh hair fall, her skin is rough;
What though her cheeks be yellow, her hair's red,
Give her thine, and she hath a maidenhead.
These things are beauty's elements; where these
Meet in one, that one must, as perfect, please.
If red and white, and each good quality
Be in thy wench, ne'er ask where it doth lie.

In buying things perfumed, we ask if there
Be musk and amber in it, but not where.
Though all her parts be not in the usual place,
She hath yet the anagram of a good face.
If we might put the letters but one way,
In that lean dearth of words, what could we say?
When by the gamut some musicians make
A perfect song, others will undertake,
By the same gamut changed, to equal it.
Things simply good can never be unfit;
She's fair as any, if all be like her;
And if none be, then she is singular.
All love is wonder; if we justly do
Account her wonderful, why not lovely too?
Love built on beauty, soon as beauty, dies;
Choose this face, changed by no deformities.
Women are all like angels; the fair be
Like those, which fell to worse: but such as she,
Like to good angels, nothing can impair:
'Tis less grief to be foul, than to have been fair.
For one night's revels silk and gold we choose,
But in long journeys cloth and leather use.
Beauty is barren oft; best husbands say,
There is best land, where there is foulest way.
Oh what a sovereign plaster will she be,
If thy past sins have taught thee jealousy!
Here needs no spies nor eunuchs, her commit
Safe to thy foes, yea, to a Marmosit.
When Belgia's cities the round country drowns,
That dirty foulness guards and arms the town;
So doth her face guard her; and so for thee,
Who, forced by business, absent oft must be;

She, whose face, like clouds, turns the day to night,
Who, mightier than the sea, makes Moors seem white;
Whom, though seven years she in the stews had laid,
A nunnery durst receive, and think a maid;
And though in childbirth's labor she did lie,
Midwives would swear, 'twere but a tympany;
Whom, if she accuse herself, I credit less
Than witches, which impossibles confess.
One like none, and liked of none, fittest were;
For things in fashion every man will wear.

ELEGY III

Change

Although thy hand and faith and good works too
Have sealed thy love, which nothing should undo;
Yea, though thou fall back, that apostasy
Confirms thy love; yet much, much I fear thee.
Women are like the arts, forced unto none,
Open to all searchers, unprized if unknown.
If I have caught a bird, and let him fly,
Another fowler, using those means as I,
May catch the same bird; and, as these things be,
Women are made for men, not him, nor me.
Foxes and goats, all beasts change, when they please,
Shall women, more hot, wily, wild, than these,
Be bound to one man? and did nature then
Idly make them apter to endure than men?
They're our clogs, not their own; if a man be
Chained to a galley, yet the galley's free.
Who hath a plough-land, casts all his seed-corn there,
And yet allows his ground more corn should bear;

Though Danuby into the sea must flow,
The sea receives the Rhine, Volga, and Po,
By nature, which gave it this liberty.
Thou lov'st, but oh! can'st thou love it and me?
Likeness glues love; and if that thou so do,
To make us like and love, must I change too?
More than thy hate, I hate it; rather let me
Allow her change, than change as oft as she;
And so not teach, but force my opinion,
To love not any one, nor every one.
To live in one land is captivity,
To run all countries a wild roguery;
Waters stink soon, if in one place they 'bide,
And in the vast sea are more putrefied:
But when they kiss one bank, and leaving this
Never look back, but the next bank do kiss,
Then are they purest; Change is the nursery
Of music, joy, life, and eternity.

ELEGY IV

The Perfume

Once, and but once, found in thy company,
All thy supposed 'scapes are laid on me;
And as a thief at bar is questioned there
By all the men that have been robbed that year,
So am I (by this traitorous means surprised)
By thy hydroptic father catechized.
Though he hath oft sworn that he would remove
Thy beauty's beauty, and food of our love,
Hope of his goods, if I with thee were seen;
Yet close and secret, as our souls, we've been.

Though thy immortal mother, which doth lie
Still buried in her bed, yet will not die,
Takes this advantage to sleep out daylight,
And watch thy entries and returns all night;
And when she takes thy hand, and would seem kind,
Doth search what rings and armlets she can find;
And kissing notes the color of thy face,
And, fearing lest thou'rt swollen, doth thee embrace;
And, to try if thou long, doth name strange meats,
And notes thy paleness, blushes, sighs, and sweats,
And politicly will to thee confess
The sins of her own youth's rank lustiness;
Yet love these sorceries did remove, and move
Thee to gull thine own mother for my love.
Thy little brethren, which like fairy sprites
Oft skipped into our chamber those sweet nights,
And kissed, and ingled on thy father's knee,
Were bribed next day to tell what they did see:
The grim eight-foot-high iron-bound serving-man,
That oft names God in oaths, and only than,
He that to bar the first gate doth as wide
As the great Rhodian Colossus stride,
Which, if in hell no other pains there were,
Makes me fear hell, because he must be there:
Though by thy father he were hired to this,
Could never witness any touch or kiss.
But, O! to common ill, I brought with me.
That, which betrayed me to mine enemy,
A loud perfume, which at my entrance cried
Ev'n at thy father's nose,—so were we spied,
When, like a tyrant king, that in his bed
Smelt gunpowder, the pale wretch shivered;

Had it been some bad smell, he would have thought
That his own feet or breath the smell had wrought;
But as we in our isle imprisoned,
Where cattle only and divers dogs are bred,
The precious unicorns strange monsters call,
So thought he sweet strange, that had none at all.
I taught my silks their whistling to forbear,
Ev'n my oppressed shoes dumb and speechless were:
Only, thou bitter sweet, whom I had laid
Next me, me traitorously hast betrayed,
And, unsuspected, hast invisibly
At once fled unto him, and stayed with me.
Base excrement of earth, which dost confound
Sense from distinguishing the sick from sound;
By thee the silly amorous sucks his death,
By drawing in a leprous harlot's breath;
By thee the greatest stain to man's estate
Falls on us, to be called effeminate;
Though you be much loved in the Prince's hall,
There things, that seem, exceed substantial.
Gods, when ye fumed on altars, were pleased well,
Because you were burnt, not that they liked your smell.
You're loathsome all, being taken simply alone,
Shall we love ill things joined, and hate each one?
If you were good, your good doth soon decay;
And you are rare, that takes the good away.
All my perfumes I give most willingly
Tenbalm thy father's corse; What? will he die?

ELEGY V

His Picture

Here take my picture; though I bid farewell:
Thine in my heart, where my soul dwells, shall dwell,
'Tis like me now, but, I dead, 'twill be more,
When we are shadows both, than 'twas before.
When weather-beaten I come back; my hand
Perhaps with rude oars torn, or sunbeams tann'd;
My face and breast of haircloth, and my head
With care's harsh sudden hoariness o'erspread;
My body a sack of bones, broken within,
And powder's blue stains scattered on my skin:
If rival fools tax thee to have loved a man
So foul and coarse, as, oh! I may seem then,
This shall say what I was: and thou shalt say,
Do his hurts reach me? doth my worth decay?
Or do they reach his judging mind, that he
Should now love less, what he did love to see?
That which in him was fair and delicate,
Was but the milk, which in love's childish state
Did nurse it: who now is grown strong enough
To feed on that, which to weak tastes seems tough.

ELEGY VI

Elegy on the Lord C.

Sorrow, who to this house scarce knew the way
Is, Oh, heir of it, all our is his prey.
This strange chance claims strange wonder, and to us
Nothing can be so strange as to weep thus;

'Tis will his life's loud speaking works deserve,
And give praise too, our cold tongues could not serve:
'Tis well, he kept tears from our eyes before,
That to it this deep all we might bare store.
Of a sweet tree climb up by a tree,
If to a paradise that transplanted be,
Or felled, and burnt for holy sacrifice,
Yet, that must wither, which by it did rise,
As we for him dead, though no family
E'er rigged a soul for heaven's discovery,
With whom more venturers more boldly dare
Venture their states, with him in joy to share.
We lose, what all friends loved, him; he gains now
But life by death, which worst foes would allow,
If he could have foes, in whose practice grew
All virtues, whose name subtle school-men knew.
What ease can hope, that we shall see him, beget;
When we must die first, and cannot die yet?
His children are his pictures; Oh! they be
Pictures of him dead; senseless, cold as he.
Here needs no marble tomb, since he is gone;
He, and about him his, are turned to stone.

ELEGY VII

Oh! let me not serve so, as those men serve,
Whom honor's smokes at once fatten and starve,
Poorly enriched with great men's words or looks;
Nor so write my name in thy loving books,
As those idolatrous flatterers, which still
Their Prince's styles with many realms fulfill,
Whence they no tribute have, and where no sway.

Such services I offer as shall pay
Themselves; I hate dead names: oh then let me
Favorite in ordinary, or no favorite be.
When my soul was in her own body sheathed,
Nor yet by oaths betrothed, nor kisses breathed
Into my purgatory, faithless thee;
Thy heart seemed wax, and steel thy constancy:
So careless flowers, strewn on the water's face,
The curled whirlpools suck, smack, and embrace,
Yet drown them; so the taper's beamy eye,
Amorously twinkling, beckons the giddy fly,
Yet burns his wings; and such the Devil is,
Scarce visiting them who are entirely his.
When I behold a stream, which from the spring
Doth with doubtful melodious murmuring,
Or in a speechless slumber calmly ride
Her wedded channel's bosom, and then chide
And bend her brows and swell, if any bough
Do but stoop down to kiss her upmost brow,
Yet if her often-gnawing kisses win
The traitorous banks to gape and let her in,
She rusheth violently and doth divorce
Her from her native and her long-kept course,
And roars and braves it and in gallant scorn,
In flattering eddies promising return,
She flouts her channel which thenceforth is dry;
I, that is she, and this am I.
Yet let not thy deep bitterness beget
Careless despair in me, for that will whet
My mind to scorn; and, oh! Love dulled with pain,
Was ne'er so wise, nor well armed, as disdain.
Then with new eyes I shall survey thee and spy

Death in thy cheeks, and darkness in thine eye:
Though hope breed faith and love, thus taught, I shall,
As nations do from Rome, from thy love fall;
My hate shall outgrow thine, and utterly
I will renounce thy dalliance: and when I
Am the recusant, in that resolute state
What hurts it me to be excommunicate?

ELEGY VIII

Nature's lay idiot, I taught thee to love,
And in that sophistry, oh! thou dost prove
Too subtle! Fool, thou didst not understand
The mystic language of the eye nor hand:
Nor could'st thou judge the difference of the air
Of sighs, and say, this lies, this sounds despair:
Nor by the eye's water know a malady
Desperately hot, or changing feverously.
I had not taught thee then the alphabet
Of flowers, how they, devicefully being set
And bound up, might with speechless secrecy
Deliver errands mutely and mutually.
Remember, since all thy words used to be
To every suitor, *Ay, if my friends agree;*
Since household charms, thy husband's name to teach,
Were all the love-tricks that thy wit could reach;
And since an hour's discourse could scarce have made
One answer in thee, and that ill-arrayed
In broken proverbs and torn sentences;
Thou art not by so many duties his,
(That, from the world's common having severed thee,
Inlaid thee, neither to be seen, nor see)

As mine, who have with amorous delicacies
Refined thee into a blissful paradise.
Thy graces and good works my creatures be,
I planted knowledge and life's tree in thee,
Which, oh! shall strangers taste? Must I, alas!
Frame and enamel plate, and drink in glass?
Chafe wax for other's seals? break a colt's force,
And leave him then being made a ready horse?

POEMS

THE STORM

To Mr. Christopher Brook, from the island voyage with the Earl of Essex

Thou, which art I ('tis nothing to be so)
Thou, which art still thyself, by this shalt know
Part of our passage; and a hand, or eye,
By Hilliard drawn, is worth a history
By a worse painter made; and (without pride)
When by thy judgment they are dignified,
My lines are such: 'tis the preëminence
Of friendship only to impute excellence.
England, to whom we owe what we be and have,
Sad that her sons did seek a foreign grave
(For Fate's or Fortune's drifts none can soothsay,
Honor and misery have one face, one way)
From out her pregnant entrails sighed a wind,
Which at the air's middle marble room did find
Such strong resistance, that itself it threw
Downward again; and so when it did view

How in the port our fleet dear time did lease,
Withering like prisoners, which lie but for fees,
Mildly it kissed our sails, and fresh and sweet,
As to a stomach starved, whose insides meet,
Meat comes, it came, and swole our sails, when we
So joyed, as Sara her swelling joyed to see:
But 'twas but so kind as our countrymen,
Which bring friends one day's way, and leave them then.
Then like two mighty kings which, dwelling far
Asunder, meet against a third to war,
The south and west winds joined, and, as they blew,
Waves like a rolling trench before them threw.
Sooner than you read this line, did the gale,
Like shot not feared till felt, our sails assail,
And what at first was called a gust, the same
Hath now a storm's, anon a tempest's name.
Jonas, I pity thee, and curse those men,
Who, when the storm raged most, did wake thee then
Sleep is pain's easiest salve, and doth fulfill
All offices of death, except to kill.
But when I waked, I saw that I saw not.
I and the Sun, which should teach me, had forgot
East, west, day, night; and I could only say,
If the world lasted, now it had been day.
Thousands our noises were, yet we amongst all
Could none by his right name, but thunder call:
Lightning was all our light, and it rained more,
Than if the sun had drunk the sea before.
Some coffined in their cabins lie equally
Grieved that they are not dead, and yet must die:
And as sin-burdened souls from graves will creep
At the last day, some forth their cabins peep,

And trembling ask what news, and do hear so
As jealous husbands, what they would not know;
Some, sitting on the hatches, would seem there
With hideous gazing to fear away fear;
There note they the ship's sicknesses, the mast
Shaked with an ague, and the hold and wast
With a salt dropsy clogged; and our tacklings
Snapping like too high-stretched treble-strings;
And from our tattered sails rags drop down so,
As from one hanged in chains a year ago;
Yea ev'n our ordnance, placed for our defense,
Strives to break loose, and scape away from thence.
Pumping hath tired our men, and what's the gain?
Seas into seas thrown, we suck in again:
Hearing hath deafed our sailors, and if they
Knew how to hear, there's none knows what to say.
Compared to these storms, death is but a qualm,
Hell somewhat lightsome, the Bermudas calm:
Darkness, light's eldest brother, his birthright
Claims o'er the world, and to heaven hath chased light:
All things are one; and that one none can be,
Since all forms uniform deformity
Doth cover; so that we, except God say
Another *Fiat*, shall have no more day;
So violent, yet long, these furies be,
That though thine absence starve me, I wish not thee.

THE CALM

Our storm is past, and that storm's tyrannous rage
A stupid calm, but nothing it, doth suage.
The fable is inverted, and far more

A block afflicts now, than a stork before.
Storms chase, and soon wear out themselves or us;
In calms Heaven laughs to see us languish thus.
As steady as I can wish that my thoughts were,
Smooth as thy mistress' glass, or what shines there,
The sea is now, and as the isles which we
Seek, when we can move, our ships rooted be.
As water did in storms, now pitch runs out,
As lead when a fired church becomes one spout;
And all our beauty and our trim decays,
Like courts removing, or like ended plays.
The fighting-place now seamen's rags supply,
And all the tackling is a frippery.
No use of lanterns; and in one place lay
Feathers and dust, to day and yesterday.
Earth's hollownesses, which the world's lungs are,
Have no more wind than the upper vault of air;
We can nor lost friends nor sought foes recover,
But meteor-like, save that we move not, hover.
Only the calenture together draws
Dear friends, which meet dead in great fishes' jaws;
And on the hatches, as on altars, lies
Each one, his own priest, and own sacrifice.
Who live, that miracle do multiply
Where walkers in hot orens do not die:
If in despite of these we swim, that hath
No more refreshing than a brimstone-bath;
But from the sea into the ship we turn,
Like parboiled wretches, on the coals to burn.
Like Bajazet encaged, the shepherds' scoff,
Or like slack-sinewed Samson, his hair off,
Languish our ships. Now as a myriad

Of ants durst the emperor's loved snake invade,
The crawling galley, sea-gulls, finny chips,
Might brave our pinnaces, now bed-rid ships:
Whether a rotten state and hope of gain,
Or to disuse me from the queasy pain
Of being beloved and loving, or the thirst
Of honor, or fair death, outpushed me first,
I lose my end; for here as well as I
A desperate may live, and coward die.
Stag, dog, and all, which from or towards flies,
Is paid with life or prey, or doing dies;
Fate grudges us all, and doth subtly lay
A scourge, 'gainst which we all forget to pray.
He that at sea prays for more wind, as well
Under the poles may beg cold, heat in hell.
What are we then? How little more, alas!
Is man now, than before he was, he was!
Nothing for us, we are for nothing fit;
Chance or ourselves still disproportion it;
We have no power, no will, no sense; I lie,
I should not then thus feel this misery.

TO SIR HENRY WOTTON

Sir, more than kisses, letters mingle souls,
For thus friends absent speak. This ease controls
The tediousness of my life: but for these
I could ideate nothing which could please;
But I should wither in one day, and pass
To a bottle of hay, that am a lock of grass.
Life is a voyage, and in our life's ways
Countries, courts, towns are rocks or remoras;

They break or stop all ships, yet our state's such
That (though than pitch they stain worse) we must touch.
If in the furnace of the event line,
Or under the adverse icy pole thou pine,
Thou know'st, two temperate regions girded in
Dwell there; but oh! what refuge canst thou win
Parched in the court, and in the country frozen?
Shall cities built of both extremes be chosen?
Can dung or garlic be a perfume? Or can
A scorpion or torpedo cure a man?
Cities are worst of all three; of all three?
(O knotty riddle) each is worst equally.
Cities are sepulchers; they who dwell there
Are carcasses, as if none such there were;
And courts are theatres, where some men play
Princes, some slaves, all to one end, of one clay.
The country is a desert, where no good
Gained, inhabits not; born's not understood;
There men become beasts, and prone to all evils;
In cities, blocks; and in a lewd court, devils.
As in the first Chaos confusedly
Each element's qualities were in the other three,
So pride, lust, covetise, being several
To these three places, yet all are in all;
And mingled thus, their issue is incestuous:
Falsehood is denizened; Virtue is barbarous.
Let no man say there, Virtue's flinty wall
Shall lock vice in me; I'll do none, but know all.
Men are sponges, which, to pour out, receive;
Who know false play, rather than lose, deceive.
For in best understanding sin began;
Angels sinned first, then devils, and then man.

Only perchance beasts sin not; wretched we
Are beasts in all but white integrity.
I think if men, which in these places live,
Durst look in themselves, and themselves retrieve,
They would like strangers greet themselves, seeing than
Utopian youth, grown old Italian.
Be thou thine own home, and in thyself dwell;
Inn anywhere; continuance maketh hell.
And seeing the snail, which everywhere doth roam,
Carrying his own house still, still is at home,
Follow (for he is easy-paced) this snail,
Be thine own palace, or the world's thy jail.
And in the world's sea, do not like cork sleep
Upon the water's face, nor in the deep
Sink like a lead without a line—but as
Fishes glide, leaving no print where they pass,
Nor making sound, so closely thy course go,
Let men dispute whether thou breathe, or no:
Only in this be no Galenist—to make
Court's hot ambitions wholesome, do not take
A dram of country's dullness; do not add
Correctives, but as chemics purge the bad;
But, Sir, I advise not you, I rather do
Say o'er those lessons, which I learned of you:
Whom, free from Germany's schisms, and lightness
Of France, and fair Italy's faithlessness,
Having from these sucked all they had of worth,
And brought home that faith which you carried forth,
I throughly love: but if myself I have won
To know my rules, I have, and you have

DONNE.

THE CROSS

Since Christ embraced the Cross itself, dare I,
His image, the image of his Cross deny?
Would I have profit by the sacrifice,
And dare the chosen altar to despise?
It bore all other sins, but is it fit
That it should bear the sin of scorning it?
Who from the picture would avert his eye,
How would he fly his pains, who there did die?
From me no pulpit, nor misgrounded law,
Nor scandal taken, shall this cross withdraw;
It shall not, for it cannot; for the loss
Of this cross were to me another cross;
Better were worse, for no affliction,
No cross is so extreme, as to have none.
Who can blot out the cross, which the instrument
Of God dewed on me in the sacrament?
Who can deny me power and liberty
To stretch mine arms, and mine own cross to be?
Swim, and at every stroke thou art thy cross;
The mast and yard make one, where seas do toss;
Look down, thou spiest out crosses in small things;
Look up, thou seest birds raised on crossed wings.
All the globe's frame and spheres is nothing else
But the meridian's crossing parallels.
Material crosses then good physic be;
But yet spiritual have chief dignity;
These for extracted chemic medicine serve,
And cure much better, and as well preserve;
Then are you your own physic, or need none,

When 'stilled or purged by tribulation:
For, when that cross ungrudged unto you sticks,
Then are you to yourself a crucifix,
As perchance carvers do not faces make,
But that away, which hid them there, do take:
Let crosses so take what hid Christ in thee,
And be his image, or not his, but he,
But as oft alchemists do coiners prove,
So may a self-despising get self-love;
And then, as worst surfeits of best meats be,
So is pride, issued from humility;
For 'tis no child, but monster: therefore cross
Your joy in crosses, else, 'tis double loss;
And cross thy senses, else both they and thou
Must perish soon, and to destruction bow.
For if the eye seek good objects, and will take
No cross from bad, we cannot 'scape a snake.
So with harsh, hard, sour, stinking, cross the rest,
Make them indifferent; call nothing best.
But most the eye needs crossing; that can roam
And move; to the others objects must come home.
And cross thy heart; for that in man alone
Pants downwards, and hath palpitation.
Cross those detorsions, when it downward tends,
And when it to forbidden heights pretends.
And as the brain through bony walls doth vent
By sutures, which a cross's form present,
So when thy brain works, ere thou utter it,
Cross and correct concupiscence of wit.
Be covetous of crosses, let none fall:
Cross no man else, but cross thyself in all.
Then doth the cross of Christ work faithfully

Within our hearts, when we love harmlessly
The Cross's pictures much, and with more care
That Cross's children, which our crosses are.

AN ELEGY ON THE LADY MARKHAM

Man is the world, and death the ocean
    To which God gives the lower parts of man.
This sea environs all, and though as yet
    God hath set marks and bounds 'twixt us and it,
Yet doth it roar and gnaw, and still pretend,
    And breaks our bank, whene'er it takes a friend:
Then our land-waters (tears of passion) vent;
    Our waters, then above our firmament,
(Tears, which our soul doth for her sins let fall)
    Take all a brackish taste, and funeral;
And even those tears, which should wash sin, are sin.
    We, after God's Noah, drown our world again.
Nothing but man, of all envenomed things,
    Doth work upon itself with inborn stings.
Tears are false spectacles; we cannot see
    Through passion's mist, what we are, or what she.
In her this sea of death hath made no breach;
    But as the tide doth wash the slimy beach,
And leaves embroidered works upon the sand,
    So is her flesh refined by death's cold hand.
As men of China, after an age's stay,
    Do take up porcelain, where they buried clay,
So at this grave, her limbec (which refines
    The diamonds, rubies, sapphires, pearls, and mines

Of which this flesh was) her soul shall inspire
    Flesh of such stuff, as God, when his last fire
Annuls this world, to recompense it, shall
    Make and name them the elixir of this all.
They say, the sea, when it gains, loseth too;
    If carnal death (the younger brother) do
Usurp the body; our soul, which subject is
    To the elder death by sin, is freed by this;
They perish both, when they attempt the just;
    For graves our trophies are, and both deaths' dust.
So, unobnoxious now, she hath buried both;
    For none to death sins, that to sin is loth,
Nor do they die, which are not loth to die;
    So hath she this and that virginity.
Grace was in her extremely diligent,
    That kept her from sin, yet made her repent.
Of what small spots pure white complains! Alas,
    How little poison cracks a crystal glass!
She sinned but just enough to let us see
    That God's word must be true, all sinners be.
So much did zeal her conscience rarefy,
    That extreme truth lacked little of a lie,
Making omissions acts, laying the touch
    Of sin on things, that sometime may be such.
As Moses' cherubins, whose natures do
    Surpass all speed, by him are winged too,
So would her soul, already in heaven, seem then
    To climb by tears, the common stairs of men.
How fit she was for God, I am content
    To speak, that Death his vain haste may repent:
How fit for us, how even and how sweet,
    How good in all her titles, and how meet

To have reformed this forward heresy,
    That women can no parts of friendship be;
How moral, how divine, shall not be told,
    Lest they, that hear her virtues, think her old;
And lest we take Death's part, and make him glad
    Of such a prey, and to his triumph add.

ELEGY ON MISTRESS BOULSTRED

Death, I recant, and say, unsaid by me
    Whate'er hath slipped, that might diminish thee:
Spiritual treason, atheism 'tis, to say,
    That any can thy summons disobey.
The earth's face is but thy table; there are set
    Plants, cattle, men, dished for Death to eat.
In a rude hunger now he millions draws
    Into his bloody, or plaguy, or starved jaws;
Now he will seem to spare, and doth more waste,
    Eating the best first, well preserved to last;
Now wantonly he spoils, and eats us not,
    But breaks off friends, and lets us piecemeal rot.
Nor will this earth serve him; he sinks the deep,
    Where harmless fish monastic silence keep,
Who (were Death dead) the roes of living sand
    Might sponge that element, and make it land.
He rounds the air, and breaks the hymnic notes
    In birds, Heaven's choristers, organic throats,
Which (if they did not die) might seem to be
    A tenth rank in the heavenly hierarchy.
O, strong and long-lived Death, how camest thou in?

And how without creation didst begin?
Thou hast, and shalt see dead, before thou diest,
All the four monarchies, and antichrist.
How could I think thee nothing, that see now
In all this all, nothing else is, but thou?
Our births and lives, vices and virtues, be
Wasteful consumptions, and degrees of thee.
For we to live, our bellows wear, and breath;
Nor are we mortal, dying, dead, but death.
And though thou beest (O mighty bird of prey)
So much reclaimed by God, that thou must lay
All, that thou kill'st, at his feet; yet doth he
Reserve but few, and leaves the most for thee.
And of those few, now thou hast overthrown
One, whom thy blow makes not ours, nor thine own;
She was more stories high: hopeless to come
To her soul, thou hast offered at her lower room.
Her soul and body was a king and court;
But thou hast both of captain missed and fort.
As houses fall not, though the kings remove,
Bodies of saints rest for their souls above.
Death gets 'twixt souls and bodies such a place
As sin insinuates 'twixt just men and grace;
Both work a separation, no divorce:
Her soul is gone to usher up her corse,
Which shall be almost another soul, for there
Bodies are purer than best souls are here.
Because in her her virtues did outgo
Her years, would'st thou, O emulous Death, do so,
And kill her young to thy loss? must the cost
Of beauty and wit, apt to do harm, be lost?
What though thou found'st her proof 'gainst sins of youth?

Oh, every age a diverse sin pursueth.
She might have proved; and such devotion
Might once have strayed to superstition.
If all her virtues must have grown, yet might
Abundant virtue have bred a proud delight.
Had she persevered just, there would have been
Some that would sin, misthinking she did sin;
Such as would call her friendship love, and feign
To sociableness a name profane;
Or sin by tempting; or, not daring that,
By wishing, though they never told her what.
Thus might'st thou have slain more souls, hadst thou not crost
Thyself, and, to triumph, thine army lost.
Yet, though these ways be lost, thou hast left one,
Which is, immoderate grief that she is gone:
But we may 'scape that sin, yet weep as much;
Our tears are due, because we are not such.
Some tears, that knot of friends, her death must cost,
Because the chain is broke, though no link lost.

TO SIR HENRY GOODYERE

Who makes the past a pattern for next year,
Turns no new leaf, but still the same things reads,
Seen things he sees again, heard things doth hear,
And makes his life but like a pair of beads.

A palace, when 'tis that which it should be,
Leaves growing, and stands such, or else decays;
But he which dwells there is not so; for he
Strives to urge upward, and his fortune raise.

So had your body her morning, hath her noon,
    And shall not better; her next change is night:
But her fair larger guest, to whom sun and moon
    Are sparks, and short-lived, claims another right.

The noble soul by age grows lustier,
    Her appetite and her digestion mend;
We must not starve, nor hope to pamper her
    With woman's milk and pap unto the end.

Provide you manlier diet; you have seen
    All libraries, which are schools, camps and courts;
But ask your garners if you have not been
    In harvests too indulgent to your sports.

Would you redeem it? Then yourself transplant
    Awhile from hence. Perchance outlandish ground
Bears no more wit than ours; but yet more scant
    Are those diversions there, which here abound.

To be a stranger hath that benefit,
    We can beginnings, but not habits choke:
Go, whither? hence; you get, if you forget;
    New faults, till they prescribe in us, are smoke.

Our soul, whose country's Heaven, and God her father,
    Into this world, corruption's sink, is sent;
Yet so much in her travel she doth gather,
    That she returns home wiser than she went.

It pays you well, if it teach you to spare,
    And make you ashamed to make your hawk's praise yours,

Which when herself she lessens in the air,
    You then first say that high enough she towers.

However, keep the lively taste you hold
    Of God; love him as now, but fear him more:
And in your afternoons think what you told
    And promised him at morning-prayer before.

Let falsehoood like a discord anger you;
    Else be not froward: but why do I touch
Things, of which none is in your practice new,
    And tables or fruit-trenchers teach as much?

But thus I make you keep your promise, Sir;
    Riding I had you, though you still stayed there,
And in these thoughts, although you never stir,
    You came with me to Micham, and are here.

TO MR. ROWLAND WOODWARD

Like one, who in her third widowhood doth profess
Herself a nun, tied to retiredness,
So affects my Muse now a chaste fallowness;

Since she to few, yet to too many, hath shown,
How love-song weeds and satiric thorns are grown,
Where seeds of better arts were early sown.

Though to use and love poetry, to me,
Betrothed to no one art, be no adultery;
Omissions of good, ill as ill deeds be.

For though to us it seem but light and thin,
Yet in those faithful scales, where God throws in
Men's works, vanity weighs as much as sin.

If our souls have stained their first white, yet we
May clothe them with faith and dear honesty,
Which God imputes as native purity.

There is no virtue but religion:
Wise, valiant, sober, just, are names which none
Want, which want not vice-covering discretion.

Seek we then ourselves in ourselves; for as
Men force the sun with much more force to pass,
By gathering his beams with a crystal glass,

So we (if we into ourselves will turn,
lowing our sparks of virtue) may outburn
The straw which doth about our hearts sojourn.

You know physicians, when they would infuse
Into any oil the souls of simples, use
Places where they may lie still warm, to choose.

So works retiredness in us; to roam
Giddily, and be everywhere but at home,
Such freedom doth a banishment become.

We are but termors of ourselves; yet may,
If we can stock ourselves and thrive, uplay
Much, much dear treasure for the great rent-day.

Manure thyself then, to thyself be approved,
And with vain outward things be no more moved,
But to know that I love thee and would be loved.

TO SIR HENRY WOTTON

Here's no more news than virtue; I may as well
Tell you Calais, or Saint Michael's tales, as tell
That vice doth here habitually dwell.

Yet as, to get stomachs, we walk up and down,
And toil to sweeten rest; so, may God frown,
If but to loathe both, I haunt court and town.

For here no one is from the extremity
Of vice by any other reason free,
But that the next to him still 's worse than he.

In this world's warfare they whom rugged Fate,
(God's commissary) doth so throughly hate,
As in the Court's squadron to marshal their state;

If they stand armed with seely honesty,
With wishing, prayers, and neat integrity,
Like Indians 'gainst Spanish hosts they be.

Suspicious boldness to this place belongs,
And to have as many ears as all have tongues;
Tender to know, tough to acknowledge wrongs.

Believe me, Sir, in my youth's giddiest days,
When to be like the court was a player's praise,
Plays were not so like courts, as courts like plays.

Then let us at these mimic antics jest,
Whose deepest projects and egregious gests
Are but dull morals of a game at chests.

But now 'tis incongruity to smile,
Therefore I end; and bid farewell a while
At court, though *from court* were the better style.

TO THE COUNTESS OF BEDFORD

Madam,
Reason is our soul's left hand, Faith her right;
By these we reach divinity—that's you:
Their loves, who have the blessing of your light,
Grew from their Reason; mine from fair Faith grew.

But as, although a squint left-handedness
Be ungracious, yet we cannot want that hand,
So would I (not to increase, but to express
My faith) as I believe, so understand.

Therefore I study you first in your saints,
Those friends, whom your election glorifies;
Then in your deeds, accesses and restraints,
And what you read, and what yourself devise.

But soon, the reasons why you're loved by all,
Grow infinite, and so pass Reason's reach,

Then back again to implicit Faith I fall,
And rest on what the catholic voice doth teach;

That you are good: and not one heretic
Denies it; if he did, yet you are so;
For rocks which high-topped and deep-rooted stick,
Waves wash, not undermine, nor overthrow.

In every thing there naturally grows
A balsamum, to keep it fresh and new,
If 'twere not injured by extrinsic blows;
Your birth and beauty are this balm in you.

But you of learning and religion
And virtue and such ingredients have made
A mithridate, whose operation
Keeps off or cures what can be done or said.

Yet this is not your physic, but your food,
A diet fit for you; for you are here
The first good angel, since the world's frame stood,
That ever did in woman's shape appear.

Since you are then God's masterpiece, and so
His factor for our loves, do as you do;
Make your return home gracious, and bestow
This life on that; so make one life of two:
For, so, God help me, I would not miss you there
For all the good which you can do me here.

TO THE COUNTESS OF BEDFORD (2)

Madam,
You have refined me; and to worthiest things,
Virtue, art, beauty, fortune, now I see
Rareness or use, not nature, value brings;
And such, as they are circumstanced, they be.
Two ills can ne'er perplex us, sin to excuse,
But of two good things we may leave or choose.

Therefore at court, which is not Virtue's clime,
Where a transcendent height (as lowness me)
Makes her not be, or not show, all my rhyme
Your virtues challenge, which there rarest be;
For as dark texts need notes, some there must be
To usher Virtue, and say, *This is she.*

So in the country's beauty; to this place
You are the season (Madam) you the day,
'Tis but a grave of spices, till your face
Exhale them, and a thick, close bud display.
Widowed and reclused else, her sweets she enshrines,
As China, when the sun at Brazil dines.

Out from your chariot morning breaks at night,
And falsifies both computations so;
Since a new world doth rise here from your light,
We your new creatures by new reckonings go:
This shows that you from nature loathly stray,
That suffer not an artificial day.

In this you've made the court the antipodes,
And willed your delegate, the vulgar sun,
To do profane autumnal offices,
Whilst here to you we sacrificers run;
And whether priests, or organs, you we obey,
We sound your influence, and your dictates say.

Yet to that deity which dwells in you,
Your virtuous soul, I now not sacrifice;
These are petitions, and not hymns; they sue
But that I may survey the edifice.
In all religions as much care hath been
Of temples' frames, and beauty, as rites within.

As all which go to Rome, do not thereby
Esteem religions, and hold fast the best,
But serve discourse and curiosity
With that which doth religion but invest,
And shun the entangling labyrinths of schools,
And make it wit to think the wiser fools;

So in this pilgrimage I would behold
You as you're Virtue's temple, not as she;
What walls of tender crystal her enfold,
What eyes, hands, bosom, her pure altars be,
And after this survey oppose to all
Babblers of chapels, you, the Escurial.

Yet not as consecrate, but merely as fair:
On these I cast a lay and country eye.
Of past and future stories, which are rare,
I find you all record and prophesy.

Purge but the book of Fate, that it admit
No sad nor guilty legends—you are it.

If good and lovely were not one, of both
You were the transcript and original,
The elements, the parent, and the growth,
And every piece of you is both their all:
So entire are all your deeds and you, that you
Must do the same things still; you cannot two.

But these (as nice thin school-divinity
Serves heresy to further or repress)
Taste of poetic rage, or flattery,
And need not, where all hearts one truth profess;
Oft from new proofs and new phrase new doubts grow,
As strange attire alienst the men we know.

Leaving them busy praise and all appeal
To higher courts, sense's decree is true;
The mine, the magazine, the commonweal,
The story of beauty, in Twicknam is and you;
Who hath seen one, would both; as who hath been
In paradise, would seek the Cherubin.

TO SIR EDWARD HERBERT

Since Lord Herbert of Cherbury, being at the siege of Juliers

Man is a lump, where all beasts kneaded be,
    Wisdom makes him an ark where all agree;
The fool, in whom these beasts do live at jar,
    Is sport to others, and a theatre:
Nor scapes he so, but is himself their prey;

All which was man in him, is eat away;
And now his beasts on one another feed,
Yet couple in anger, and new monsters breed:
How happy is he, which hath due place assigned
To his beasts! and disaforested his mind,
Impaled himself to keep them out, not in;
Can sow, and dares trust corn, where they have been;
Can use his horse, goat, wolf, and every beast,
And is not ass himself to all the rest!
Else man not only is the herd of swine,
But he's those devils, too, which did incline
Them to a headlong rage and made them worse;
For man can add weight to heaven's heaviest curse.
As souls (they say) by our first touch take in
The poisonous tincture of original sin,
So to the punishments which God doth fling,
Our apprehension contributes the sting.
To us, as to his chickens, he doth cast
Hemlock; and we, as men, his hemlock taste,
We do infuse to what he meant for meat
Corrosiveness, or intense cold or heat:
For God no such specific poison hath
As kills, we know not how; his fiercest wrath
Hath no antipathy, but may be good
At least for physic, if not for our food.
Thus man, that might be his pleasure, is his rod;
And is his devil, that might be his God.
Since then our business is to rectify
Nature to what she was, we're led awry
By them who man to us in little show;
Greater than due no form we can bestow
On him; for man into himself can draw

All; all his faith can swallow, or reason chaw;
All that is filled, and all that which doth fill,
All the round world, to man is but a pill;
In all it works not, but it is in all
Poisonous, or purgative, or cordial.
For knowledge kindles calentures in some,
And is to others icy opium.
As brave as true is that profession than,
Which you do use to make; that you know man.
This makes it credible, you've dwelt upon
All worthy books, and now are such a one;
Actions are authors, and of those in you
Your friends find every day a mart of new.

TO THE COUNTESS OF BEDFORD (3)

To have written then, when you writ, seemed to me
Worst of spiritual vices, simony;
And not to have written then, seems little less
Than worst of civil vices, thanklessness.
In this my debt I seemed loath to confess,
In that I seemed to shun beholdingness:
But 'tis not so: Nothings, as I am, may
Pay all they have, and yet have all to pay.
Such borrow in their payments, and owe more
By having leave to write so, than before.
Yet, since rich mines in barren grounds are shown,
May not I yield, not gold, but coal or stone?
Temples were not demolished, though profane;
Here Peter Jove's, there Paul hath Dian's fane.

So whether my hymns you admit or choose,
 In me you've hallowed a pagan muse,
And denizened a stranger, who, mistaught
 By blamers of the times they marred, hath sought
Virtues in corners, which now bravely do
 Shine in the world's best part, or all in you.
I have been told that virtue in courtier's hearts
 Suffers an ostracism and departs.
Profit, ease, fitness, plenty bid it go,
 But whither, only knowing you, I know;
You, or your virtue, to vast uses serves,
 It ransoms one sex and one court preserves;
There's nothing but your worth, which being true
 Is known to any other, not to you;
And you can never know it; to admit
 No knowledge of your worth, is some of it.
But since to you your praises discords be,
 Stoop other's ills to meditate with me.
Oh, to confess we know not what we would
 Is half excuse, we know not what we should.
Lightness depresseth us, emptiness fills;
 We sweat and faint, yet still go down the hills;
As new philosophy arrests the sun,
 And bids the passive earth about it run,
So we have dulled our mind, it hath no ends;
 Only the body is busy and pretends.
As dead low earth eclipses and controls
 The quick high moon, so doth the body souls:
In none but us are such mixed engines found,
 As hands of double office; for the ground
We till with them, and them to heaven we raise;
 Who prayerless labors, or without this prays,

Doth but one half; that's none; he which said, *Plough,*
  And look not back, to look up doth allow.
Good seed degenerates, and oft obeys
  The soil's disease, and into cockle strays:
Let the mind's thoughts be but transplanted so
  Into the body, and bastardly they grow.
What hate could hurt our bodies like our love?
  We, but no foreign tyrants, could remove
These, not engraved, but inborn dignities
  Caskets of souls, temples and palaces.
For bodies shall from death redeemed be,
  Souls but preserved, born naturally free;
As men to our prisons now, souls to us are sent,
  Which learn vice there, and come in innocent.
First seeds of every creature are in us;
  Whate'er the world hath bad or precious,
Man's body can produce: hence hath it been,
  That stones, worms, frogs and snakes in man are seen:
But who e'er saw, though nature can work so,
  That pearl, or gold, or corn in man did grow?
We have added to the world Virginia, and sent
  Two new stars lately to the firmament;
Why grudge we us (not heaven) the dignity
  To increase with ours those fair souls' company?
But I must end this letter; though it do
  Stand on two truths, neither is true to you.
Virtue hath some perverseness; for she will
  Neither believe her good, nor other's ill.
Even in you, virtue's best paradise,
  Virtue hath some, but wise, degrees of vice.
Too many virtues, or too much of one
  Begets in you unjust suspicion,

And ignorance of vice makes virtue less,
  Quenching compassion of our wretchedness.
But these are riddles: some aspersion
  Of vice becomes well some complexion.
Statesmen purge vice with vice, and may corrode
  The bad with bad, a spider with a toad;
For so ill thralls not them, but they tame ill,
  And make her do much good against her will;
But in your commonwealth, or world in you,
  Vice hath no office or good work to do.
Take then no vicious purge, but be content
  With cordial virtue, your known nourishment.

TO THE COUNTESS OF BEDFORD (4)

On New Year's Day

This twilight of two years, not past, nor next,
  Some emblem is of me, or I of this,
Who meteor-like, of stuff and form perplext,
  Whose what and where in disputation is)
  If I should call me anything, should miss.

I sum the years and me, and find me not
  Debtor to the old, nor creditor to the new:
That cannot say, my thanks I have forgot;
  Nor trust I this with hopes; and yet scarce true
  This bravery is; since these times showed me you.

In recompense I would show future times
  What you were, and teach them to urge towards such.
Verse embalms virtue; and tombs or thrones of rhymes

Preserve frail transitory fame, as much
As spice doth bodies from corrupt air's touch.

Mine are short-lived; the tincture of your name
Creates in them, but dissipates as fast,
New spirit; for strong agents with the same
Force, that doth warm and cherish us, do waste;
Kept hot with strong extracts no bodies last.

So my verse, built of your just praise, might want
Reason and likelihood, the firmest base,
And, made of miracle, now faith is scant,
Will vanish soon, and so possess no place;
And you and it too much grace might disgrace.

When all (as truth commands assent) confess
All truth of you, yet they will doubt how I
(One corn of one low ant-hill's dust, and less)
Should name, know, or express a thing so high,
And (not an inch) measure infinity.

I cannot tell them, nor myself, nor you,
But leave, lest truth be endangered by my praise,
And turn to God, who knows I think this true,
And useth oft, when such a heart missays,
To make it good; for such a praiser prays.

He will best teach you, how you should lay out
His stock of *beauty, learning, favor, blood;*
He will perplex security with doubt,
And clear those doubts; hide from you, and show you good,
And so increase your appetite and food.

He will teach you that good and bad have not
    One latitude in cloisters and in court;
Indifferent there the greatest space hath got;
    Some pity's not good there, some vain disport,
    On this side sin, with that place may comport.

Yet he, as he bounds seas, will fix your hours,
    Which pleasure and delight may not ingress;
And though what none else lost, be truliest yours,
    He will make you, what you did not, possess,
    By using other's (not vice, but) weakness.

He will make you speak truths, and credibly,
    And make you doubt that others do not so;
He will provide you keys and locks, to spy,
    And scape spies; to good ends; and he will show
    What you may not acknowledge, what not know.

For your own conscience he gives innocence,
    But for your fame a discreet wariness,
And (though to 'scape than to revenge offence
    Be better) he shows both, and to repress
    Joy, when your state swells, sadness, when 'tis less.

From need of tears he will defend your soul,
    Or make a rebaptizing of one tear;
He cannot (that's, he will not) disenroll
    Your name; and when with active joy we hear
    This private gospel, then 'tis our new year.

TO THE COUNTESS OF HUNTINGDON

Madam,
Man to God's image, Eve to man's was made,
  Nor find we that God breathed a soul in her;
Canons will not church-functions you invade,
  Nor laws to civil office you prefer.

Who vagrant transitory comets sees,
  Wonders because they're rare; but a new star
Whose motion with the firmament agrees,
  Is miracle; for there no new things are.

In woman so perchance mild innocence
  A seldom comet is; but active good
A miracle, which reason 'scapes and sense;
  For Art and Nature this in them withstood.

As such a star the Magi led to view
  The manger-cradled infant, God below,
By virtue's beams by fame derived from you
  May apt souls, and the worst may virtue know.

If the world's age and death be argued well
  By the sun's fall, which now towards earth doth bend,
Then we might fear that virtue, since she fell
  So low as woman, should be near her end.

But she's not stooped, but raised; exiled by men,
  She fled to heaven, that's heavenly things, that's you

She was in all men thinly scattered then
    But now a mass contracted in a few.

She gilded us, but you are gold; and she
    Informed us, but transubstantiates you:
Soft dispositions, which ductile be,
    Elixir-like, she makes not clean, but new.

Though you a wife's and mother's name retain,
    'Tis not as woman, for all are not so;
But virtue, having made you virtue, is fain
    To adhere in these names, her and you to show.

Else, being alike pure, we should neither see,
    As water being into air rarefied,
Neither appear, till in one cloud they be,
    So for our sakes you do low names abide.

Taught by great constellations, (which, being framed
    Of the most stars, take low names *Crab* and *Bull*,
When single planets by the gods are named)
    You covet not great names, of great things full.

So you, as woman, one doth comprehend,
    And in the veil of kindred others see;
To some you are revealed, as in a friend,
    And as a virtuous prince far off, to me.

To whom, because from you all virtues flow,
    And 'tis not none to dare contemplate you,
I, which do so, as your true subject owe
    Some tribute for that; so these lines are due.

If you can think these flatteries, they are;
    For then your judgment is below my praise;
If they were so, oft flatteries work as far
    As counsels, and as far the endeavor raise.

So my ill, reaching you, might there grow good,
    But I remain a poisoned fountain still;
But not your beauty, virtue, knowledge, blood
    Are more above all flattery than my will.

And if I flatter any, 'tis not you,
    But my own judgment, who did long ago
Pronounce that all these praises should be true,
    And virtue should your beauty and birth outgrow.

Now that my prophecies are all fulfilled,
    Rather than God should not be honored too,
And all these gifts confessed, which he instilled,
    Yourself were bound to say that which I do.

So I but your recorder am in this,
    Or mouth, and speaker of the universe,
A ministerial notary; for 'tis
    Not I, but you and fame, that make this verse,

I was your prophet in your younger days,
    And now your chaplain, God in you to praise.

TO MR. I. W.

All hail, sweet Poet, more full of more strong fire,
        Than hath or shall enkindle any spirit!
    I loved what nature gave thee; but thy merit

Of wit and art I love not, but admire;
Who have before or shall write after thee,
Their works, though toughly labored, will be
Like infancy or age to man's firm stay,
Or early and late twilights to mid-day.

Men say, and truly, that they better be,
    Which be envied than pitied; therefore I,
    Because I wish thee best, do thee envy:
O would'st thou by like reason pity me,
But care not for me, I, that ever was
In Nature's and in Fortune's gifts, alas!
    (Before by thy grace got in the Muse's school)
    A monster and a beggar, am a fool.

Oh how I grieve, that late-born modesty
    Hath got such root in easy waxen hearts,
    That men may not themselves their own good parts
Extol, without suspect of surquedry;
For, but thyself, no subject can be found
Worthy thy quill, nor any quill resound
    Thy worth but thine: how good it were to see
    A poem in thy praise, and writ by thee!

Now if this song be too harsh for rhyme, yet as
    The painter's bad god made a good devil,
    'Twill be good prose, although the verse be evil.
If thou forget the rhyme, as thou dost pass,
Then write, that I may follow, and so be
    Thy echo, thy debtor, thy foil, thy zany.
    I shall be thought (if mine like thine I shape)
All the world's lion, though I be thy ape.

TO MR. T. W.

Haste thee, harsh verse, as fast as thy lame measure
Will give thee leave, to him; my pain and pleasure
I've given thee, and yet thou art too weak
Feet and a reasoning soul, and tongue to speak.
Tell him all questions, which men have defended
Both of the place and pains of hell are ended;
And 'tis decreed, our hell is but privation
Of him, at least in this earth's habitation:
And 'tis where I am, where in every street
Infections follow, overtake and meet.
Live I or die, by you my love is sent;
You are my pawns, or else my Testament.

TO MR. T. W. (2)

Pregnant again with the old twins, Hope and Fear,
Oft have I asked for thee, both how and where
Thou wert, and what my hopes of letters were;

As in our streets sly beggars narrowly
Watch motions of the giver's hand or eye,
And evermore conceive some hope thereby.

And now thy alms is given, thy letter's read,
The body risen again, the which was dead,
And thy poor starveling bountifully fed.

After this banquet my soul doth say grace,
And praise thee for't, and zealously embrace

Thy love; though I think thy love in this case
 To be as gluttons', which say 'midst their meat,
 They love that best, of which they most do eat.

At once from hence my lines and I depart,
I to my soft still walks, they to my heart;
I to the nurse, they to the child of art.

Yet as a firm house, though the carpenter
Perish, doth stand; as an ambassador
Lies safe, howe'er his king be in danger,

So, though I languish, pressed with melancholy,
My verse, the strict map of my misery,
Shall live to see that, for whose want I die.

Therefore I envy them, and do repent,
That from unhappy me things happy are sent;
Yet as a picture, or bare sacrament,
 Accept these lines, and if in them there be
 Merit of love, bestow that love on me.

TO MR. C. B.

Thy friend, whom thy deserts to thee enchain,
  Urged by this unexcusable occasion,
 Thee and the saint of his affection
Leaving behind, doth of both wants complain;
And let the love I bear to both sustain
 No blot nor maim by this division;
 Strong is this love, which ties our hearts in one,
And strong that love pursued with amorous pain:

But though beside thyself I leave behind
Heaven's liberal and earth's thrice-fair sun,
Going to where starved winter aye doth won;
Yet love's hot fires, which martyr my sad mind,
Do send forth scalding sighs which have the art
To melt all ice, but that which walls her heart.

TO MR. S. B.

O Thou, which to search out the secret parts
Of the India, or rather paradise
Of knowledge, hast with courage and advice
Lately launched into the vast sea of arts,
Disdain not in thy constant travailing
To do as other voyagers, and make
Some turns into less creeks, and wisely take
Fresh water at the Heliconian spring.
I sing not Siren-like to tempt; for I
Am harsh; nor as those schismatics with you,
Which draw all wits of good hope to their crew;
But seeing in you bright sparks of poetry,
I, though I brought no fuel, had desire
With these articulate blasts to blow the fire.

TO MR. B. B.

Is not thy sacred hunger of science
Yet satisfied? is not thy brain's rich hive
Fulfilled with honey, which thou dost derive
From the art's spirits and their quintessence?
Then wean thyself at last, and thee withdraw

From Cambridge, thy old nurse; and, as the rest,
Here toughly chew and sturdily digest
The immense vast volumes of our common law;
And begin soon, lest my grief grieve thee too,
Which is that that, which I should have begun
In my youth's morning, now late must be done;
And I, as giddy travelers must do,
Which stray or sleep all day, and having lost
Light and strength, dark and tired must then ride post.

If thou unto thy Muse be married,
Embrace her ever, ever multiply;
Be far from me that strange adultery
To tempt thee, and procure her widowhood;
My Muse (for I had one) because I'm cold,
Divorced herself, the cause being in me;
That I can take no new in bigamy,
Not my will only, but power doth withhold;
Hence comes it that these rhymes, which never had
Mother, want matter; and they only have
A little form, the which their father gave:
They are profane, imperfect, oh! too bad
To be counted children of poetry,
Except confirmed and bishoped by thee.

TO MR. R. W.

If, as mine is, thy life a slumber be,
Seem, when thou read'st these lines, to dream of me;
Never did Morpheus, nor his brother, wear
Shapes so like those shapes, whom they would appear,
As this my letter is like me; for it

Hath my name, words, hand, feet, heart, mind, and wit;
It is my deed of gift of me to thee,
    It is my will, myself the legacy.
So thy retirings I love, yea, envy,
    Bred in thee by a wise melancholy,
That I rejoice that, unto where thou art,
    Though I stay here, I can thus send my heart,
As kindly as any enamored patient
    His picture to his absent love hath sent.

All news I think sooner reach thee than me;
    Havens are heavens, and ships winged angels be,
The which both gospel and stern threatenings bring;
    Guiana's harvest is nipped in the spring,
I fear; and with us (methinks) Fate deals so,
    As with the Jew's guide God did; he did show
Him the rich land, but barred his entry in:
    Our slowness is our punishment and sin.
Perchance, these Spanish businesses being done,
    (Which, as the earth between the moon and sun,
Eclipse the light which Guiana would give)
    Our discontinued hopes we shall retrieve:
But if (as all the all must) hopes smoke away,
    Is not almighty Virtue an India?

If men be worlds, there is in every one
    Something to answer in some proportion
All the world's riches: and in good men this
    Virtue our form's form, and our soul's soul is.

TO MR. I. L.

Of that short roll of friends writ in my heart,
Which with thy name begins, since their depart,
Whether in the English provinces they be,
Or drink of Po, Sequan or Danuby,
There's none, that sometimes greets us not; and yet
Your Trent is Lethe, that past, us you forget.
You do not duties of societies,
If from the embrace of a loved wife you rise,
View your fat beasts, stretched barns, and labored fields,
Eat, play, ride, take all joys, which all day yields,
And then again to your embracements go;
Some hours on us your friends, and some bestow
Upon your Muse; else both we shall repent,
I, that my love; she, that her gifts on you are spent.

TO MR. I. P.

Blest are your North parts, for all this long time
My sun is with you, cold and dark 's our clime.
Heaven's sun, which stayed so long from us this year,
Stayed in your North (I think) for she was there,
And hither by kind Nature drawn from thence,
Here rages, chafes and threatens pestilence;
Yet I, as long as she from hence doth stay,
Think this no South, no summer, nor no day.
With thee my kind and unkind heart is run,
There sacrifice it to that beauteous sun:
So may thy pastures with their flowery feasts,
As suddenly as lard, fat thy lean beasts;

So may thy woods oft polled yet ever wear
    A green, and (when she list) a golden hair;
So may all thy sheep bring forth twins; and so
    In chase and race may thy horse all out-go;
So may thy love and courage ne'er be cold;
    Thy son ne'er ward; thy loved wife ne'er seem old;
But may'st thou wish great things, and them attain,
    As thou tell'st her, and none but her, my pain.

TO THE EARL OF DONCASTER WITH SIX HOLY SONNETS

See, Sir, how as the sun's hot masculine flame
    Begets strange creatures on Nile's dirty slime,
    In me your fatherly yet lusty rhyme
(For these songs are their fruits) have wrought the same;
But though the engendering force, from whence they came,
    Be strong enough, and nature doth admit
    Seven to be born at once, I send as yet
But six; they say the seventh hath still some maim:
    I choose your judgment, which the same degree
    Doth with her sister, your invention, hold,
As fire these drossy rhymes to purify,
    Or as elixir to change them to gold;
You are that alchemist, which always had
Wit, whose one spark could make goods things of bad.

TO SIR HENRY WOTTON (2)

At his going ambassador to Venice

After those reverend papers, whose soul is
  Our good and great king's loved hand and feared name,
By which to you he derives much of his,
  And (how he may) makes you almost the same,

A taper of his torch, a copy writ
  From his original, and a fair beam
Of the same warm and dazzling sun, though it
  Must in another sphere his virtue stream;

After those learned papers, which your hand
  Hath stored with notes of use and pleasure too,
From which rich treasury you may command
  Fit matter, whether you will write or do;

After those loving papers, where friends send,
  With glad grief to your sea-ward steps, farewell,
Which thicken on you now, as prayers ascend
  To heaven in troops at a good man's passing-bell;

Admit this honest paper, and allow
  It such an audience as yourself would ask;
What you must say at Venice, this means now,
  And hath for nature, what you have for task,

To swear much love, not to be changed before
  Honor alone will to your fortune fit;
Nor shall I then honor your fortune more,
  Than I have done your honor wanting it.

But 'tis an easier load (though both oppress)
  To want than govern greatness; for we are
In that, our own and only business;
  In this, we must for other's vices care.

'Tis therefore well your spirits now are placed
  In their last furnace, in activity;
Which fits them (schools and courts and wars o'erpast)
  To touch and test in any best degree.

For me, (if there be such a thing as I)
  Fortune (if there be such a thing as she)
Spies that I bear so well her tyranny,
  That she thinks nothing else so fit for me.

But though she part us, to hear my oft prayers
  For your increase, God is as near me here;
And to send you what I shall beg, his stairs
  In length and ease are alike everywhere.

TO MRS. M. H.

Mad paper, stay, and grudge not here to burn
  With all those sons, whom thy brain did create;
At least lie hid with me, till thou return
  To rags again, which is thy native state.

What though thou have enough unworthiness
  To come unto great place as others do,
That's much; emboldens, pulls, thrusts, I confess;
  But 'tis not all, thou shouldst be wicked too.

And that thou canst not learn, or not of me;
    Yet thou wilt go; go, since thou goest to her
Who lacks but faults to be a prince, for she
    Truth, whom they dare not pardon, dares prefer.

But when thou com'st to that perplexing eye,
    Which equally claims love and reverence,
Thou wilt not long dispute it, thou wilt die,
    And having little now, have then no sense.

Yet when her warm redeeming hand (which is
    A miracle, and made such to work more)
Doth touch thee (sapless leaf) thou grow'st by this
    Her creature, glorified more than before.

Then, as a mother which delights to hear
    Her early child misspeak half-uttered words,
Or, because majesty doth never fear
    Ill or bold speech, she audience affords.

And then, cold speechless wretch, thou diest again,
    And wisely; what discourse is left for thee?
From speech of ill and her thou must abstain,
    And is there any good which is not she?

Yet may'st thou praise her servants, though not her
    And Wit and Virtue and Honor her attend,
And since they're but her clothes, thou shalt not err,
    If thou her shape and beauty and grace commend.

Who knows thy destiny? when thou hast done,
    Perchance her cabinet may harbor thee,

Whither all noble ambitious wits do run,
  A nest almost as full of good as she.

When thou art there, if any, whom we know,
  Were saved before, and did that heaven partake,
When she revolves his papers, mark what show
  Of favor she, alone, to them doth make.

Mark if, to get them, she o'erskip the rest;
  Mark if she read them twice, or kiss the name;
Mark if she do the same that they protest;
  Mark if she mark whither her woman came.

Mark if slight things be objected, and o'erblown;
  Mark if her oaths against him be not still
Reserved, and that she grieve she's not her own,
  And chides the doctrine that denies free-will.

I bid thee not do this to be my spy,
  Nor to make myself her familiar;
But so much I do love her choice, that I
  Would fain love him, that shall be loved of her.

TO THE COUNTESS OF BEDFORD (5)

Honor is so sublime perfection,
And so refined, that when God was alone,
And creatureless at first, himself had none;

But as of the elements these which we tread,
Produce all things with which we're joyed or fed,
And those are barren both above our head,

So from low persons doth all honor flow;
Kings, whom they would have honored, to us show,
And but *direct* our honor, not *bestow.*

For when from herbs the pure part must be won
From gross by stilling, this is better done
By despised dung, than by the fire or sun:

Care not then, Madam, how low your praises lie;
In laborers' ballads oft more piety
God finds, than in *Te Deum's* melody;

And ordnance raised on towers so many mile
Send not their voice, nor last so long a while,
As fires from the earth's low vaults in Sicil isle.

Should I say I lived darker than were true,
Your radiation can all clouds subdue
But one; 'tis best light to contemplate you,

You, for whose body Goa made better clay,
Or took soul's stuff, such as shall late decay,
Or such as needs small change at the last day.

This, as an amber drop enwraps a bee,
Covering discovers your quick soul; that we
May in your through-shine front our heart's thought see.

You teach (though we learn not) a thing unknown
To our late times, the use of specular stone,
Through which all things within without were shown.

Of such were temples; so, and such you are;
Being and seeming is your equal care;
And virtue's whole sum is but *know* and *dare*.

Discretion is a wise man's soul, and so
Religion is a Christian's, and you know
How these are one; her *yea* is not her *no*.

But, as our souls of growth and souls of sense
Have birthright of our reason's soul, yet hence
They fly not from that, nor seek precedence,

Nature's first lesson so, discretion,
Must not grudge zeal a place, nor yet keep none,
Not banish itself, nor religion.

Nor may we hope to solder still and knit
These two, and dare to break them; nor must wit
Be colleague to Religion, but be it.

In those poor types of God (round circles) so
Religion's types the pieceless centers flow,
And are in all the lines which all ways go.

If either ever wrought in you alone,
Or principally, then religion
Wrought your ends, and your ways discretion.

Go thither still, go the same way you went;
Whoso would change, doth covet or repent;
Neither can reach you, great and innocent.

TO THE COUNTESS OF BEDFORD (6)

Begun in France, but never perfected

Though I be dead and buried, yet I have
    (Living in you) court enough in my grave;
As oft as there I think myself to be,
    So many resurrections waken me;
That thankfulness your favors have begot
    In me, embalms me that I do not rot:
This season, as 'tis Easter, as 'tis spring,
    Must both to growth and to confession bring
My thoughts disposed unto your influence; so
    These verses bud, so these confessions grow;
First I confess I have to others lent
    Your stock, and over-prodigally spent
Your treasure, for since I had never known
    Virtue and beauty, but as they are grown
In you, I should not think or say they shine,
    (So as I have) in any other mine;
Next I confess this confession;
    For 'tis some fault thus much to touch upon
Your praise to you, where half-rights, seem too much
    And make your mind's sincere complexion blush.
Next I confess my impenitence; for I
    Can scarce repent my first fault, since thereby
Remote low spirits, which shall ne'er read you,

May in less lessons find enough to do,
By studying copies, not originals;
Desunt caetera.

A LETTER TO THE LADY CARY, AND MRS. ESSEX RICH, FROM AMIENS

Madam,
Here, where by all All-saints invoked are,
'Twere too much schism to be singular,
And 'gainst good practice general to war.

Yet turning to saints, should my humility
To other saint than you directed be,
That were to make my schism heresy.

Nor would I be a convertite so cold,
As not to tell it; if this be too bold,
Pardons are in this market cheaply sold.

Where, because faith is in too low degree,
I thought it some apostleship in me
To speak things, which by faith alone I see;

That is, of you, who are a firmament
Of virtues, where no one is grown or spent;
They are your materials, not your ornament.

Others, whom we call virtuous, are not so
In their whole substance; but their virtues grow

But in their humors, and at seasons show.
For when through tasteless flat humility
In dough-baked men some harmlessness we see,
'Tis but his phlegm that's virtuous, and not he:

So is the blood sometimes; who ever ran
To danger unimportuned, he was than
No better than a sanguine-virtuous man.

So cloisteral men, who, in pretense of fear,
All contributions to this life forbear,
Have virtue in melancholy, and only there.

Spiritual choleric critics, which in all
Religions find faults, and forgive no fall,
Have through this zeal virtue but in their gall.

We are thus but parcel-gilt; to gold we are grown,
When virtue is our soul's complexion;
Who knows his virtue's name or place, hath none.

Virtue's but aguish, when 'tis several,
By occasion waked and circumstantial;
True Virtue is *soul*, always in all deeds *All.*

This virtue thinking to give dignity
To your soul, found there no infirmity;
For your soul was as good Virtue as she.

She therefore wrought upon that part of you,
Which is scarce less than soul, as she could do,
And so hath made your beauty virtue too.

Hence comes it, that your beauty wounds not hearts,
As others, with profane and sensual darts,
But as an influence virtuous thoughts imparts.

But if such friends by the honor of your sight
Grow capable of this so great a light,
As to partake your virtues and their might,

What must I think that influence must do,
Where it finds sympathy and matter too,
Virtue and beauty of the same stuff as you?

Which is your noble worthy sister; she,
Of whom, if what in this my ecstasy
And revelation of you both I see,

I should write here, (as in short galleries
The master at the end large glasses ties,
So to present the room twice to our eyes)

So I should give this letter length, and say
That which I said of you; there is no way
From either, but by the other, not to stray.

May therefore this be enough to testify
My true devotion, free from flattery;
He that believes himself, doth never lie.

TO THE COUNTESS OF SALISBURY

AUGUST, 1614

Fair, great, and good, since seeing you we see
What Heaven can do, what any earth can be;
Since now your beauty shines, now when the sun,
Grown stale, is to so low a value run,
That his disheveled beams and scattered fires
Serve but for ladies' periwigs and tiars
In lover's sonnets; you come to repair
God's book of creatures, teaching what is fair.
Since now, when all is withered, shrunk and dried,
All virtues ebbed out to a dead-low tide,
All the world's frame being crumbled into sand,
Where every man thinks by himself to stand,
Integrity, friendship and confidence,
(Cements of greatness) being vapored hence,
And narrow man being filled with little shares,
Courts, city, church, are all shops of small-wares,
All having blown to sparks their noble fire,
And drawn their sound gold ingot into wire,
All trying by a love of littleness
To make abridgments and to draw to less
Even that nothing which at first we were;
Since in these times your greatness doth appear,
And that we learn by it that Man, to get
Towards him that's infinite, must first be great;
Since in an age so ill, as none is fit
So much as to accuse, much less mend it,
(For who can judge or witness of those times,

Where all alike are guilty of the crimes?
Where he, that would be good, is thought by all
A monster, or at best fantastical?)
Since now you durst be good, and that I do
Discern, by daring to contemplate you,
That there may be degrees of fair, great, good,
Through your light, largeness, virtue, understood;
If, in this sacrifice of mine, be shown
Any small spark of these, call it your own;
And if things like these have been said by me
Of others, call not that idolatry.
For had God made man first, and man had seen
The third day's fruits and flowers, and various green,
He might have said the best that he could say
Of those fair creatures which were made that day;
And when next day he had admired the birth
Of sun, moon, stars, fairer than late praised earth,
He might have said the best that he could say,
And not be chid for praising yesterday;
So, though some things are not together true,
As, that another is worthiest, and that you,
Yet to say so doth not condemn a man,
If, when he spoke them, they were both true than.
How fair a proof of this in our soul grows!
We first have souls of growth, and sense; and those,
When our last soul, our soul immortal, came,
Were swallowed into it and have no name;
Nor doth he injure those souls, which doth cast
The power and praise of both them on the last;
No more do I wrong any; I adore
The same things now, which I adored before,
The subject changed, and measure; the same thing

In a low constable and in the king
I reverence,—his power to work on me;
So did I humbly reverence each degree
Of fair, great, good; but more now I am come
From having found their walks, to find their home.
And, as I owe my first soul's thanks, that they
For my last soul did fit and mold my clay,
So am I debtor unto them whose worth
Enabled me to profit, and take forth
This new great lesson, thus to study you,
Which none, not reading others first, could do.
Nor lack I light to read this book, though I
In a dark cave, yea, in a grave do lie;
For as your fellow-angels, so you do
Illustrate them who come to study you.
The first, whom we in histories do find
To have professed all arts, was one born blind:
He lacked those eyes beasts have as well as we,
Not those by which angels are seen and see;
So, though I am born without those eyes to live,
Which Fortune, who hath none herself, doth give,
Which are fit means to see bright courts and you,
Yet may I see you thus, as now I do;
I shall by that all goodness have discerned,
And, though I burn my library, be learned.

AN EPITHALAMION

On Frederick Count Palatine of the Rhine, and the Lady Elizabeth, being married on St. Valentine's Day

I.

Hail, Bishop Valentine, whose day this is,
All the air is thy diocese,
And all the chirping choristers
And other birds are thy parishioners:
Thou marriest every year
The lyric lark, and the grave whispering dove;
The sparrow, that neglects his life for love;
The household bird with the red stomacher;
Thou mak'st the blackbird speed as soon
As doth the goldfinch or the halcyon;
The husband cock looks out, and straight is sped,
And meets his wife, which brings her feather-bed;
This day more cheerfully than ever shine,
This day, which might inflame thyself, old Valentine.

II.

Till now thou warm'dst with multiplying loves
Two larks, two sparrows, or two doves;
All that is nothing unto this,
For thou this day couplest two phenixes.
Thou mak'st a taper see
What the sun never saw, and what the ark
(Which was of fowl and beasts the cage and park)
Did not contain, one bed contains, through thee;
Two phoenixes, whose joined breasts
Are unto one another mutual nests;
Where motion kindles such fires as shall give
Young phenixes, and yet the old shall live:
Whose love and courage never shall decline,
But make the whole year through thy day, O Valentine.

III.

Up then, fair phenix bride, frustrate the sun;
Thyself from thine affection
Tak'st warmth enough, and from thine eye
All lesser birds will take their jollity.
Up, up, fair bride, and call
Thy stars from out their several boxes, take
Thy rubies, pearls, and diamonds forth, and make
Thyself a constellation of them all:
And by their blazing signify,
That a great princess falls, but doth not die;
Be thou a new star, that to us portends
Ends of much wonder; and be thou those ends.
Since thou dost this day in new glory shine,
May all men date records from this day, Valentine.

IV.

Come forth, come forth, and as one glorious flame,
Meeting another, grows the same,
So meet thy Frederick, and so
To an inseparable union go;
Since separation
Falls not on such things as are infinite,
Nor things, which are but one, can disunite,
You're twice inseparable, great, and one.
Go then to where the bishop stays,
To make you one, his way, which divers ways
Must be effected; and when all is past,
And that ye are one, by hearts and hands made fast,
You two have one way left yourselves to entwine,
Besides this bishop's knot, O Bishop Valentine.

V.

But oh! what ails the sun, that here he stays
Longer today than other days?
Stays he new light from these to get?
And finding here such stores, is loath to set?
And why do you two walk
So slowly paced in this procession?
Is all your care but to be looked upon,
And be to others spectacle and talk?
The feast with gluttonous delays
Is eaten, and too long their meat they praise;
The masquers come late, and I think will stay,
Like fairies, till the cock crow them away.
Alas! did not antiquity assign
A night, as well as day, to thee, O Valentine?

VI.

They did, and night is come: and yet we see
Formalities retarding thee.
What mean these ladies, which (as though
They were to take a clock in pieces) go
So nicely about the bride?
A bride, before a good-night could be said,
Should vanish from her clothes into her bed,
As souls from bodies steal, and are not spied.
But now she is laid: what though she be?
Yet there are more delays; for where is he?
He comes, and passes through sphere after sphere;
First her sheets, then her arms, then anywhere.
Let not this day, then, but this night be thine,
Thy day was but the eve to this, O Valentine.

VII.

Here lies a she sun, and a he moon here;
She gives the best light to his sphere,
Or each is both, and all, and so
They unto one another nothing owe;
And yet they do, but are
So just and rich in that coin which they pay,
That neither would, nor needs, forbear nor stay;
Neither desires to be spared, nor to spare:
They quickly pay their debt, and then
Take no acquittances, but pay again;
They pay, they give, they lend, and so let fall
No such occasion to be liberal.
More truth, more courage in these two do shine,
Than all thy turtles have and sparrows, Valentine.

VIII.

And by this act of these two phoenixes
Nature again restored is;
For since these two are two no more,
There's but one phenix still, as was before.
Rest now at last, and we
(As Satyrs watch the sun's uprise) will stay
Waiting when your eyes opened let out day,
Only desired, because your face we see;
Others near you shall whispering speak,
And wagers lay, at which side day will break,
And win by observing then whose hand it is,
That opens first a curtain, hers or his;
This will be tried to-morrow after nine,
Till which hour we thy day enlarge, O Valentine.

ECLOGUE

DECEMBER 26, 1613

Allophanes finding Idios in the Country in Christmas time, reprehends his absence from Court, at the Marriage of the Earl of Somerset; Idios gives an account of his purpose therein, and of his actions there.

Allophanes.

Unseasonable man, statue of ice,
What could to country's solitude entice
Thee, in this year's cold and decrepit time?
        Nature's instinct draws to the warmer clime
Ev'n smaller birds, who by that courage dare
        In numerous fleets sail through their sea, the air.
What delicacy can in fields appear,
        Whilst Flora herself doth a frieze jerkin wear?
Whilst winds do all the trees and hedges strip
        Of leaves, to furnish rods enough to whip
Thy madness from thee, and all springs by frost
        Have taken cold, and their sweet murmurs lost?
If thou thy faults or fortunes would'st lament

With just solemnity, do it in Lent:
At court the spring already advanced is,
The sun stays longer up; and yet not his
The glory is; far other, other fires:
First zeal to prince and state; then love's desires
Burn in one breast, and like heaven's two great lights,
The first doth govern days, the other nights.
And then that early light, which did appear
Before the sun and moon created were,
The prince's favor, is diffused o'er all,
From which all fortunes, names, and natures fall;
Then from those wombs of stars, the bride's bright eyes,
At every glance a constellation flies,
And sows the court with stars, and doth prevent
In light and power the all-eyed firmament.
First her eyes kindle other ladies' eyes,
Then from their beams their jewels' lusters rise,
And from their jewels torches do take fire;
And all is warmth and light and good desire.
Most other courts, alas! are like to hell,
Where in dark plots fire without light doth dwell:
Or but like stoves, for lust and envy get
Continual but artificial heat;
Here zeal and love, grown one, all clouds digest,
And make our court an everlasting east.
And canst thou be from thence?

Idios. No, I am there:
As heaven, to men disposed, is ev'ry where,
So are those courts, whose princes animate,
Not only all their house, but all their state.
Let no man think, because he's full, he hath all;

Kings (as their pattern, God) are liberal
Not only in fulness but capacity,
    Enlarging narrow men to feel and see,
And comprehend, the blessings they bestow.
    So reclused hermits oftentimes do know
More of heaven's glory, than a worldling can.
    As man is of the world, the heart of man
Is an epitome of God's great book
    Of creatures, and man need no further look;
So's the country of courts, where sweet peace doth,
    As their own common soul, give life to both.
And am I then from court?

ALLOPHANES. Dreamer thou art.
    Think'st thou, fantastic, that thou hast a part
In the Indian fleet, because thou hast
    A little spice or amber in thy taste?
Because thou art not frozen, art thou warm?
    Seest thou all good, because thou seest no harm?
The earth doth in her inner bowels hold
    Stuff well disposed, and which would fain be gold:
But never shall, except it chance to lie
    So upward, that heaven gild it with his eye;
As for divine things, faith comes from above,
    So, for best civil use, all tinctures move
From higher powers; from God, religion springs;
    Wisdom and honor, from the use of kings;
Then unbeguile thyself, and know with me,
    That angels, though on earth employed they be,
Are still in heaven; so is he still at home
    That doth abroad to honest actions come.
Chide thyself then, O fool, which yesterday

Might'st have read more than all thy books bewray:
Hast thou a history, which doth present
A court, where all affections do assent
Unto the king's, and that, that kings are just?
And where it is no levity to trust,
Where there is no ambition but to obey,
Where men need whisper nothing, and yet may;
Where the king's favors are so placed, that all
Find that the king therein is liberal
To them, in him, because his favors bend
To virtue, to the which they all pretend?
Thou hast no such; yet here was this, and more,
An earnest lover, wise then, and before.
Our little Cupid hath sued livery,
And is no more in his minority;
He is admitted now into that breast
Where the king's counsels and his secrets rest.
What hast thou lost, O ignorant man?

Idios. I knew
All this, and only therefore I withdrew.
To know and feel all this, and not to have
Words to express it, makes a man a grave
Of his own thoughts; I would not therefore stay
At a great feast, having no grace to say.
And yet I 'scaped not here; for being come
Full of the common joy, I uttered some.
Read then this nuptial song, which was not made
Either the court or men's hearts to invade;
But since I am dead and buried, I could frame
No epitaph, which might advance my fame,
So much as this poor song, which testifies

I did unto that day some sacrifice.

I. The Time Of Marriage

Thou art reprieved, old year, thou shalt not die,
    Though thou upon thy death-bed lie,
    And should'st within five days expire;
Yet thou art rescued from a mightier fire,
    Than thy old soul, the sun,
When he doth in his largest circle run.
The passage of the West or East would thaw,
And open wide their easy liquid jaw
To all our ships, could a Promethean art
Either unto the northern pole impart
The fire of these inflaming eyes, or of this loving heart.

II. Equality of Persons

But undiscerning Muse, which heart, which eyes,
    In this new couple dost thou prize,
    When his eye as inflaming is
As hers, and her heart loves as well as his?
    Be tried by beauty, and than
The bridegroom is a maid, and not a man;
If by that manly courage they be tried,
Which scorns unjust opinion, then the bride
Becomes a man: should chance or envy's art
Divide these two, whom nature scarce did part,
Since both have the inflaming eye, and both the loving heart?

III. Raising of the Bridegroom

Though it be some divorce to think of you
    Single, so much one are you two,
    Let me here contemplate thee

First, cheerful bridegroom, and first let me see,
  How thou prevent'st the sun,
And his red foaming horses dost outrun;
How, having laid down in thy sovereign's breast
All businesses, from thence to reinvest
Them, when these triumphs cease, thou forward art
To show to her, who doth the like impart,
The fire of thy inflaming eyes, and of thy loving heart.

IV. Raising of the Bride

But now to thee, fair bride, it is some wrong,
  To think thou wert in bed so long:
  Since soon thou liest down first, 'tis fit
Thou in first rising should allow for it.
  Powder thy radiant hair,
Which if without such ashes thou would'st wear,
Thou who, to all which come to look upon,
Wert meant for Phoebus, would'st be Phaeton.
For our ease give thine eyes the unusual part
Of joy, a tear; so quenched, thou may'st impart,
To us that come, thy inflaming eyes; to him, thy loving heart.

V. Her Apparelling

Thus thou descend'st to our infirmity,
  Who can the sun in water see;
  So dost thou, when in silk and gold
Thou cloud'st thyself; since we, which do behold,
  Are dust and worms, 'tis just
Our objects be the fruits of worms and dust.
Let every jewel be a glorious star;
Yet stars are not so pure as their spheres are.
And though thou stoop to appear to us in part,

Still, in that picture thou entirely art,
Which thy inflaming eyes have made within his loving heart.

VI. Going to the Chapel

Now from your east you issue forth, and we,
 As men, which through a cypress see
 The rising sun, do think it two,
So, as you go to church, do think of you
 But that veil being gone,
By the church-rites you are from thenceforth one.
The church triumphant made this match before,
And now the militant doth strive no more.
Then, reverend priest, who God's recorder art,
Do from his dictates to these two impart
All blessings which are seen, or thought, by angel's eye or heart.

VII. The Benediction

Blest pair of swans, O may you interbring
 Daily new joys, and never sing:
 Live, till all grounds of wishes fail,
Till honor, yea till wisdom grow so stale,
 That new great heights to try,
It must serve your ambition, to die;
Raise heirs, and may here to the world's end live
Heirs from this king to take thanks; you, to give.
Nature and grace do all, and nothing art;
May never age or error overthwart
With any west these radiant eyes, with any north this heart.

VIII. Feasts and Revels

But you are over-blest. Plenty this day
 Injures; it causeth time to stay;

The tables groan, as though this feast
Would, as the flood, destroy all fowl and beast.
And were the doctrine new
That the earth moved, this day would make it true,
For every part to dance and revel goes,
They tread the air, and fall not where they rose.
Though six hours since the sun to bed did part
The masks and banquets will not yet impart
A sunset to these weary eyes, a center to this heart.

IX. The Bride's Going to Bed

What mean'st thou, bride, this company to keep?
To sit up, till thou fain would sleep?
Thou may'st not, when thou'rt laid, do so.
Thyself must to him a new banquet grow,
And you must entertain,
And do all this day's dances o'er again.
Know, that if sun and moon together do
Rise in one point, they do not set so too.
Therefore thou may'st, fair bride, to bed depart;
Thou art not gone being gone; where'er thou art,
Thou leav'st in him thy watchful eyes, in him thy loving heart.

X. The Bridegroom's Coming

As he that sees a star fall, runs apace
And finds a jelly in the place,
So doth the bridegroom haste as much,
Being told this star is fall'n, and finds her such.
And as friends may look strange
By a new fashion, or apparel's change,
Their souls, though long acquainted they had been,
These clothes, their bodies, never yet had seen.

Therefore at first she modestly might start,
But must forthwith surrender every part
As freely, as each to each before gave either hand or heart.

XI. The Good-Night

Now, as in Tullia's tomb one lamp burnt clear,
Unchanged for fifteen hundred year,
May these love-lamps we here enshrine,
In warmth, light, lasting, equal the divine.
Fire ever doth aspire,
And makes all like itself, turns all to fire,
But ends in ashes; which these cannot do,
For none of these is fuel, but fire too.
This is joy's bonfire, then, where love's strong arts
Make of so noble individual parts
One fire of four inflaming eyes, and of two loving hearts.
Idios. As I have brought this song, that I may do
A perfect sacrifice, I'll burn it too.
Allophanes. No, Sir, this paper I have justly got,
For in burnt incense the perfume is not
His only, that presents it, but of all;
Whatever celebrates this festival
Is common, since the joy thereof is so.
Nor may yourself be priest: but let me go
Back to the court, and I will lay't upon
Such altars as prize your devotion.

EPITHALAMION MADE AT LINCOLN'S INN

The sunbeams in the east are spread,
Leave, leave, fair bride, your solitary bed;
No more shall you return to it alone;
It nurseth sadness; and your body's print,
Like to a grave, the yielding down doth dint.
You and your other you meet there anon;
Put forth, put forth, that warm balm-breathing thigh,
Which when next time you in these sheets will smother,
There it must meet another,
Which never was, but must be oft more nigh;
Come glad from thence; go gladder than you came,
Today put on perfection, and a woman's name.

Daughters of London, you which be
Our golden mines, and furnished treasury;
You which are angels, yet still bring with you
Thousands of angels on your marriage-days,
Help with your presence, and devise to praise
These rites, which also unto you grow due.
Conceitedly dress her, and be assigned

By you fit place for every flower and jewel,
Make her for love fit fuel
As gay as Flora, and as rich as Ind;
So may she fair and rich, in nothing lame,
Today put on perfection, and a woman's name.

And you, frolic patricians,
Sons of those senators, wealth's deep oceans;
Ye painted courtiers, barrels of others' wits;
Ye countrymen, who but your beasts love none;
Ye of those fellowships, whereof he's one,
Of study and play made strange hermaphrodites,
Here shine; this bridegroom to the Temple bring.
Lo, in yon path, which store of strewed flowers graceth,
The sober virgin paceth;
Except my sight fail, 'tis no other thing.
Weep not, nor blush, here is no grief nor shame;
Today put on perfection, and a woman's name.

Thy two-leaved gates, fair temple, unfold,
And these two in thy sacred bosom hold,
Till, mystically joined, but one they be;
Then may thy lean and hunger-starved womb
Long time expect their bodies, and their tomb,
Long after their own parents fatten thee.
All elder claims, and all cold barrenness,
All yielding to new loves, be far forever,
Which might these two dissever;
Always all the other may each one possess;
For the best bride, best worthy of praise and fame,
Today puts on perfection, and a woman's name.

Winter days bring much delight,
Not for themselves, but for they soon bring night;
    Other sweets wait thee than these diverse meats,
Other disports than dancing jollities,
Other love-tricks than glancing with the eyes,
    But that the sun still in our half-sphere sweats;
    He flies in winter, but he now stands still;
Yet shadows turn; noon-point he hath attained,
    His steeds will be restrained,
        But gallop lively down the western hill:
Thou shalt, when he hath run the heaven's half frame,
To-night put on perfection, and a woman's name.

The amorous evening star is rose;
Why then should not our amorous star enclose
    Herself in her wished bed? Release your strings,
Musicians, and dancers, take some truce
With these your pleasing labors, for great use
    As much weariness as perfection brings.
    You, and not only you, but all toiled beasts,
Rest duly; at night all their toils are dispensed;
    But in their beds commenced
        Are other labors, and more dainty feasts.
She goes a maid, who, lest she turn the same,
To-night puts on perfection, and a woman's name.

Thy virgin's girdle now untie,
And in thy nuptial bed (love's altar) lie
    A pleasing sacrifice; now dispossess
Thee of these chains and robes, which were put on
To adorn the day, not thee; for thou alone,
    Like virtue and truth, art best in nakedness;

This bed is only to virginity
A grave, but to a better state a cradle.
Till now thou wast but able
To be what now thou art; then that by thee
No more be said, *I may be,* but *I am,*
To-night put on perfection, and a woman's name.

Even like a faithful man content,
That this life for a better should be spent,
So she a mother's rich style doth prefer,
And at the bridegroom's wished approach doth lie
Like an appointed lamb, when tenderly
The priest comes on his knees to embowel her.
Now sleep or watch with more joy; and oh light
Of heaven, to-morrow rise thou hot and early;
This sun will love so dearly
Her rest, that long, long we shall want her sight.
Wonders are wrought, for she, which had no maim,
To-night puts on perfection, and a woman's name.

LETTER TO THE COUNTESS OF BEDFORD

Madame, I have learned by those laws, wherein I am little conversant, that he which bestows any cost upon the dead, obliges him which is dead, but not his heir; I do not therefore send this paper to your Ladyship, that you should thank me for it, or think that I thank you in it; your favors and benefits to me are so much above my merits, that they are even above my gratitude, if that were to be judged by words, which must express it. But, Madam, since your noble brother's fortune being yours, the evidences also concerning it are yours; so his virtues being yours, the evidences concerning that belong also to you, of which by your acceptance this may be one piece; in which quality I humbly present it, and as a testimony how entirely your family possesseth Your Ladyship's Most humble and thankful servant, John Donne

OBSEQUIES

To the Lord Harrington's Brother & To the Countess of Bedford

Fair soul, which wast not only as all souls be,
Then when thou wast infused, harmony,
But didst continue so, and now dost bear
A part in God's great organ, this whole sphere;
If looking up to God, or down to us,
Thou find that any way is pervious
'Twixt heaven and earth, and that men's actions do
Come to your knowledge and affections too,
See, and with joy, me to that good degree
Of goodness grown, that I can study thee,
And by these meditations refined,
Can unapparel and enlarge my mind,
And so can make by this soft ecstasy,
This place a map of heaven, myself of thee.
Thou seest me here at midnight, now all rest;
Time's dead-low water, when all minds divest
To-morrow's business; when the laborers have
Such rest in bed, that their last church-yard grave,

Subject to change, will scarce be a type of this;
Now when the client, whose last hearing is
To-morrow, sleeps; when the condemned man,
(Who, when he opes his eyes, must shut them than
Again by death) although sad watch he keep,
Doth practice dying by a little sleep;
Thou at this midnight seest me, and as soon
As that sun rises to me, midnight's noon;
All the world grows transparent, and I see
Through all, both Church and State, in seeing thee;
And I discern by favor of this light
Myself, the hardest object of the sight.
God is the glass; as thou, when thou dost see
Him who sees all, seest all concerning thee,
So, yet unglorified, I comprehend
All in these mirrors of thy ways and end.
Though God be our true glass, through which we see
All, since the being of all things is he,
Yet are the trunks, which do to us derive
Things in proportion, fit by perspective,
Deeds of good men: for by their being here,
Virtues, indeed remote, seem to be near.
But where can I affirm or where arrest
My thoughts on his deeds? which shall I call best?
For fluid virtue cannot be looked on,
Nor can endure a contemplation.
As bodies change, and as I do not wear
Those spirits, humors, blood, I did last year;
And as, if on a stream I fix mine eye,
That drop which I looked on, is presently
Pushed with more waters from my sight, and gone;
So in this sea of virtues, can no one

Be insisted on; virtues as rivers pass,
Yet still remains that virtuous man there was.
And as, if man feed on man's flesh, and so
Part of his body to another owe,
Yet at the last two perfect bodies rise,
Because God knows where every atom lies,
So, if one knowledge were made of all those,
Who knew his minutes well, he might dispose
His virtues into names, and ranks; but I
Should injure Nature, Virtue, and Destiny,
Should I divide and discontinue so
Virtue, which did in one entireness grow.
For as he that should say, spirits are framed
Of all the purest parts that can be named,
Honors not spirits half so much as he,
Which says they have no parts, but simple be,
So is it of virtue; for a point and one
Are much entirer than a million.
And had Fate meant to have had his virtues told,
It would have let him live to have been old.
So then that virtue in season, and then this,
We might have seen, and said that now he is
Witty, now wise, now temperate, now just:
In good short lives, virtues are fain to thrust,
And to be sure betimes to get a place,
When they would exercise, lack time and space.
So was it in this person, forced to be,
For lack of time, his own epitome;
So to exhibit in few years as much
As all the long-breathed chronicles can touch.
As when an angel down from heaven doth fly,
Our quick thought cannot keep him company;

We cannot think, now he is at the sun,
Now through the moon, now through the air doth run,
Yet when he's come, we know he did repair
To all 'twixt heaven and earth, sun, moon, and air;
And as this angel in an instant knows,
And yet we know this sudden knowledge grows
By quick amassing several forms of things,
Which he successively to order brings,
When they, whose slow-paced lame thoughts cannot go
So fast as he, think that he doth not so,
(Just as a perfect reader doth not dwell
On every syllable, nor stay to spell,
Yet without doubt he doth distinctly see,
And lay together every A and B)
So in short-lived good men is not understood
Each several virtue, but the compound good;
For they all virtue's paths in that pace tread,
As angels go and know, and as men read.
O, why should then these men, these lumps of balm,
Sent hither the world's tempest to becalm,
Before by deeds they are diffused and spread,
And so make us alive, themselves be dead?
O soul! O circle! why so quickly be
Thy ends, thy birth, and death closed up in thee?
Since one foot of thy compass still was placed
In heaven, the other might securely have paced
In the most large extent through every path,
Which the whole world, or man, the abridgment, hath.
Thou know'st, that though the tropic circles have
(Yea, and those small ones, which the poles engrave)
All the same roundness, evenness, and all
The endlessness of the equinoctial,

Yet when we come to measure distances,
How here, how there the sun affected is,
When he doth faintly work, and when prevail,
Only great circles then can be our scale;
So, though thy circle to thyself express
All tending to thy endless happiness,
And we, by our good use of it, may try
Both how to live well (young) and how to die,
Yet, since we must be old, and age endures
His torrid zone at court, and calentures
Of hot ambition, irreligion's ice,
Zeal's agues, and by hydroptic avarice,
(Infirmities, which need the scale of truth,
As well as lust and ignorance of youth);
Why didst thou not for these give medicines too,
And by thy doing set us what to do?
Though, as small pocket-clocks, whose every wheel
Doth each mis-motion and distemper feel,
Whose hands gets shaking palsies, and whose string
(His sinews) slackens, and whose soul, the spring,
Expires or languishes, whose pulse, the flee,
Either beats not, or beats unevenly,
Whose voice, the bell, doth rattle or grow dumb,
Or idle, as men, which to their last hours come,
If these clocks be not wound, or be wound still,
Or be not set, or set at every will,
So youth is easiest to destruction,
If then we follow all, or follow none.
Yet as in great clocks, which in steeples chime,
Placed to inform whole towns to employ their time,
An error doth more harm, being general,
When small clocks' faults only on the wearer fall,

So work the faults of age, on which the eye
Of children, servants, or the state rely;
Why would'st not thou then, which hadst such a soul,
A clock so true, as might the sun control,
And daily hadst from him, who gave it thee,
Instructions, such, as it could never be
Disordered, stay here, as a general
And great sun-dial, to have set us all?
Oh why wouldest thou be an instrument
To this unnatural course? or why consent
To this, not miracle, but prodigy,
That when the ebbs longer than flowings be,
Virtue, whose flood did with thy youth begin,
Should so much faster ebb out than flow in?
Though her flood were blown in by thy first breath,
All is at once sunk in the whirlpool, death;
Which word I would not name, but that I see
Death, else a desert, grown a court by thee.
Now I am sure that if a man would have
Good company, his entry is a grave.
Methinks all cities now but ant-hills be,
Where when the several laborers I see
For children, house, provision, taking pain,
They're all but ants, carrying eggs, straw, and grain:
And church-yards are our cities, unto which
The most repair, that are in goodness rich;
There is the best concourse and confluence,
There are the holy suburbs, and from thence
Begins God's city, new Jerusalem,
Which doth extend her utmost gates to them:
At that gate then, triumphant soul, dost thou
Begin thy triumph. But since laws allow

That at the triumph-day the people may,
All that they will, 'gainst the triumpher say,
Let me here use that freedom, and express
My grief, though not to make the triumph less.
By law to triumphs none admitted be,
Till they, as magistrates, get victory;
Though then to thy force all youth's foes did yield,
Yet till fit time had brought thee to that field,
To which thy rank in this state destined thee,
That there thy counsels might get victory,
And so in that capacity remove
All jealousies 'twixt prince and subject's love,
Thou could'st no title to this triumph have,
Thou didst intrude on death, usurp a grave.
Then (though victoriously) thou hadst fought as yet
But with thine own affections, with the heat
Of youth's desires, and colds of ignorance,
But till thou should'st successfully advance
Thine arms 'gainst foreign enemies, which are
Both envy, and acclamations popular,
(For both these engines equally defeat,
Though by a divers mine, those which are great)
Till then thy war was but a civil war,
For which to triumph none admitted are;
No more are they, who, though with good success,
In a defensive war their power express.
Before men triumph, the dominion
Must be enlarged, and not preserved alone;
Why should'st thou then, whose battles were to win
Thyself from those straits nature put thee in,
And to deliver up to God that state,
Of which he gave thee the vicariate,

(Which is thy soul and body) as entire
As he, who takes indentures, doth require,
But didst not stay, to enlarge his kingdom too,
By making others, what thou didst, to do;
Why should'st thou triumph now, when heaven no more
Hath got, by getting thee, than it had before?
For heaven and thou, even when thou livedst here,
Of one another in possession were.
But this from triumph most disables thee,
That that place, which is conquered, must be
Left safe from present war, and likely doubt
Of imminent commotions to break out;
And hath he left us so? or can it be
His territory was no more than he?
No, we were all his charge; the diocese
Of every exemplar man the whole world is;
And he was joined in commission
With tutelar angels, sent to every one.
But though this freedom to upbraid, and chide
Him who triumphed, were lawful, it was tied
With this, that it might never reference have
Unto the senate who this triumph gave;
Men might at Pompey jest, but they might not
At that authority by which he got
Leave to triumph, before by age he might;
So though, triumphant soul, I dare to write
Moved with a reverential anger, thus
That thou so early would'st abandon us,
Yet I am far from daring to dispute
With that great sovereignty, whose absolute
Prerogative hath thus dispensed with thee
'Gainst nature's laws, which just impugners be

Of early triumphs: and I though with pain
Lessen our loss, to magnify thy gain
Of triumph, when I say it was more fit
That all men should lack thee, than thou lack it.
Though then in our times be not suffered
That testimony of love unto the dead,
To die with them and in their graves be hid,
As Saxon Wives, and French Soldarii did;
And though in no degree I can express
Grief in great Alexander's great excess,
Who at his friend's death made whole towns divest
Their walls and bulwarks, which became them best;
Do not, fair soul, this sacrifice refuse,
That in thy grave I do inter my Muse,
Which by my grief, great as thy worth, being cast
Behindhand, yet hath spoke, and spoke her last.

ELEGIES

ELEGY VIII

The Comparison

As the sweet sweat of roses in a still,
As that which from chafed musk cat's pores doth trill,
As the almighty balm of th' early east,
Such are the sweat drops of my mistress' breast;
And on her neck her skin such luster sets,
They seem no sweat drops, but pearl coronets.
Rank sweaty froth thy mistress' brow defiles,
Like spermatic issue of ripe menstruous boils,
Or like the scum, which, by need's lawless law
Enforced, Sanserra's starvèd men did draw
From parboil'd shoes and boots, and all the rest
Which were with any sovereign fatness blest;
And like vile lying stones in saffron'd tin,
Or warts, or wheals, it hangs upon her skin.
Round as the world's her head, on every side,
Like to the fatal ball which fell on Ide;
Or that whereof God had such jealousy,
As for the ravishing thereof we die.

Thy head is like a rough-hewn statue of jet,
Where marks for eyes, nose, mouth, are yet scarce set;
Like the first chaos, or flat seeming face
Of Cynthia, when th' earth's shadows her embrace.
Like Proserpine's white beauty-keeping chest,
Or Jove's best fortune's urn, is her fair breast.
Thine's like worm-eaten trunks, clothed in seal's skin,
Or grave, that's dust without, and stink within.
And like that slender stalk, at whose end stands
The woodbine quivering, are her arms and hands.
Like rough-bark'd elm-boughs, or the russet skin
Of men late scourged for madness, or for sin,
Like sun-parch'd quarters on the city gate,
Such is thy tann'd skin's lamentable state;
And like a bunch of ragged carrots stand
The short swollen fingers of thy gouty hand.
Then like the chemic's masculine equal fire,
Which in the limbec's warm womb doth inspire
Into th' earth's worthless dirt a soul of gold,
Such cherishing heat her best loved part doth hold.
Thine's like the dread mouth of a fired gun,
Or like hot liquid metals newly run
Into clay molds, or like to that Aetna,
Where round about the grass is burnt away.
Are not your kisses then as filthy, and more,
As a worm sucking an envenom'd sore?
Doth not thy fearful hand in feeling quake,
As one which gathering flowers still fears a snake?
Is not your last act harsh and violent,
As when a plough a stony ground doth rent?
So kiss good turtles, so devoutly nice
Are priests in handling reverent sacrifice,

And such in searching wounds the surgeon is,
As we, when we embrace, or touch, or kiss.
Leave her, and I will leave comparing thus,
She and comparisons are odious.

ELEGY IX

The Autumnal

No Spring, nor Summer's beauty hath such grace,
    As I have seen in one autumnal face.
Young beauties force our loves, and that's a rape;
    This doth but counsel, yet you cannot 'scape.
If 'twere a shame to love, here 'twere no shame:
    Affections here take Reverence's name.
Were her first years the golden age? that's true;
    But now she's gold oft tried, and ever new.
That was her torrid and inflaming time;
    This is her habitable tropic clime.
Fair eyes, who asks more heat than comes from hence,
    He in a fever wishes pestilence.
Call not these wrinkles graves: if graves they were,
    They were Love's graves; or else he is nowhere.
Yet lies not Love dead here, but here doth sit
    Vowed to this trench, like an anachorit.
And here, till her's, which must be his death, come,
    He doth not dig a grave, but build a tomb.
Here dwells he; though he sojourn everywhere
    In progress, yet his standing-house is here;
Here, where still evening is, not noon nor night,
    Where no voluptuousness, yet all delight.
In all her words, unto all hearers fit,
    You may at revels, you at councils sit.

This is love's timber, youth his underwood;
  There he, as wine in June, enrages blood,
Which then comes seasonablest, when our taste
  And appetite to other things is past.
Xerxes's strange Lydian love, the platane tree,
  Was loved for age, none being so old as she,
Or else because, being young, nature did bless
  Her youth with age's glory, barrenness.
If we love things long sought, age is a thing,
  Which we are fifty years in compassing;
If transitory things, which soon decay,
  Age must be loveliest at the latest day.
But name not winter-faces, whose skin's slack;
  Lank as an unthrift's purse; but a soul's sack;
Whose eyes seek light within, for all here's shade;
  Whose mouths are holes, rather worn out than made;
Whose every tooth to a several place is gone
  To vex the soul at resurrection;
Name not these living death-heads unto me,
  For these not ancient but antique be:
I hate extremes: yet I had rather stay
  With tombs than cradles, to wear out the day.
Since such love's natural station is, may still
  My love descend, and journey down the hill;
Not panting after growing beauties; so
  I shall ebb on with them, who homeward go.

ELEGY X

The Dream

Image of her, whom I love more than she,
  Whose fair impression in my faithful heart

Makes me her medal, and makes her love me,
    As kings do coins, to which their stamps impart
The value: go, and take my heart from hence,
    Which now is grown too great and good for me.
Honors oppress weak spirits, and our sense
    Strong objects dull; the more, the less we see.
When you are gone, and reason gone with you,
    Then Phantasy is queen, and soul, and all;
She can present joys meaner than you do
    Convenient, and more proportional.
So if I dream I have you, I have you,
    For all our joys are but fantastical.
And so I 'scape the pain, for pain is true;
    And sleep, which locks up sense, doth lock out all.
After a such fruition I shall wake,
    And, but the waking, nothing shall repent;
And shall to Love more thankful sonnets make,
    Than if more honor, tears, and pains were spent.
But dearest heart, and dearer image, stay,
    Alas! true joys at best are dreams enough;
Though you stay here, you pass too fast away:
    For even at first life's taper is a snuff.
Filled with her love, may I be rather grown
    Mad with much heart, than idiot with none.

AN ELEGY ON THE UNTIMELY DEATH OF THE INCOMPARABLE PRINCE HENRY

Look to me, faith, and look to my faith, God;
For both my centers feel this period.

Of weight one center, one of greatness is;
And reason is that center, faith is this;
For into our reason flow, and there do end,
All that this natural world doth comprehend,
Quotidian things, and equidistant hence,
Shut in for man in one circumference;
But for the enormous greatnesses, which are
So disproportioned, and so angular,
As is God's essence, place, and providence,
Where, how, when, what souls do, departed hence,
These things (eccentric else) on faith do strike;
Yet neither all, nor upon all, alike.
For Reason, put to her best extension,
Almost meets Faith, and makes both centers one;
And nothing ever came so near to this,
As contemplation of that Prince we miss.
For all, that Faith might credit mankind could,
Reason still seconded that this prince would.
If then least moving of the center make
More, than if whole hell belched, the world to shake,
What must this do, centers distracted so,
That we see not what to believe or know?
Was it not well believed till now, that he,
Whose reputation was an ecstasy
On neighbor states, which knew not why to wake,
Till he discovered what ways he would take;
For whom, what princes angled, when they tried,
Met a torpedo and were stupefied;
And others' studies, how he would be bent;
Was his great father's greatest instrument,
And activest spirit, to convey and tie
This soul of peace to Christianity?

Was it not well believed, that he would make
This general peace the Eternal overtake
And that his times might have stretched out so far,
As to touch those, of which they emblems are?
For to confirm this just belief, that now
The last days came, we saw heaven did allow,
That, but from his aspect and exercise,
In peaceful times rumors of wars should rise.
But now this faith is heresy: we must
Still stay, and vex our great grandmother, Dust.
Oh, is God prodigal? hath he spent his store
Of plagues on us; and only now, when more
Would ease us much, doth he grudge misery,
And will not let's enjoy our curse, to die?
As for the earth, thrown lowest down of all,
'Twere an ambition to desire to fall;
So God, in our desire to die, doth know
Our plot for ease, in being wretched so;
Therefore we live, though such a life we have,
As but so many mandrakes on his grave.
What had his growth and generation done,
When, what we are, his putrefaction
Sustains in us, earth, which griefs animate?
Nor hath our world now other soul than that.
And could grief get so high as heaven, that choir,
Forgetting this their new joy, would desire
(With grief to see him) he had stayed below,
To rectify our errors they foreknow.
Is the other center, Reason, faster then?
Where should we look for that, now we're not men?
For if our Reason be our connection
Of causes, now to us there can be none.

For, as if all the substances were spent,
'Twere madness to inquire of accident,
So is it to look for Reason, he being gone,
The only subject Reason wrought upon.
If Fate have such a chain, whose divers links
Industrious man discerneth, as he thinks,
When miracle doth come, and so steal in
A new link, man knows not where to begin;
At a much deader fault must reason be,
Death having broke off such a link as he.
But now, for us with busy proof to come,
That we've no Reason, would prove we had some;
So would just lamentations: therefore we
May safelier say, that we are dead, than he.
So, if our griefs we do not well declare,
We've double excuse; he's not dead, and we are.
Yet I would not die yet; for though I be
Too narrow to think him, as he is he,
(Our soul's best baiting and mid-period,
In her long journey of considering God)
Yet, (no dishonor) I can reach him thus,
As he embraced the fires of love, with us.
Oh may I, (since I live) but see or hear,
That she-intelligence which moved this sphere,
I pardon fate my life; who e'er thou be,
Which hast the noble conscience, thou art she:
I conjure thee by all the charms he spoke,
By the oaths which only you two never broke,
By all the souls ye sighed, that if you see
These lines, you wish I knew your history;
So much as you two mutual heavens were here,
I were an angel, singing what you were.

PSALM 137

I.

By Euphrates' flowery side
We did bide,
From dear Judah far absented,
Tearing the air with our cries,
And our eyes
With their streams his stream augmented.

II.

When poor Sion's doleful state,
Desolate,
Sacked, burned, and enthralled;
And the Temple spoiled, which we
Ne'er should see,
To our mirthless minds we called:

III.

Our mute harps, untuned, unstrung,
Up we hung
On green willows near beside us;
Where we sitting all forlorn,

Thus in scorn
Our proud spoilers 'gan deride us.

IV.

Come, sad captives, leave your moans,
And your groans
Under Sion's ruins bury;
Tune your harps, and sing us lays
In the praise
Of your God, and let's be merry.

V.

Can, ah! can we leave our moans?
And our groans
Under Sion's ruins bury?
Can we in this land sing lays
In the praise
Of our God, and here be merry?

VI.

No; dear Sion, if I yet
Do forget
Thine affliction miserable,
Let my nimble joints become
Stiff and numb,
To touch warbling harp unable.

VII.

Let my tongue lose singing skill,
Let it still
To my parched roof be glued;
If in either harp or voice

I rejoice,
Till thy joys shall be renewed.

VIII.

Lord, curse Edom's traitorous kind,
Bear in mind,
In our ruins how they reveled:
Sack, kill, burn, they cried out still,
Sack, burn, kill,
Down with all, let all be levelled!

IX.

And thou, Babel, when the tide
Of thy pride,
Now aflowing, grows to turning;
Victor now, shall then be thrall,
And shall fall
To as low an ebb of mourning.

X.

Happy he, who shall thee waste,
As thou hast
Us without all mercy wasted,
And shall make thee taste and see,
What poor we
By thy means have seen and tasted.

XI.

Happy, who thy tender barns
From the arms
Of their wailing mothers tearing,
'Gainst the walls shall dash their bones,

Ruthless stones
With their brains and blood besmearing.

FURTHER POEMS

RESURRECTION, IMPERFECT

Sleep, sleep, old sun, thou canst not have re-past
As yet the wound, thou took'st on Friday last;
Sleep then, and rest, the world may bear thy stay;
A better sun rose before thee today,
Who, not content t' enlighten all that dwell
On the earth's face, as thou, enlightened hell,
And made the dark fires languish in that vale,
As at thy presence here our fires grow pale;
Whose body having walked on earth, and now
Hastening to Heaven, would, that he might allow
Himself unto all stations, and fill all,
For these three days become a mineral.
He was all gold, when he lay down, but rose
All tincture; and doth not alone dispose
Leaden and iron wills to good, but is
Of power to make even sinful flesh like his.
Had one of those, whose credulous piety
Thought that a soul one might discern and see
Go from a body, at this sepulcher been,

And issuing from the sheet this body seen,
He would have justly thought this body a soul,
If not of any man, yet of the whole.
Desunt caetera

A HYMN TO THE SAINTS, AND TO MARQUESS HAMILTON

Whether that soul, which now comes up to you,
Fill any former rank, or make a new,
Whether it take a name named there before,
Or be a name itself, and order more
Than was in heaven till now; (for may not he
Be so, if every several angel be
A kind alone) whatever order grow
Greater by him in heaven, we do not so.
One of your orders grows by his access,
But by his loss grow all our orders less:
The name of father, master, friend, the name
Of subject and of prince, in one is lame;
Fair mirth is damp and conversation black,
The household widowed, and the Garter slack;
The chapel wants an ear, council a tongue,
Story a theme, and music lacks a song.
Blest order, that hath him! the loss of him
Gangrened all orders here; all lost a limb!
Never made body such haste to confess
What a soul was; all former comeliness
Fled in a minute, when the soul was gone,
And, having lost that beauty, would have none:
So fell our monasteries, in an instant grown,

Not to less houses, but to heaps of stone;
So sent his body that fair form it wore,
Unto the sphere of forms, and doth (before
His soul shall fill up his sepulchral stone)
Anticipate a resurrection;
For, as in his fame, now, his soul is here,
So in the form thereof his body is there.
And if, fair soul, not with first innocents
Thy station be, but with the penitents;
(And who shall dare to ask then, when I am
Dyed scarlet in the blood of that pure Lamb,
Whether that color, which is scarlet then,
Were black or white before in eyes of men?)
When thou rememberest what sins thou didst find
Amongst those many friends now left behind,
And seest such sinners as they are, with thee
Got thither by repentance, let it be
Thy wish to wish all there, to wish them clean:
With him a David, her a Magdalen.

TO SIR ROBERT CARR

Sir, I presume you rather try what you can do in me, than what I can do in verse; you know my uttermost when it was best, and even then I did best, when I had least truth for my subjects. In this present case there is so much truth, as it defeats all poetry. Call therefore this paper by what name you will, and if it be not worthy of him, nor of you, nor of me, smother it, and be that the sacrifice. If you had commanded me to have waited on his body to Scotland and preached there, I would have embraced the obligation with more alacrity; But I thank you, that you would command me that, which I was lother to do, for even that hath given a tincture of merit to the obedience of

Your poor friend and servant in Christ Jesus, J. DONNE

AN EPITAPH ON SHAKSPEARE

Renowned Chaucer, lie a thought more nigh
To rare Beaumont; and learned Beaumont lie
A little nearer Spenser, to make room
For Shakespeare in your threefold fourfold tomb;
To lie all four in one bed make a shift,
For until doomsday hardly shall a fift
Betwixt this day and that be slain,
For whom your curtains need be drawn again;
But if precedency in death doth bar
A fourth place in your sacred sepulcher,
Under this curled marble of thine own,
Sleep, rare tragedian! Shakespeare, sleep alone,
That unto us and others it may be
Honor hereafter to be laid by thee!

SAPPHO TO PHILAENIS

Where is that holy fire, which verse is said
  To have? is that enchanting force decayed?
Verse, that draws nature's works from nature's law,
  Thee, her best work, to her work cannot draw.
Have my tears quenched my old poetic fire?
  Why quenched they not as well that of desire?
Thoughts, my mind's creatures, often are with thee,
  But I, their maker, want their liberty:
Only thine image in my heart doth sit;
  But that is wax, and fires environ it.
My fires have driven, thine have drawn it hence,
  And I am robbed of picture, heart, and sense.

Dwells with me still mine irksome memory,
    Which both to keep and lose grieves equally.
That tells how fair thou art; thou art so fair,
    As gods, when gods to thee I do compare,
Are graced thereby; and to make blind men see,
    What things gods are, I say they are like to thee.
For if we justly call each silly man
    A little world, what shall we call thee than?
Thou art not soft, and clear, and straight, and fair,
    As down, as stars, cedars and lilies are;
But thy right hand, and cheek, and eye only
    Are like thy other hand, and cheek, and eye.
Such was my Phao awhile, but shall be never
    As thou wast, art, and, oh! may'st thou be ever!
Here lovers swear in their idolatry,
    That I am such; but grief discolors me:
And yet I grieve the less, lest grief remove
    My beauty, and make me unworthy of thy love.
Plays some soft boy with thee? oh! there wants yet
    A mutual feeling, which should sweeten it.
His chin a thorny hairy unevenness
    Doth threaten, and some daily change possess.
Thy body is a natural paradise,
    In whose self, unmanured, all pleasure lies,
Nor needs perfection; why should'st thou then
    Admit the tillage of a harsh rough man?
Men leave behind them that, which their sin shows,
    And are as thieves traced, which rob when it snows;
But of our dalliance no more signs there are,
    Than fishes leave in streams, or birds in air.
And between us all sweetness may be had;
    All, all that nature yields, or art can add.

My two lips, eyes, thighs differ from thy two,
But so, as thine from one another do:
And, oh! no more; the likeness being such,
Why should they not alike in all parts touch?
Hand to strange hand, lip to lip none denies;
Why should they breast to breast, or thighs to thighs?
Likeness begets such strange self-flattery,
That touching myself, all seems done to thee.
Myself I embrace, and mine own hands I kiss,
And amorously thank myself for this.
Me in my glass I call thee; but, alas!
When I would kiss, tears dim mine eyes and glass.
O, cure this loving madness, and restore
Me to me; thee my half, my all, my more.
So may thy cheek's red outwear scarlet dye,
And their white, whiteness of the Galaxy;
So may thy mighty amazing beauty move
Envy in all women, and in all men love;
And so be change and sickness far from thee,
As thou, by coming near, keep'st them from me.

THE ANNUNCIATION AND PASSION

Tamely, frail body, abstain today; today
My soul eats twice, Christ hither and away;
She sees him man, so like God made in this,
That of them both a circle emblem is,
Whose first and last concur; this doubtful day
Of feast or fast Christ came, and went away.
She sees him nothing twice at once, who's all;

She sees a cedar plant itself, and fall;
Her Maker put to making, and the head
Of life, at once not yet alive, and dead;
She sees at once the Virgin-mother stay
Reclused at home, public at Golgotha.
Sad and rejoiced she's seen at once, and seen
At almost fifty and at scarce fifteen:
At once a son is promised her, and gone;
Gabriel gives Christ to her, He her to John:
Not fully a mother, she's in orbity,
At once receiver and the legacy.
All this, and all between, this day hath shown,
The abridgment of Christ's story, which makes one
(As in plain maps the furthest West is East)
Of the angel's Ave, and *consummatum est.*
How well the Church, God's Court of Faculties,
Deals in sometimes and seldom joining these!
As by the self-fixed Pole we never do
Direct our course, but the next star thereto,
Which shows where the other is, and which we say
(Because it strays not far) doth never stray,
So God by his Church, nearest to him, we know,
And stand firm, if we by her motion go;
His Spirit as his fiery pillar doth
Lead, and his Church as cloud; to one end both.
This Church, by letting those days join, hath shown
Death and conception in mankind are one;
Or 'twas in him the same humility,
That he would be a man and leave to be.
Or as creation he hath made, as God,
With the last judgment but one period,
His imitating spouse would join in one

Manhood's extremes: *he shall come, he is gone.*
Or as, though one blood-drop which thence did fall,
Accepted, would have served, he yet shed all,
So, though the least of his pains, deeds, or words,
Would busy a life, she all this day affords.
This treasure then in gross, my soul, up-lay,
And in my life retail it every day.

GOOD FRIDAY, 1613, RIDING WESTWARD

Let man's soul be a sphere, and then in this
The intelligence that moves, devotion is;
And as the other spheres, by being grown
Subject to foreign motion, lose their own,
And being by others hurried every day,
Scarce in a year their natural form obey,
Pleasure or business so our souls admit
For their first mover, and are whirled by it.
Hence is't, that I am carried towards the West
This day, when my soul's form bends towards the East;
There I should see a sun by rising set,
And, by that setting, endless day beget.
But that Christ on this cross did rise and fall,
Sin had eternally benighted all;
Yet dare I almost be glad I do not see
That spectacle of too much weight for me.
Who sees God's face, that is self-life, must die;
What a death were it then to see God die?
It made his own lieutenant, Nature, shrink,
It made his footstool crack, and the sun wink.

Could I behold those hands which span the poles
And tune all spheres at once, pierced with those holes
Could I behold that endless height which is
Zenith to us, and our antipodes,
Humbled below us? or that blood which is
The seat of all our souls, if not of his,
Made dirt of dust? or that flesh, which was worn
By God for his apparel, ragg'd and torn?
If on these things I durst not look, durst I
On his distressed mother cast mine eye,
Who was God's partner here, and furnished thus
Half of that sacrifice, which ransomed us?
Though these things, as I ride, be from mine eye,
They're present yet unto my memory,
For that looks towards them; and thou look'st towards me,
O Savior, as thou hang'st upon the tree;
I turn my back to thee, but to receive
Corrections, till thy mercies bid thee leave.
O think me worth thine anger, punish me,
Burn off my rusts, and my deformity;
Restore thine image so much by thy grace,
That thou may'st know me, and I'll turn my face.

THE LITANY

1. The Father

Father of Heaven, and him by whom
    It, and us for it, and all else for us
    Thou mad'st and govern'st ever, come,
And recreate me, now grown ruinous:
        My heart is by dejection clay,
        And by self-murder red.

From this red earth, O, Father, purge away
All vicious tinctures, that new fashioned
I may rise up from death, before I am dead.

II. The Son

O Son of God, who seeing two things,
Sin and Death, crept in, which were never made,
By bearing one, triedst with what stings
The other could thine heritage invade;
O, be thou nailed unto my heart,
And crucified again;
Part not from it, though it from thee would part,
But let it be, by applying so thy pain,
Drowned in thy blood, and in thy passion slain.

III. The Holy Ghost

O Holy Ghost, whose temple I
Am, but of mud walls and condensed dust,
And being sacrilegiously
Half-wasted with youth's fires, of pride and lust,
Must with new storms be weather-beat,
Double in my heart thy flame,
Which let devout sad tears intend; and let
(Though this glass lantern, flesh, do suffer maim)
Fire, sacrifice, priest, altar be the same.

IV. The Trinity

O blessed, glorious Trinity,
Bones to Philosophy, but milk to Faith,
Which, as wise serpents, diversely
Most slipperiness, yet most entanglings hath,
As you distinguished (undistinct)

By power, love, knowledge be,
Give me a such self-different instinct,
Of these let all me elemented be,
Of power to love, to know you, upnumbered Three.

V. The Virgin Mary

For that fair, blessed, mother-maid,
Whose flesh redeemed us—That she-cherubin,
Which unlocked Paradise, and made
One claim for innocence, and disseized sin,
Whose womb was a strange heaven, for there
God clothed himself, and grew,
Our zealous thanks we pour.
As her deeds were Our helps, so are her prayers; nor can she sue
In vain, who hath such titles unto you.

VI. The Angels

And since this life our nonage is,
And we in wardship to thine angels be,
Native in heaven's fair palaces,
Where we shall be but denizened by thee;
As the earth, conceiving by the sun,
Yields fair diversity,
Yet never knows which course that light doth run,
So let me study, that mine actions be
Worthy their sight, though blind in how they see.

VII. The Patriarchs

And let thy patriarchs' desire
(Those great-grandfathers of thy Church, which saw
More in the cloud, than we in fire,
Whom Nature cleared more than us grace and law,

And now in heaven still pray, that we
May use our new helps right)
Be satisfied, and fructify in me;
Let not my mind be blinder by more light,
Nor Faith, by Reason added, lose her sight.

VIII. The Prophets

Thy eagle-sighted prophets, too,
(Which were thy Church's organs, and did sound
That harmony, which made of two
One law, and did unite, but not confound—
Those heavenly poets, which did see
Thy will, and it express
In rhythmic feet) in common pray for me,
That I by them excuse not my excess
In seeking secrets, or poeticness.

IX. The Apostles

And thy illustrious zodiac
Of twelve apostles, which engirt this All,
(From whom whosoe'er do not take
Their light, to dark deep pits thrown down do fall)
As through their prayers thou hast let me know,
That their books are divine,
May they pray still, and be heard, that I go
The old broad way in applying; O, decline
Me, when my comment would make thy word mine.

X. The Martyrs

And since thou so desirously
Didst long to die, that long before thou could'st,
And long since thou no more could'st die,

Thou in thy scattered mystic body would'st
In Abel die, and ever since
In thine; let their blood come
To beg for us a discreet patience
Of death, or of worse life; for, oh! to some
Not to be martyrs is a martyrdom.

XI. The Confessions

Therefore with thee triumpheth there
A virgin squadron of white confessors,
Whose bloods betrothed, not married, were;
Tendered, not taken by those ravishers:
They know, and pray, that we may know;
In every Christian
Hourly tempestuous persecutions grow;
Temptations martyr us alive; a man
Is to himself a Diocletian.

XII. The Virgins

The cold, white, snowy nunnery,
(Which, as thy mother, their high abbess, sent
Their bodies back again to thee,
As thou hadst lent them, clean and innocent)
Though they have not obtained of thee,
That or thy Church, or I,
Should keep, as they, our first integrity,
Divorce thou sin in us, or bid it die,
And call chaste widowhead virginity.

XIII. The Doctor

Thy sacred academe above
Of doctors, whose pains have unclasped and taught

Both books of life to us, (for love
To know thy scriptures tells us, we are wrote
In thy other book) pray for us there,
That what they have misdone,
Or missaid, we to that may not adhere;
Their zeal may be our sin. Lord, let us run
Mean ways, and call them stars, but not the sun.

XIV.

And whilst this universal choir
(That church in triumph, this in warfare here,
Warmed with one all-partaking fire
Of love, that none be lost, which cost thee dear)
Prays ceaselessly, and thou hearken too,
(Since to be gracious
Our task is treble, to pray, bear, and do)
Hear this prayer, Lord; O Lord, deliver us
From trusting in those prayers, though poured out thus.

XV.

From being anxious, or secure,
Dead clods of sadness, or light squibs of mirth,
From thinking, that great courts immure
All or no happiness, or that this earth
Is only for our prison framed,
Or that thou 'rt covetous
To them thou lovest, or that they are maimed,
From reaching this world's sweets, who seek thee thus
With all their might, good Lord, deliver us.

XVI.

From needing danger to be good,
From owing thee yesterday's tears today,
From trusting so much to thy blood,
That in that hope we wound our souls away
From bribing thee with alms, t' excuse
Some sin more burdenous,
From light affecting, in religion, news,
From thinking us all foul, neglecting thus
Our mutual duties, Lord, deliver us.

XVII.

From tempting Satan to tempt us,
By our connivance, or slack company,
From measuring ill by vicious,
Neglecting to choke sin's spawn, vanity,
From indiscreet humility,
Which might be scandalous,
And cast reproach on Christianity,
From being spies, or to spies pervious,
From thirst or scorn of fame, deliver us.

XVIII.

Deliver us through thy descent
Into the Virgin, whose womb was a place
Of middle kind, and thou being sent
To ungracious us, strayed'st as her full grace—
And through thy poor birth, where first thou
Glorified'st poverty,
And yet soon after riches didst allow,
By accepting kings' gifts in the Epiphany,
Deliver, and make us to both ways free.

XIX.

And through that bitter agony,
Which still is the agony of pious wits,
Disputing what distorted thee,
And interrupted evenness with fits,
And through thy free confession,
Though thereby they were then
Made blind, so that thou might'st from them have gone,
Good Lord, deliver us, and teach us when
We may not, and we may, blind unjust men.

XX.

Through thy submitting all to blows
Thy face, thy robes to spoil, thy fame to scorn,
All ways, which rage or justice knows,
And by which thou could'st show that thou wast born,
And through thy gallant humbleness,
Which thou in death didst show,
Dying before thy soul they could express,
Deliver us from death, by dying so
To this world, ere this world do bid us go.

XXI.

When senses, which thy soldiers are,
We arm against thee, and they fight for sin,
When want, sent but to tame, doth war,
And work Despair a breach to enter in,
When plenty, God's image and seal,
Makes us idolatrous,
And love it, not him whom it should reveal,
When we are moved to seem religious,
Only to vent wit, Lord, deliver us.

XXII.

In Churches when the infirmity
Of him which speaks, diminishes the Word,
When magistrates do misapply
To us, as we judge, lay or ghostly sword,
When plague, which is thine angel, reigns,
Or wars, thy champions, sway,
When Heresy, thy second deluge, gains,
In the hour of death, the eve of last judgment day,
Deliver us from the sinister way.

XXIII.

Hear us, O hear us, Lord: to thee
A sinner is more music, when he prays,
Than spheres, or angels' praises be
In panegyric *Allelujas,*
Hear us; for till thou hear us, Lord,
We know not what to say:
Thine ear to our sighs, tears, thoughts, gives voice and word.
O thou, who Satan heard'st in Job's sick day,
Hear thyself now, for thou in us dost pray.

XXIV.

That we may change to evenness
This intermitting aguish piety—
That snatching cramps of wickedness,
And apoplexies of fast sin may die,
That music of thy promises,
Not threats in thunder, may
Awaken us to our just offices,
What in thy book thou dost, or creatures say,
That we may hear, Lord, hear us, when we pray.

XXV.

That out ears' sickness we may cure,
And rectify those labyrinths aright,
That we by hearkening not procure
Our praise, nor others' dispraise so invite,
That we get not a slipperiness,
And senselessly decline,
From hearing bold wits jest at kings' excess,
To admit the like of majesty divine,
That we may lock our ears, Lord, open thine.

XXVI.

That living law, the magistrate,
Which, to give us and make us physic, doth
Our vices often aggravate,
That preachers, taxing sin before her growth,
That Satan, and envenomed men,
Which will, if we starve, dine,
When they do most accuse us, may see then
Us to amendment hear them thee decline,
That we may open our ears, Lord, lock thine.

XXVII.

That learning, thine ambassador,
From thine allegiance we never tempt,
That beauty, paradise's flower,
For physic made, from poison be exempt,
That wit, born apt high good to do,
By dwelling lazily
On Nature's nothing, be not nothing too,
That our affections kill us not, nor die,
Hear us, weak echoes, O, thou ear, and cry.

XXVIII.

Son of God, hear us; and since thou,
By taking our blood, ow'st it us again,
Gain to thyself and us allow;
And let not both us and thyself be slain.
O Lamb of God, which took'st our sin,
Which could not stick to thee,
O let it not return to us again;
But patient and physician being free,
As sin is nothing, let it nowhere be.

THE MESSAGE

Send home my long-strayed eyes to me,
Which (oh) too long have dwelt on thee;
But if they there have learned such ill,
Such forced fashions
And false passions,
That they be
Made by thee
Fit for no good sight, keep them still.

Send home my harmless heart again,
Which no unworthy thought could stain;
Which if it be taught by thine
To make jestings
Of protestings,
And break both
Word and oath,
Keep it, for then 'tis none of mine.

Yet send me back my heart and eyes,
That I may know and see thy lies,
And may laugh and joy, when thou
Art in anguish,
And dost languish
For some one,
That will none,
Or prove as false as thou art now.

A NOCTURNAL UPON ST. LUCY'S DAY, BEING THE SHORTEST DAY

'Tis the year's midnight, and it is the day's,
Lucy's, who scarce seven hours herself unmasks;
The sun is spent, and now his flasks
Send forth light squibs, no constant rays;
The world's whole sap is sunk:
The general balm the hydroptic earth hath drunk,
Whither, as to the beds-feet, life is shrunk,
Dead and interred; yet all these seem to laugh,
Compared with me, who am their epitaph.

Study me then, you who shall lovers be
At the next world, that is, at the next spring:
For I am a very dead thing,
In whom Love wrought new alchemy.
For his art did express
A quintessence even from nothingness,
From dull privations, and lean emptiness:
He ruined me, and I am rebegot
Of absence, darkness, death, things which are not.

All others from all things draw all that 's good,
Life, soul, form, spirit, whence they being have;
I, by Love's limbec, am the grave
Of all, that's nothing. Oft a flood
Have we two wept, and so
Drowned the whole world, us two; oft did we grow
To be two Chaos's, when we did show
Care to aught else; and often absences
Withdrew our souls, and made us carcasses.

But I am by her death (which word wrongs her)
Of the first nothing the elixir grown;
Were I a man, that I were one,
I needs must know; I should prefer,
If I were any beast,
Some ends, some means; yea, plants, yea, stones detest
And love; all, all some properties invest.
If I an ordinary nothing were,
As shadow, a light and body must be here.

But I am none; nor will my sun renew:
You lovers, for whose sake the lesser sun
At this time to the Goat is run
To fetch new lust, and give it you,
Enjoy your summer all,
Since she enjoys her long night's festival,
Let me prepare towards her, and let me call
This hour her vigil and her eve, since this
Both the year's, and the day's deep midnight is.

WITCHCRAFT BY A PICTURE

I fix mine eye on thine, and there
Pity my picture burning in thine eye;
My picture drowned in a transparent tear,
When I look lower, I espy;
Hadst thou the wicked skill,
By pictures made and marred, to kill
How many ways might'st thou perform thy will!

But now I've drunk thy sweet salt tears,
And though thou pour more, I'll depart:
My picture vanished, vanish all fears,
That I can be endamaged by that art:
Though thou retain of me
One picture more, yet that will be,
Being in thine own heart, from all malice free.

THE BAIT

Come live with me, and be my love,
And we will some new pleasures prove
Of golden sands, and crystal brooks,
With silken lines and silver hooks.

There will the river whispering run
Warmed by thine eyes, more than the sun;
And there the enamored fish will stay,
Begging themselves they may betray.

When thou wilt swim in that live bath,
Each fish, which every channel hath,
Will amorously to thee swim,
Gladder to catch thee, than thou him.

If thou to be so seen be'st loath
By sun or moon, thou darkenest both;
And if myself have leave to see,
I need not their light, having thee.

Let others freeze with angling reeds,
And cut their legs with shells and weeds,
Or treacherously poor fish beset,
With strangling snare, or windowy net:

Let coarse bold hands from slimy nest
The bedded fish in banks outwrest,
Or curious traitors, sleave-silk flies,
Bewitch poor fishes' wandering eyes:

For thee, thou need'st no such deceit,
For thou thyself art thine own bait;
That fish, that is not catched thereby,
Alas! is wiser far than I.

THE APPARITION

When by thy scorn, O murderess, I am dead,
            And that thou think'st thee free
Of all solicitation from me,
Then shall my ghost come to thy bed,
And thee feigned vestal in worse arms shall see;

Then thy sick taper will begin to wink,
And he, whose thou art then, being tired before,
Will, if thou stir, or pinch to wake him, think
Thou call'st for more,
And in a false sleep even from thee shrink.
And then, poor aspen wretch, neglected thou
Bathed in a cold quicksilver sweat wilt lie
A verier ghost than I;
What I will say, I will not tell thee now,
Lest that preserve thee: and since my love is spent,
I'd rather thou should'st painfully repent,
Than by my threatenings rest still innocent.

THE BROKEN HEART

He is stark mad, whoever says,
That he hath been in love an hour;
Yet not that love so soon decays,
But that it can ten in less space devour;
Who will believe me, if I swear
That I have had the plague a year?
Who would not laugh at me, if I should say,
I saw a flash of powder burn a day?

Ah! what a trifle is a heart,
If once into Love's hands it come!
All other griefs allow a part
To other griefs, and ask themselves but some.
They come to us, but us love draws,
He swallows us, and never chaws:
By him, as by chained shot, whole ranks do die;
He is the tyrant pike, our hearts the fry.

If 'twere not so, what did become
Of my heart, when I first saw thee?
I brought a heart into the room,
But from the room I carried none with me:
If it had gone to thee, I know
Mine would have taught thy heart to show
More pity unto me: but Love, alas,
At one first blow did shiver it as glass.

Yet nothing can to nothing fall,
Nor any place be empty quite,
Therefore I think my breast hath all
Those pieces still, though they be not unite:
And now, as broken glasses show
A hundred lesser faces, so
My rags of heart can like, wish, and adore,
But after one such Love can love no more.

A VALEDICTION FORBIDDING MOURNING

As virtuous men pass mildly away,
And whisper to their souls to go,
Whilst some of their sad friends, do say,
The breath goes now, and some say no;

So let us melt, and make no noise,
No tear-floods, nor sigh-tempests move,
'Twere profanation of our joys,
To tell the laity our love.

Moving of the earth brings harms and fears,
Men reckon what it did and meant;
But trepidation of the spheres,
Though greater far, is innocent.

Dull sublunary Lovers' love
(Whose soul is sense) cannot admit
Absence, because it doth remove
Those things which elemented it.

But we by a love so much refined,
That ourselves know not what it is,
Inter-assured of the mind,
Care less eyes, lips, and hands to miss.

Our two souls, therefore, which are one,
Though I must go, endure not yet
A breach, but an expansion,
Like gold to airy thinness beat.

If they be two, they are two so
As stiff twin compasses are two;
Thy soul, the fixt foot, makes no show
To move, but doth if the other do.

And though it in the center sit,
Yet when the other far doth roam,
It leans and hearkens after it,
And grows erect, as that comes home.

Such wilt thou be to me, who must,
Like the other foot, obliquely run.

Thy firmness makes my circle just,
And makes me end where I begun.

THE GOOD-MORROW

I wonder, by my troth, what thou and I,
Did, till we loved? were we not weaned till then
But sucked on country pleasures childishly?
Or slumbered we in the Seven Sleepers' den?
'twas so; but this, all pleasures fancies be:
If ever any beauty I did see,
Which I desired and got, 'twas but a dream of thee.

And now good-morrow to our waking souls,
Which watch not one another out of fear;
For lore all love of other sights controls,
And makes one little room an everywhere.
Let sea-discoverers to new worlds have gone,
Let maps to other, worlds on worlds have shown,
Let us possess one world; each hath one, and is one.

My face in thine eye, thine in mine appears,
And true plain hearts do in the faces rest;
Where can we find two fitter hemispheres
Without sharp north, without declining west?
Whatever dies, was not mixed equally;
If our two loves be one, both thou and I
Love just alike in all, none of these loves can die.

SONG

Go and catch a falling star,
Get with child a mandrake root,
Tell me where all years past are,
Or who cleft the devil's foot,
Teach me to hear mermaid's singing,
Or to keep off envy's stinging,
And find,
What wind
Serves to advance an honest mind.

If thou be'st born to strange sights,
Things invisible go see,
Ride ten thousand days and nights,
Till age snow white hairs on thee;
Thou, when thou return'st, wilt tell me
All strange wonders that befell thee,
And swear,
Nowhere
Lives a woman true and fair.

If thou find'st one, let me know,
Such a pilgrimage were sweet;
Yet do not: I would not go,
Though at next door we might meet;
Though she were true when you met her,
And last till you write your letter,
Yet she
Will be
False, ere I come, to two or three.

WOMAN'S CONSTANCY

Now thou hast loved me one whole day,
To-morrow when thou leav'st, what wilt thou say?
Wilt thou then antedate some new-made vow?
Or say that now
We are not just those persons which we were?
Or that oaths made in reverential fear
Of Love and his wrath, any may forswear?
Or, as true deaths true marriages untie,
So lovers' contracts, images of those,
Bind but till Sleep, Death's image, them unloose?
Or, your own end to justify,
For having purposed change and falsehood, you
Can have no way but falsehood to be true?
Vain lunatic, against these scapes I could
Dispute and conquer, if I would;
Which I abstain to do,
For by to-morrow I may think so too.

THE UNDERTAKING

I have done one braver thing,
Than all the Worthies did;
And yet a braver thence doth spring,
Which is, to keep that hid.

It were but madness now to impart
The skill of specular stone,
When he, which can have learned the art
To cut it, can find none.

So, if I now should utter this,
Others (because no more
Such stuff to work upon there is)
Would love but as before:

But he who loveliness within
Hath found, all outward loathes;
For he who color loves and skin,
Loves but their oldest clothes.

If, as I have, you also do
Virtue in woman see,
And dare love that, and say so too,
And forget the He and She;

And if this love, though placed so,
From profane men you hide,
Which will no faith on this bestow,
Or, if they do, deride;

Then you have done a braver thing,
Than all the Worthies did,
And a braver thence will spring,
Which is, to keep that hid.

THE SUN-RISING

Busy old fool, unruly sun,
Why dost thou thus,
Through windows and through curtains call on us?
Must to thy motions lovers' seasons run?
Saucy pedantic wretch, go chide

Late school-boys, and sour 'prentices,
Go tell court-huntsmen, that the King will ride,
Call country ants to harvest offices;
Love, all alike, no season knows nor clime,
Nor hours, days, months, which are the rags of time.

Thy beams so reverend and strong,
Dost thou not think
I could eclipse and cloud them with a wink,
But that I would not lose her sight so long?
If her eyes have not blinded thine,
Look, and to-morrow late tell me
Whether both the Indias of spice and mine
Be where thou left them, or lie here with me;
Ask for those kings, whom thou saw'st yesterday;
And thou shalt hear all here in one bed lay.

She's all states, and all princes I,
Nothing else is.
Princes do but play us; compared to this,
All honor's mimic, all wealth alchemy;
Thou sun art half as happy as we,
In that the world's contracted thus;
Thine age asks ease, and since thy duties be
To warm the world, that's done in warming us.
Shine here to us, and thou art everywhere;
This bed thy center is, these walls thy sphere.

THE INDIFFERENT

I can love both fair and brown;
Her whom abundance melts, and her whom want betrays;

Her who loves loneness best, and her who sports and plays;
Her whom the country formed, and whom the town;
Her who believes, and her who tries;
Her who still weeps with spongy eyes,
And her who is dry cork, and never cries;
I can love her, and her, and you, and you,
I can love any, so she be not true.

Will no other vice content you?
Will it not serve your turn to do as did your mothers?
Or have you all old vices spent, and now would find out others?
Or doth a fear that men are true torment you?
Oh, we are not, be not you so;
Let me; and do you twenty know.

Rob me, but bind me not, and let me go;
Must I, who came to travel thorough you,
Grow your fixed subject, because you are true?

Venus heard me sing this song,
And by Love's sweetest part, variety, she swore,
She heard not this till now; it should be so no more.
She went, examined, and returned ere long,
And said, Alas! some two or three
Poor heretics in love there be,
Which think to 'stablish dangerous constancy;
But I have told them, since you will be true,
You shall be true to them, who are false to you.

LOVE'S USURY

For every hour that thou wilt spare me now,
I will allow,
Usurious God of Love, twenty to thee,
When with my brown my gray hairs equal be;
Till then, Love, let my body range, and let
Me travel, sojourn, snatch, plot, have, forget,
Resume my last year's relict, think that yet
We had never met.

Let me think any rival's letter mine,
And at next nine
Keep midnight's promise; mistake by the way
The maid, and tell the lady of that delay;
Only let me love none, no not the sport;
From country grass to comfitures of court,
Or city's *quelque-choses,* let not report
My mind transport.

This bargain's good; if when I'm old, I be
Inflamed by thee,
If thine own honor, or my shame or pain,
Thou covet most, at that age thou shalt gain;
Do thy will then, then subject and degree
And fruit of love, Love, I submit to thee;
Spare me till then, I'll bear it, though she be
One that loves me.

CANONIZATION

For God's sake hold your tongue, and let me love,
Or chide my palsy, or my gout,
My true gray hairs, or ruined fortunes flout;
With wealth your state, your mind with arts improve.
Take you a course, get you a place,
Observe his Honor or his Grace,
Or the King's real, or his stamped face
Contemplate; what you will, approve,
So you will let me love.

Alas, alas, who's injured by my love?
What merchant's ships have my sighs drowned?
Who says my tears have overflowed his ground?
When did my colds a forward spring remove?
When did the heats which my veins fill
Add one more to the plaguy bill?
Soldiers find wars, and lawyers find out still
Litigious men which quarrels move,
Though she and I do love.

Call's what you will, we are made such by love;
Call her one, me another fly;
We're tapers too, and at our own cost die;
And we in us find the eagle and the dove;
The phoenix-riddle hath more wit
By us; we two being one, are it:
So to one neutral thing both sexes fit.
We die and rise the same, and prove
Mysterious by this love.

We can die by it, if not live by love.
    And if unfit for tomb or hearse
Our legend be, it will be fit for verse;
    And if no piece of chronicle we prove,
        We'll build in sonnets pretty rooms.
        As well a well-wrought urn becomes
The greatest ashes, as half-acre tombs;
    And by those hymns all shall approve
    Us canonized for love,

And thus invoke us: "You whom reverend love
    Made one another's hermitage;
You to whom love was peace, that now is rage,
    Who did the whole world's soul contract, and drove
        Into the glasses of your eyes,
        So made such mirrors and such spies,
That they did all to you epitomize;
    Countries, towns, courts, beg from above
    A pattern of your love."

THE TRIPLE FOOL

I am two fools, I know,
For loving, and for saying so
In whining poetry;
But where's that wise man, that would not be I,
If she would not deny?
Then as the earth's inward narrow crooked lanes
Do purge sea-water's fretful salt away,
I thought, if I could draw my pains
Through rhyme's vexation, I should them allay.
Grief, brought to numbers cannot be so fierce,
For he tames it that fetters it in verse.

But when I have done so,
Some man, his art and voice to show,
Doth set and sing my pain,
And, by delighting many, frees again
Grief, which verse did restrain.
To love and grief tribute of verse belongs,
But not of such as pleases when 'tis read,
Both are increased by such songs;
For both their triumphs so are published,
And I, which was two fools, do so grow three:
Who are a little wise, the best fools be.

LOVER'S INFINITENESS

If yet I have not all thy love,
Dear, I shall never have it all;
I cannot breathe one other sigh to move,
Nor can entreat one other tear to fall;
And all my treasure, which should purchase thee,
Sighs, tears, and oaths, and letters I have spent,
Yet no more can be due to me,
Than at the bargain made was meant:
If then thy gift of love were partial,
That some to me, some should to others fall,
    Dear, I shall never have it all.

Or, if then thou gav'st me all,
All was but all, which thou hadst then:
But if in thy heart since there be, or shall
New love created be by other men,
Which have their stocks entire, and can in tears,
In sighs, in oaths, in letters outbid me,

This new love may beget new fears;
For this love was not vowed by thee,
And yet it was, thy gift being general;
The ground, thy heart, was mine, whatever shall
  Grow there, dear, I should have it all.

Yet, I would not have all yet,
He that hath all can have no more;
And since my love doth every day admit
New growth, thou should'st have new rewards in store;
Thou canst not every day give me thy heart,
If thou canst give it, then thou never gav'st it:
Love's riddles are that, though thy heart depart,
It stays at home, and thou with losing sav'st it:
But we will love a way more liberal
Than changing hearts,—to join them; so we shall
  Be one, and one another's All.

SONG (2)

Sweetest Love, I do not go,
For weariness of thee,
Nor in hope the world can show
  A fitter Love for me;
    But since that I
At the last must part, 'tis best,
To use myself in jest
  Thus by feigned deaths to die;

Yesternight the sun went hence,
  And yet is here today,
He hath no desire nor sense,

Nor half so short a way:
Then fear not me,
But believe that I shall make
Speedier journeys, since I take
More wings and spurs than he.

O how feeble is man's power,
That, if good fortune fall,
Cannot add another hour,
Nor a lost hour recall!
But come bad chance,
And we join to it our strength,
And we teach it art and length,
Itself o'er us to advance.

When thou sigh'st thou sigh'st no wind,
But sigh'st my soul away;
When thou weep'st, unkindly kind,
My life's blood doth decay.
It cannot be
That thou lov'st me, as thou say'st,
If in thine my life thou waste,
That art the best of me.

Let not thy divining heart
Forethink me any ill,
Destiny may take thy part,
And may thy fears fulfill;
But think that we
Are but turned aside to sleep:
They, who one another keep
Alive, ne'er parted be.

THE LEGACY

When I died last (and, Dear, I die
As often as from thee I go,
Though it be but an hour ago,
And lovers' hours be full eternity)
I can remember yet, that I
Something did say, and something did bestow,
Though I be dead, which meant me, I should be
Mine own executor, and legacy.

I heard me say, Tell her anon,
That myself, that is you, not I,
Did kill me; and when I felt me die,
I bid me send my heart, when I was gone,
But I, alas! could there find none.
When I had ripped, and searched where hearts should lie,
It killed me again, that I, who still was true
In life, in my last will should cozen you.

Yet I found something like a heart,
But colors it and corners had,
It was not good, it was not bad,
It was entire to none, and few had part:
As good, as could be made by art,
It seemed, and therefore for our loss as sad;
I meant to send that heart instead of mine,
But oh! no man could hold it, for 'twas thine.

A FEVER

You do not die, for I shall hate
  All women so, when thou art gone,
That thee I shall not celebrate,
  When I remember thou wast one.

But yet thou canst not die, I know;
  To leave this world behind, is death;
But when thou from this world wilt go,
  The whole world vapors in thy breath.

Or if, when thou, the world's soul, go'st,
  It stay, 'tis but thy carcass then;
The fairest woman, but thy ghost;
  But corrupt worms, the worthiest men.

O wrangling schools, that search what fire
Shall burn this world, had none the wit
Unto this knowledge to aspire,
  That this her fever might be it?

And yet she cannot waste by this,
  Nor long bear this torturing wrong,
For more corruption needful is,
  To fuel such a fever long.

These burning fits but meteors be,
  Whose matter in thee soon is spent;
Thy beauty, and all parts, which are thee,
  Are an unchangeable firmament.

Yet 'twas of my mind, seizing thee,
    Though it in thee cannot persever;
For I had rather owner be
    Of thee one hour, than all else ever.

AIR AND ANGELS

    Twice or thrice had I loved thee,
Before I knew thy face or name;
So in a voice, so in a shapeless flame,
Angels affect us oft, and worshipped be:
    Still when, to where thou wast, I came,
Some lovely glorious nothing I did see;
    But since my soul, whose child love is,
Takes limbs of flesh, and else could nothing do,
    More subtle than the parent is,
Love must not be, but take a body too;
    And therefore what thou wast, and who,
        I bid love ask, and now,
That it assume thy body, I allow,
And fix itself in thy lip, eye, and brow.

Whilst thus to ballast love I thought,
And so more steadily to have gone,
With wares which would sink admiration
I saw, I had Love's pinnace overfraught;
    Every thy hair for love to work upon
Is much too much, some fitter must be sought;
    For, nor in nothing, nor in things
Extreme, and scattering-bright, can love inhere;
    Then as an angel face and wings
Of air, not pure as it, yet pure doth wear,

So thy love may be my love's sphere;
Just such disparity
As is, twixt air's and angel's purity,
'Twixt women's love, and men's will ever be.

BREAK OF DAY

'Tis true, 'tis day; what though it be?
O wilt thou therefore rise from me?
Why should we rise, because 'tis light?
Did we lie down, because 'twas night?
Love, which in spite of darkness brought us hither,
Should in despite of light keep us together.

Light hath no tongue, but is all eye;
If it could speak as well as spy,
This were the worst that it could say,
That being well, I fain would stay,
And that I loved my heart and honor so,
That I would not from him, that had them, go.

Must business thee from hence remove?
Oh, that's the worst disease of love;
The poor, the foul, the false, Love can
Admit, but not the busied man.
He which hath business, and makes love, doth do
Such wrong, as when a married man should woo.

THE ANNIVERSARY

All Kings, and all their favorites,
All glory of honors, beauties, wits,

The sun itself (which makes times, as these pass)
Is elder by a year now, than it was,
When thou and I first one another saw:
All other things to their destruction draw;
    Only our love hath no decay:
This no to-morrow hath, nor yesterday;
Running, it never runs from us away,
But truly keeps his first-last-everlasting day.

    Two graves must hide thine and my corse;
    If one might, death were no divorce;
Alas! as well as other princes, we,
(Who prince enough in one another be)
Must leave at last in death these eyes, and ears,
Oft fed with true oaths, and with sweet salt tears.
    But souls where nothing dwells but love,
(All other thoughts being inmates) then shall prove
This, or a love increased, there above,
When bodies to their graves, souls from their graves remove.

    And then we shall be throughly blest:
    But now no more than all the rest.
Here upon earth we are kings, and none but we
Can be such kings, nor of such subjects be;
Who is so safe as we, where none can do
Treason to us, except one of us two?
    True and false fears let us refrain:
Let us love nobly, and live, and add again
Years and years unto years, till we attain
To write threescore: this is the second of our reign.

A VALEDICTION OF MY NAME IN THE WINDOW

I.

My name engraved herein,
Doth contribute my firmness to this glass,
Which, ever since that charm, hath been
As hard as that which graved it was;
Thine eye will give it price enough to mock
The diamonds of either rock.

II.

'Tis much that glass should be
As all-confessing and through-shine as I;
'Tis more that it shows thee to thee,
And clear reflects thee to thine eye.
But all such rules Love's magic can undo,
Here you see me, and I am you.

III.

As no one point nor dash,
Which are but accessories to this name,
The showers and tempests can outwash,
So shall all times find me the same;
You this entireness better may fulfill,
Who have the pattern with you still.

IV.

Or if too hard and deep
This learning be, for a scratched name to teach,
It as a given death's-head keep,
Lovers' mortality to preach;

Or think this ragged bony name to be
My ruinous anatomy.

V.

Then as all my souls be
Emparadised in you (in whom alone
I understand, and grow, and see)
The rafters of my body, bone,
Being still with you, the muscle, sinew, and vein,
Which tile this house, will come again.

VI.

Till my return, repair
And recompact my scattered body so,
As all the virtuous powers, which are
Fixed in the stars, are said to flow
Into such characters as graved be,
When those stars had supremacy.

VII.

So since this name was cut,
When love and grief their exaltation had,
No door 'gainst this name's influence shut;
As much more loving, as more sad,
'Twill make thee; and thou should'st, till I return,
Since I die daily, daily mourn.

VIII.

When thy inconsiderate hand
Flings ope this casement, with my trembling name,
To look on one, whose wit or land
New battery to thy heart may frame,

Then think this name alive, and that thou thus
In it offend'st my Genius.

IX.

And when thy melted maid,
Corrupted by thy lover's gold or page,
His letter at thy pillow hath laid,
Disputed it, and tamed thy rage,
And thou begin'st to thaw toward him for this,
May my name step in, and hide his.

X.

And if this treason go
To an overt act, and that thou write again:
In superscribing, my name flow
Into thy fancy from the pen,
So in forgetting thou rememberest right,
And unaware to me shalt write.

XI.

But glass and lines must be
No means our firm substantial love to keep;
Near death inflicts this lethargy,
And thus I murmur in my sleep;
Impute this idle talk to that I go;
For dying men talk often so.

TWICKENHAM GARDEN

Blasted with sighs, and surrounded with tears,
Hither I come to seek the spring,
And at mine eyes, and at mine ears,

Receive such balm as else cures every thing:
    But O, self-traitor, I do bring
The spider Love, which transubstantiates all,
    And can convert manna to gall,
And that this place may thoroughly be thought
True Paradise, I have the serpent brought.

'Twere wholesomer for me, that winter did
    Benight the glory of this place,
    And that a grave frost did forbid
These trees to laugh, and mock me to my face;
    But that I may not this disgrace
Endure, nor leave this garden, Love, let me
    Some senseless piece of this place be;
Make me a mandrake, so I may grow here,
Or a stone fountain weeping out the year.

Hither with crystal vials, lovers, come,
    And take my tears, which are Love's wine,
    And try your mistress' tears at home,
For all are false, that taste not just like mine;
    Alas! hearts do not in eyes shine,
Nor can you more judge women's thoughts by tears,
    Than by her shadow, what she wears.
O, perverse sex, where none is true but she,
Who's therefore true, because her truth kills me.

VALEDICTION TO HIS BOOK

I'll tell thee now (dear love) what thou shalt do
    To anger destiny, as she doth us;
    How I shall stay, though she eloign me thus,

And how posterity shall know it too;
How thine may out-endure
Sibyl's glory, and obscure
Her, who from Pindar could allure,
And her, through whose help Lucan is not lame,
And her, whose book (they say) Homer did find and name.

Study our manuscripts, those myriads
Of letters, which have past 'twixt thee and me,
Thence write our annals, and in them will be
To all, whom love's subliming fire invades,
Rule and example found;
There, the faith of any ground
No schismatic will dare to wound,
That sees, how love this grace to us affords,
To make, to keep, to use, to be these his records.

This book as long-lived as the elements,
Or as the world's form, this all-graved tome,
In cipher writ, or new-made idiom;
We for Love's clergy only are instruments;
When this book is made thus,
Should again the ravenous
Vandals and Goths invade us,
Learning were safe in this our universe,
Schools might learn sciences, spheres music, angels verse.

Here Love's divines (since all divinity
Is love or wonder) may find all they seek,
Whether abstract spiritual love they like,
Their souls exhaled with what they do not see;
Or, loath so to amuse

Faith's infirmity, they choose
Something, which they may see and use;
For though mind be the heaven, where Love doth sit,
Beauty a convenient type may be to figure it.

Here more than in their books may lawyers find,
Both by what titles mistresses are ours,
And how prerogative these states devours,
Transferred from Love himself to womankind,
Who, though from heart and eyes
They exact great subsidies,
Forsake him, who on them relies,
And for the cause honor or conscience give,
Chimeras, vain as they, or their prerogative.

Here statesmen (or of them they which can read)
May of their occupation find the grounds,
Love and their art alike it deadly wounds,
If to consider what 'tis, one proceed;
In both they do excel,
Who the present govern well,
Whose weakness none doth, or dares tell;
In this thy book such will their nothing see,
As in the Bible some can find out alchemy.

Thus vent thy thoughts; abroad I'll study thee,
As he removes far off, that great heights takes:
How great love is, presence best trial makes,
But absence tries, how long this love will be;
To take a latitude,
Sun, or stars, are fitliest viewed
At their brightest; but to conclude

Of longitudes, what other way have we,
But to mark when, and where the dark eclipses be?

COMMUNITY

Good we must love, and must hate ill,
For ill is ill, and good good still;
But there are things indifferent,
Which we may neither hate nor love,
But one, and then another prove,
As we shall find our fancy bent.

If then at first wise nature had
Made women either good or bad,
Then some we might hate, and some choose,
But since she did them so create,
That we may neither love nor hate,
Only this rests, all all may use.

If they were good, it would be seen;
Good is as visible as green,
And to all eyes itself betrays;
If they were bad, they could not last,
Bad doth itself and others waste,
So they deserve nor blame nor praise.

But they are ours, as fruits are ours,
He that but tastes, he that devours,
And he that leaves all, doth as well;
Changed loves are but changed sorts of meat,
And, when he hath the kernel eat,
Who doth not fling away the shell?

LOVE'S GROWTH

I scarce believe my love to be so pure
As I had thought it was,
Because it doth endure
Vicissitude and season, as the grass;
Methinks I lied all winter, when I swore
My love was infinite, if spring make it more.

But if this medicine Love, which cures all sorrow
With more, not only be no quintessence,
But mixt of all stuffs, vexing soul or sense,
And of the sun his active vigor borrow,
Love's not so pure an abstract, as they use
To say, which have no mistress but their muse;
But, as all else, being elemented too,
Love sometimes would contemplate, sometimes do.

And yet no greater, but more eminent
Love by the spring is grown;
As in the firmament
Stars by the sun are not enlarged, but shown.
Gentle love-deeds, as blossoms on a bough,
From Love's awakened root do bud out now.
If, as in water stirred, more circles be
Produced by one, Love such additions take,
Those, like so many spheres, but one heaven make,
For they are all concentric unto thee;

And though each spring do add to love new heat,
As princes do in times of action get

New taxes, and remit them not in peace,
No winter shall abate this spring's increase.

LOVE'S EXCHANGE

Love, any devil else but you
Would for a given soul give something too;
At court, your fellows every day
Give the art of rhyming, huntsmanship, or play
For them which were their own before;
Only I've nothing, which gave more,
But am, alas! by being lowly, lower.
I ask no dispensation now
To falsify a tear, a sigh, a vow,
I do not sue from thee to draw
A non obstante on nature's law;
These are prerogatives, they inhere
In thee and thine; none should forswear,
Except that he Love's minion were.

Give me thy weakness, make me blind
Both ways, as thou and thine, in eyes and mind:
Love, let me never know that this
Is love, or that love childish is.
Let me not know that others know
That she knows my pains, lest that so
A tender shame make me mine own new woe.

If thou give nothing, yet thou art just,
Because I would not thy first motions trust:
Small towns which stand stiff, till great shot
Enforce them, by war's law condition not;

Such in love's warfare is my case,
I may not article for grace,
Having put Love at last to show this face.

This face, by which he could command
And change the idolatry of any land;
This face, which, wheresoe'er it comes,
Can call vowed men from cloisters, dead from tombs,
And melt both poles at once, and store
Deserts with cities, and make more
Mines in the earth, than quarries were before.

For this Love is enraged with me,
Yet kills not: if I must example be
To future rebels, if the unborn
Must learn, by my being cut up and torn;
Kill and dissect me, Love; for this
Torture against thine own end is,
Racked carcasses make ill anatomies.

CONFINED LOVE

Some man unworthy to be possessor
Of old or new love, himself being false or weak,
Thought his pain and shame would be lesser
If on womankind he might his anger wreak,
And thence a law did grow,
One might but one man know;
But are other creatures so?

Are sun, moon, or stars by law forbidden
To smile where they list, or lend away their light?
Are birds divorced, or are they chidden

If they leave their mate, or lie abroad all night?
Beasts do no jointures lose,
Though they new lovers choose,
But we are made worse than those.

Whoe'er rigged fair ships to lie in harbors,
And not to seek new lands, or not to deal with all?
Or build fair houses, set trees and arbors,
Only to lock up, or else to let them fall?
Good is not good, unless
A thousand it possess,
But doth waste with greediness.

THE DREAM

Dear Love, for nothing less than thee
Would I have broke this happy dream;
It was a theme
For reason, much too strong for fantasy,
Therefore thou waked'st me wisely; yet
My dream thou brok'st not, but continued'st it:
Thou art so true, that thoughts of thee suffice
To make dreams truths, and fables histories;
Enter these arms, for since thou thought'st it best
Not to dream all my dream, let's act the rest.

As lightning or a taper's light,
Thine eyes, and not thy noise waked me;
Yet I thought thee
(For thou lov'st truth) an angel at first sight;
But when I saw thou saw'st my heart,
And knew'st my thoughts beyond an angel's art,

When thou knew'st what I dreamt, then thou knew'st when
Excess of joy would wake me, and cam'st then;
I must confess, it could not choose but be
Profane to think thee any thing but thee.

Coming and staying showed thee thee;
But rising makes me doubt that now
Thou art not thou.
That Love is weak, where fear's as strong as he;
'Tis not all spirit, pure and brave,
If mixture it of fear, shame, honor, have.
Perchance as torches, which must ready be,
Men light and put out, so thou deal'st with me,
Thou cam'st to kindle, goest to come: then I
Will dream that hope again, but else would die.

A VALEDICTION OF WEEPING

Let me pour forth
My tears before thy face, whilst I stay here,
For thy face coins them, and thy stamp they bear:
And by this mintage they are something worth,
For thus they be
Pregnant of thee;
Fruits of much grief they are, emblems of more;
When a tear falls, that Thou fallst, which it bore;
So thou and I are nothing then, when on a divers shore.

On a round ball
A workman, that hath copies by, can lay
A Europe, Afric, and an Asia,
And quickly make that, which was nothing, all:

So doth each tear,
Which thee doth wear,
A globe, yea, world by that impression grow,
Till thy tears mixed with mine do overflow
This world, by waters sent from thee, my hear'n dissolved so.

O more than moon,
Draw not up seas to drown me in thy sphere;
Weep me not dead in thine arms, but forbear
To teach the sea, what it may do too soon;
Let not the wind
Example find
To do me more harm, than it purposeth:
Since thou and I sigh one another's breath,
Whoe'er sighs most, is cruellest, and hastes the other's death.

LOVE'S ALCHEMY

Some that have deeper digged Love's mine than I,
Say, where his centric happiness doth lie:
I've loved, and got, and told,
But should I love, get, tell, till I were old,
I should not find that hidden mystery;
Oh, 'tis imposture all:
And as no chemic yet the Elixir got,
But glorifies his pregnant pot,
If by the way to him befall
Some odoriferous thing, or medicinal,
So lovers dream a rich and long delight,
But get a winter-seeming summer's night.
Our ease, our thrift, our honor, and vur day
Shall we for this vain bubble's shadow pay?

Ends love in this, that any man
Can be as happy as I can, if he can
Endure the short scorn of a bridegroom's play?
That loving wretch that swears,
'Tis not the bodies marry, but the minds,
Which he in her angelic finds,
Would swear as justly, that he hears,
In that day's rude hoarse minstrelsy, the spheres:
Hope not for mind in women; at their best
Sweetness and wit, they're but mummy, possest.

THE FLEA

Mark but this flea, and mark in this,
How little that which thou deniest me is;
Me it sucked first, and now sucks thee,
And in this flea our two bloods mingled be;
Confess it. This cannot be said
A sin, or shame, or loss of maidenhead,
Yet this enjoys, before it woo,
And pampered swells with one blood made of two,
And this, alas! is more than we could do.

Oh stay, three lives in one flea spare,
Where we almost, nay, more than married are.
This flea is you and I, and this
Our marriage-bed, and marriage-temple is;
Though parents grudge, and you, we are met,
And cloistered in these living walls of jet.
Though use make you apt to kill me,
Let not to that self-murder added be,
And sacrilege, three sins in killing three.

Cruel and sudden, hast thou since
Purpled thy nail in blood of innocence?
Wherein could this flea guilty be,
Except in that blood which it sucked from thee?
Yet thou triumph'st, and say'st that thou
Find'st not thyself, nor me the weaker now;
'Tis true; then learn how false fears be:
Just so much honor, when thou yield'st to me,
Will waste, as this flea's death took life from thee.

THE CURSE

Whoever guesses, thinks, or dreams he knows
Who is my mistress, wither by this curse;
His only for his purse
May some dull whore to love dispose,
And then yield unto all that are his foes;
May he be scorned by one, whom all else scorn,
Forswear to others, what to her he hath sworn,
With fear of missing, shame of getting, torn.

Madness his sorrow, gout his cramp may he
Make, by but thinking who hath made him such:
And may he feel no touch
Of conscience, but of fame, and be
Anguished, not that 'twas sin, but that 'twas she:
In early and long scarceness may he rot,
For land which had been his, if he had not
Himself incestuously an heir begot.

May he dream treason, and believe that he
Meant to perform it, and confess, and die,

And no record tell why:
His sons, which none of his may be,
Inherit nothing but his infamy:
Or may he so long parasites have fed,
That he would fain be theirs, whom he hath bred,
And at the last be circumcised for bread.

The venom of all step-dames, gamester's gall,
What tyrants and their subjects interwish,
What plants, mine, beasts, fowl, fish
Can contribute, all ill, which all
Prophets or poets spake; and all, which shall
Be annexed in schedules unto this by me,
Fall on that man; for if it be a she,
Nature beforehand hath outcursed me.

AN ANATOMY OF THE WORLD

Wherein, by occasion of the untimely death of Misress Elizabeth Drury, the frailty and the decay of this whole world is represented

THE FIRST ANNIVERSARY

To the Praise of the Dead, and the Anatomy

Well died the world, that we might live to see
This world of wit in his anatomy:
No evil wants his good; so wilder heirs
Bedew their fathers' tombs with forced tears,
Whose state requites their loss: while thus we gain,
Well may we walk in blacks, but not complain.
Yet how can I consent the world is dead,
While this Muse lives? which in his spirit's stead
Seems to inform a world, and bids it be,
In spite of loss or frail mortality?
And thou the subject of this well-born thought,
Thrice-noble maid, could'st not have found nor sought
A fitter time to yield to thy sad fate,

Than while this spirit lives, that can relate
Thy worth so well to our last nephews' eyne,
That they shall wonder both at his and thine:
Admired match, where strives in mutual grace
The cunning pencil and the comely face!
A task, which thy fair goodness made too much
For the bold pride of vulgar pens to touch:
Enough is us to praise them that praise thee,
And say that but enough those praises be,
Which, hadst thou lived, had hid their fearful head
From the angry checkings of thy modest red:
Death bars reward and shame; when envy's gone,
And gain, 'tis safe to give the dead their own.
As then the wise Egyptians wont to lay
More on their tombs than houses (these of clay,
But those of brass or marble were) so we
Give more unto thy ghost than unto thee.
Yet what we give to thee, thou gavest to us,
And may'st but thank thyself, for being thus:
Yet what thou gav'st and wert, O, happy maid,
Thy grace professed all due, where 'tis repaid.
So these high songs, that to thee suited been,
Serre but to sound thy Maker's praise and thine;
Which thy dear soul as sweetly sings to him
Amid the choir of saints and seraphim,
As any angels' tongues can sing of thee;
The subjects differ, though the skill agree:
For as by infant years men judge of age,
Thy early love, thy virtues did presage
What high part thou bear'st in those best of songs,
Whereto no burden, nor no end belongs.
Sing on, thou virgin soul, whose lossful gain

Thy love-sick parents have bewailed in vain;
Ne'er may thy name be in our songs forgot,
Till we shall sing thy ditty and thy note.

When that rich soul, which to her heaven is gone,
Whom all do celebrate, who know they've one,
(For who is sure he hath a soul, unless
It see and judge and follow worthiness,
And by deeds praise it? he who doth not this,
May lodge an inmate soul, but 'tis not his)
When that queen ended here her progress-time,
And as to her standing-house to heaven did climb,
Where, loth to make the saints attend her long,
She's now a part both of the choir and song;
This world in that great earthquake languished;
For in a common bath of tears it bled,
Which drew the strongest vital spirits out,
But succored them with a perplexed doubt,
Whether the world did lose, or gain in this;
Because (since now no other way there is
But goodness, to see her, whom all would see,
All must endeavor to be good as she)
This great consumption to a fever turned,
And so the world had fits; it joyed, it mourned;
And, as men think that agues physic are,
And the ague being spent, give over care,
So thou, sick world, mistak'st thyself to be
Well, when alas thou art in a lethargy:
Her death did wound and tame thee then, and than
Thou might'st have better spared the sun, or man,
That wound was deep; but 'tis more misery,
That thou hast lost thy sense and memory.

'Twas heavy then to hear thy voice of moan,
But this is worse, that thou art speechless grown.
Thou hast forgot thy name thou hadst; thou wast
Nothing but she, and her thou hast o'erpast.
For as a child kept from the font until
A prince, expected long, come to fulfill
The ceremonies, thou unnamed hadst laid,
Had not her coming thee her palace made:
Her name defined thee, gave thee form and frame,
And thou forget'st to celebrate thy name.
Some months she hath been dead (but being dead,
Measures of time are all determined)
But long she hath been away, long, long: yet none
Offers to tell us, who it is that's gone;
But as in states doubtful of future heirs,
When sickness without remedy impairs
The present prince, they're loth it should be said,
The prince doth languish, or the prince is dead,
So mankind, feeling now a general thaw,
A strong example gone, equal to law,
The cement, which did faithfully compact
And glue all virtues, now resolved and slacked,
Thought it some blasphemy to say she was dead,
Or that our weakness was discovered
In that confession; therefore spoke no more
Than tongues, the soul being gone, the loss deplore
But, though it be too late to succor thee,
Sick world, yea, dead, yea, putrefied, since she,
Thy intrinsic balm and thy preservative,
Can never be renewed, thou never live,
I (since no man can make thee live) will try
What we may gain by thy anatomy.

Her death hath taught us dearly that thou art
Corrupt and mortal in thy purest part.
Let no man say, the world itself being dead,
'Tis labor lost to have discovered
The world's infirmities, since there is none
Alive to study this dissection;
For there's a kind of world remaining still;
Though she, which did inanimate and fill
The world, be gone, yet in this last long night
Her ghost doth walk, that is, a glimmering light,
A faint weak love of virtue, and of good
Reflects from her on them which understood
Her worth; and though she have shut in all day,
The twilight of her memory doth stay,
Which, from the carcass of the old world free,
Creates a new world, and new creatures be
Produced: the matter and the stuff of this
Her virtue, and the form our practice is:
And though to be thus elemented arm
These creatures from home-born intrinsic harm,
(For all assumed unto this dignity,
So many weedless paradises be,
Which of themselves produce no venomous sin,
Except some foreign serpent bring it in)
Yet, because outward storms the strongest break,
And strength itself by confidence grows weak,
This new world may be safer, being told
The dangers and diseases of the old;
For with due temper men do then forego
Or covet things, when they their true worth know.
There is no health; physicians say that we
At best enjoy but a neutrality;

And can there be worse sickness than to know,
That we are never well, nor can be so?
We are born ruinous: poor mothers cry,
That children come not right nor orderly,
Except they headlong come and fall upon
An ominous precipitation.
How witty is ruin, how importunate
Upon mankind! it labored to frustrate
Even God's purpose, and made woman, sent
For man's relief, cause of his languishment;
They were to good ends, and they are so still,
But accessary, and principal in ill;
For that first marriage was our funeral;
One woman at one blow then killed us all;
And singly one by one they kill us now.
We do delightfully ourselves allow
To that consumption, and, profusely blind,
We kill ourselves to propagate our kind;
And yet we do not that; we are not men:
There is not now that mankind, which was then,
Whenas the sun and man did seem to strive,
(Joint-tenants of the world) who should survive;
When stag and raven, and the long-lived tree,
Compared with man, died in minority;
When, if a slow-paced star had stolen away
From the observer's marking, he might stay
Two or three hundred years to see it again,
And then make up his observation plain;
When, as the age was long, the size was great;
Man's growth confessed and recompensed the meat;
So spacious and large, that every soul
Did a fair kingdom and large realm control;

And when the very stature thus erect,
Did that soul a good way towards heaven direct;
Where is this mankind now? who lives to age,
Fit to be made Methusalem his page;
Alas! we scarce live long enough to try
Whether a true-made clock run right or lie.
Old grandsires talk of yesterday with sorrow,
And for our children we reserve to-morrow.
So short is life, that every peasant strives,
In a torn house, or field, to have three lives.
And, as in lasting, so in length, is man
Contracted to an inch, who was a span;
For had a man at first in forests strayed
Or shipwracked in the sea, one would have laid
A wager, that an elephant or whale
That met him, would not hastily assail
A thing so equal to him; now alas!
The fairies and the pigmies well may pass
As credible; mankind decays so soon,
We're scarce our fathers' shadows cast at noon:
Only death adds to our length; nor are we grown
In stature to be men, till we are none.
But this were light, did our less volume hold
All the old text, or had we changed to gold
Their silver, or disposed into less glass
Spirits of virtue, which then scattered was:
But 'tis not so: we're not retired but damped;
And, as our bodies, so our minds are cramped:
'Tis shrinking, not close weaving, that hath thus
In mind and body both bedwarfed us.
We seem ambitious God's whole work to undo;
Of nothing he made us, and we strive, too,

To bring ourselves to nothing back; and we
Do what we can to do it so soon as he:
With new diseases on ourselves we war,
And with new physic, a worse engine far.
This Man, this world's vice-emperor, in whom
All faculties, all graces are at home,
And if in other creatures they appear,
They're but man's ministers and legates there,
To work on their rebellions, and reduce
Them to civility and to man's use;
This man, whom God did woo, and, loth to attend
Till man came up, did down to man descend;
This man so great, that all that is is his,
Oh what a trifle and poor thing he is!
If man were any thing, he's nothing now;
Help, or at least some time to waste, allow
To his other wants, yet when he did depart
With her whom we lament, he lost his heart.
She, of whom the ancients seemed to prophesy,
When they called virtues by the name of *She;*
She, in whom virtue was so much refined,
That for alloy unto so pure a mind
She took the weaker sex; she, that could drive
The poisonous tincture and the stain of Eve
Out of her thoughts and deeds, and purify
All by a true religious alchemy;
She, she is dead; she's dead: when thou know'st this,
Thou know'st how poor a trifling thing man is,
And learn'st thus much by our anatomy,
The heart being perished, no part can be free,
And that except thou feed (not banquet) on
The supernatural food, religion,

Thy better growth grows withered and scant;
Be more than Man, or thou 'rt less than an ant.
Then as mankind, so is the world's whole frame
Quite out of joint, almost created lame:
For before God had made up all the rest,
Corruption entered and depraved the best;
It seized the Angels, and then first of all
The world did in her cradle take a fall,
And turned her brains, and took a general maim,
Wronging each joint of the universal frame.
The noblest part, Man, felt it first; and then
Both beasts and plants, curst in the curse of man;
So did the world from the first hour decay,
That evening was beginning of the day;
And now the springs and summers which we see,
Like sons of women after fifty be.
And new philosophy calls all in doubt,
The element of fire is quite put out;
The sun is lost, and the earth; and no man's wit
Can well direct him where to look for it.
And freely men confess that this world's spent,
When in the planets and the firmament
They seek so many new; they see that this
Is crumbled out again to his atomies.
'Tis all in pieces, all coherence gone,
All just supply, and all relation:
Prince, subject, father, son, are things forgot,
For every man alone thinks he hath got
To be a phoenix, and that there can be
None of that kind, of which he is, but he.
This is the world's condition now, and now
She, that should all parts to reunion bow;

She, that had all magnetic force alone
To draw and fasten sundered parts in one;
She, whom wise nature had invented then,
When she observed that every sort of men
Did in their voyage in this world's sea stray,
And needed a new compass for their way;
She, that was best and first original
Of all fair copies, and the general
Steward to fate; she, whose rich eyes and breast
Gilt the West-Indies, and perfumed the East;
Whose having breathed in this world did bestow
Spice on those isles, and bade them still smell so;
And that rich India which doth gold inter,
Is but as single money coined from her;
She, to whom this world must itself refer,
As suburbs, or the microcosm of her;
She, she is dead; she's dead: when thou know'st this
Thou know'st how lame a cripple this world is,
And learn'st thus much by our anatomy,
That this world's general sickness doth not lie
In any humor, or one certain part,
But as thou saw'st it rotten at the heart,
Thou seest a hectic fever hath got hold
Of the whole substance, not to be controlled;
And that thou hast but one way not to admit
The world's infection, to be none of it.
For the world's subtlest immaterial parts
Feel this consuming wound, and age's darts.
For the world's beauty is decayed or gone,
Beauty, that's color and proportion.
We think the Heavens enjoy their spherical,
Their round proportion embracing all,

But yet their various and perplexed course,
Observed in divers ages, doth enforce
Men to find out so many eccentric parts,
Such divers downright lines, such overthwarts,
As disproportion that pure form; it tears
The firmament in eight-and-forty-shares,
And in these constellations then arise
New stars, and old do vanish from our eyes;
As though heaven suffered earthquakes, peace or war,
When new towers rise, and old demolished are.
They have impaled within a zodiac
The free-born sun, and keep twelve signs awake
To watch his steps; the Goat and Crab control
And fright him back, who else to either pole
(Did not these Tropics fetter him) might run;
For his course is not round, nor can the sun
Perfect a circle, or maintain his way
One inch direct, but where he rose to day
He comes no more, but with a cozening line,
Steals by that point, and so is serpentine,
And seeming weary of his reeling thus,
He means to sleep, being now fallen nearer us.
So of the stars, which boast that they do run
In circle still, none ends where he begun:
All their proportion's lame, it sinks, it swells;
For of meridians and parallels,
Man hath weaved out a net, and this net thrown
Upon the Heavens; and now they are his own.
Loth to go up the hill, or labor thus
To go to heaven, we make heaven come to us;
We spur, we rein the stars, and in their race
They're diversely content to obey our peace.

But keeps the earth her round proportion still?
Doth not a Tenarus or higher hill
Rise so high like a rock, that one might think
The floating moon would shipwrack there and sink?
Seas are so deep, that whales being struck today,
Perchance to-morrow scarce at middle way
Of their wished journey's end, the bottom, die:
And men, to sound depths, so much line untie,
As one might justly think that there would rise
At end thereof one of the antipodes:
If under all a vault infernal be,
(Which sure is spacious, except that we
Invent another torment, that there must
Millions into a strait hot room be thrust)
Then solidness and roundness have no place:
Are these but warts and pockholes in the face
Of the earth? Think so; but yet confess, in this
The world's proportion disfigured is;
That those two legs whereon it doth rely,
Reward and punishment, are bent awry:
And, oh! it can no more be questioned,
That beauty's best, proportion, is dead,
Since even grief itself, which now alone
Is left us, is without proportion.
She, by whose lines proportion should be
Examined, measure of all symmetry,
Whom had that ancient seen, who thought souls made
Of harmony, he would at next have said
That harmony was she, and thence infer
That souls were but resultances from her,
And did from her into our bodies go,
As to our eyes the forms from objects flow;

She, who, if those great doctors truly said
That the ark to man's proportion was made,
Had been a type for that, as that might be
A type of her in this, that contrary
Both elements and passions lived at peace
In her, who caused all civil war to cease;
She, after whom what form soe'er we see,
Is discord and rude incongruity;
She, she is dead, she's dead! when thou know'st this
Thou know'st how ugly a monster this world is;
And learn'st thus much by our anatomy,
That here is nothing to enamor thee;
And that not only faults in inward parts,
Corruptions in our brains, or in our hearts,
Poisoning the fountains, whence our actions spring,
Endanger us; but that if every thing
Be not done fitly and in proportion,
To satisfy wise and good lookers on,
Since most men be such as most think they be,
They are loathsome too by this deformity.
For Good and Well must in our actions meet;
Wicked is not much worse than indiscreet.
But beauty's other second element,
Color, and luster, now is as near spent;
And had the world his just proportion,
Were it a ring still, yet the stone is gone;
As a compassionate turquoise which doth tell,
By looking pale, the wearer is not well,
As gold falls sick, being stung with mercury,
All the world's parts of such complexion be.
When nature was most busy, the first week,
Swaddling the new-born earth, God seemed to like

That she should sport herself sometimes in play,
To mingle and vary colors every day;
And then, as though she could not make enow,
Himself his various rainbow did allow.
Sight is the noblest sense of any one,
Yet sight hath only color to feed on,
And color is decayed; summer's robe grows
Dusky, and like an oft-died garment shows.
Our blushing red, which used in cheeks to spread,
Is inward sunk, and only our souls are red.
Perchance the world might have recovered,
If she, whom we lament, had not been dead;
But she, in whom all white, and red, and blue
(Beauty's ingredients) voluntary grew,
As in an unvexed paradise; from whom
Did all things' verdure and their luster come;
Whose composition was miraculous,
Being all color, all diaphanous,
(For air and fire but thick gross bodies were,
And liveliest stones but drowsy and pale to her)
She, she is dead; she's dead: when thou know'st this,
Thou know'st how wan a ghost this our world is;
And learn'st thus much by our anatomy,
That it should more affright than pleasure thee;
And that, since all fair color then did sink,
'Tis now but wicked vanity to think
To color vicious deeds with good pretense,
Or with bought colors to illude men's sense.
Nor in aught more this world's decay appears,
Than that her influence the heaven forbears,
Or that the elements do not feel this,
The father or the mother barren is.

The clouds conceive not rain, or do not pour,
In the due birth-time, down the balmy shower;
The air doth not motherly sit on the earth,
To hatch her seasons, and give all things birth;
Spring-times were common cradles, but are tombs;
And false conceptions fill the general wombs;
The air shows such meteors, as none can see
Not only what they mean, but what they be;
Earth such new worms, as would have troubled much
The Egyptian Magi to have made more such.
What artist now dares boast that he can bring
Heaven hither, or constellate anything,
So as the influence of those stars may be
Imprisoned in an herb, or charm, or tree,
And do by touch all which those stars could do?
The art is lost, and correspondence too;
For heaven gives little, and the earth takes less,
And man least knows their trade and purposes.
If this commerce 'twixt heaven and earth were not
Embarred, and all this traffic quite forgot,
She, for whose loss we have lamented thus,
Would work more fully and powerfully on us;
Since herbs and roots by dying lose not all,
But they, yea ashes too, are medicinal,
Death could not quench her virtue so, but that
It would be (if not followed) wondered at,
And all the world would be one dying swan,
To sing her funeral praise, and vanish than.
But as some serpents' poison hurteth not,
Except it be from the live serpent shot,
So doth her virtue need her here, to fit
That unto us; she working more than it.

But she, in whom to such maturity
Virtue was grown past growth, that it must die;
She, from whose influence all impression came,
But by receiver's impotences lame;
Who, though she could not transubstantiate
All states to gold, yet gilded every state,
So that some princes have some temperance,
Some counsellors some purpose to advance
The common profit, and some people have
Some stay, no more than kings should give, to crave,
Some women have some taciturnity,
Some nunneries some grains of chastity,
She, that did thus much, and much more could do,
But that our age was iron, and rusty too;
She, she is dead; she's dead! when thou know'st this,
Thou know'st how dry a cinder this world is,
And learn'st thus much by our anatomy,
That 'tis in vain to dew or mollify
It with thy tears, or sweat, or blood: nothing
Is worth our travail, grief, or perishing,
But those rich joys, which did possess her heart,
Of which she is now partaker, and a part.
But, as in cutting up a man that's dead,
The body will not last out, to have read
On every part, and therefore men direct
Their speech to parts that are of most effect,
So the world's carcass would not last, if I
Were punctual in this anatomy;
Nor smells it well to hearers, if one tell
Them their disease, who fain would think they are well.
Here therefore be the end; and, blessed maid,
Of whom is meant whatever hath been said,

Or shall be spoken well by any tongue,
Whose name refines coarse lines, and makes prose song,
Accept this tribute, and his first year's rent,
Who, till his dark short taper's end he spent,
As oft as thy feast sees this widowed earth,
Will yearly celebrate thy second birth,
That is, thy death; for though the soul of man
Be got when man is made, 'tis born but than,
When man doth die; our body's as the womb,
And, as a midwife, death directs it home;
And you her creatures, whom she works upon,
And have your last and best concoction
From her example and her virtue, if you
In reverence to her do think it due,
That no one should her praises thus rehearse,
As matter fit for chronicle, not verse;
Vouchsafe to call to mind that God did make
A last, and lasting'st piece, a song. He spake
To Moses to deliver unto all,
That song, because he knew they would let fall
The law, the prophets, and the history,
But keep the song still in their memory:
Such an opinion in due measure, made
Me this great office boldly to invade;
Nor could incomprehensibleness deter
Me from thus trying to imprison her;
Which when I saw that a strict grave could do,
I saw not why verse might not do so too.
Verse hath a middle nature; heaven keeps souls,
The grave keeps bodies, verse the fame enrolls.

A FUNERAL ELEGY

'Tis loss to trust a tomb with such a guest,
Or to confine her in a marble chest;
Alas! what's marble, jet, or porphyry,
Prized with the chrysolite of either eye,
Or with those pearls and rubies which she was?
Join the two Indies in one tomb, 'tis glass;
And so is all to her materials,
Though every inch were ten Escurials;
Yet she's demolished; can we keep her then
In works of hands, or of the wits of men?
Can these memorials, rags of paper, give
Life to that name, by which name they must live?
Sickly, alas! short-lived, abortive be
Those carcass verses, whose soul is not she;
And can she, who no longer would be she,
(Being such a tabernacle) stoop to be
In paper wrapped, or, when she would not lie
In such an house, dwell in an elegy?
But 'tis no matter; we may well allow
Verse to live so long as the world will now,
For her death wounded it. The world contains
Princes for arms, and counsellors for brains;
Lawyers for tongues; divines for hearts, and more;
The rich for stomachs, and for backs the poor;
The officers for hands; merchants for feet,
By which remote and distant countries meet;
But those fine spirits, which do tune and set
This organ, are those pieces which beget
Wonder and love; and these were she; and she

Being spent, the world must needs decrepit be:
For since death will proceed to triumph still,
He can find nothing after her to kill,
Except the world itself, so great was she.
Thus brave and confident may nature be;
Death cannot give her such another blow,
Because she cannot such another show.
But must we say she's dead? may it not be said,
That as a sundered clock is piecemeal laid,
Not to be lost, but by the maker's hand
Repolished, without error then to stand,
Or, as the Afric Niger stream enwombs
Itself into the earth, and after comes
(Having first made a natural bridge, to pass
For many leagues) far greater than it was,
May it not be said, that her grave shall restore
Her greater, purer, firmer than before?
Heaven may say this, and joy in 't; but can, we,
Who live, and lack her here, this 'vantage see?
What is 't to us, alas! if there have been
An Angel made a Throne or Cherubin?
We lose by it; and, as aged men are glad,
Being tasteless grown, to joy in joys they had,
So now the sick-starved world must feed upon
This joy, that we had her, who now is gone.
Rejoice then, Nature and this world, that you,
Fearing the last fire's hastening to subdue
Your force and vigor, ere it were near gone,
Wisely bestowed and laid it all on one;
One, whose clear body was so pure and thin,
Because it need disguise no thought within,
'Twas but a through-light scarf her mind to enroll,

Or exhalation breathed out from her soul;
One, whom all men, who durst no more, admired,
And whom, who'er had worth enough, desired,
As, when a temple is built, saints emulate
To which of them it shall be consecrate.
But as when heaven looks on us with new eyes,
Those new stars every artist exercise;
What place they should assign to them, they doubt,
Argue, and agree not, till those stars go out;
So the world studied whose this piece should be,
Till she can be no body's else, nor she:
But like a lamp of balsamum, desired
Rather to adorn than last, she soon expired,
Clothed in her virgin-white integrity;
For marriage, though it doth not stain, doth die.
To 'scape the infirmities which wait upon
Woman, she went away before she was one;
And the world's busy noise to overcome,
Took so much death as served for opium;
For though she could not, nor could choose to die,
She hath yielded to too long an ecstasy.
He which, not knowing her sad history,
Should come to read the book of destiny,
How fair and chaste, humble and high she had been,
Much promised, much performed at not fifteen,
And measuring future things by things before,
Should turn the leaf to read, and read no more,
Would think that either destiny mistook,
Or that some leaves were torn out of the book;
But 'tis not so: Fate did but usher her
To years of reason's use, and then infer
Her destiny to herself, which liberty

She took, but for this much, thus much to die;
Her modesty not suffering her to be
Fellow-commissioner with destiny,
She did no more but die; if after her
Any shall live, which dare true good prefer,
Every such person is her delegate,
To accomplish that which should have been her fate.
They shall make up that book, and shall have thanks
Of fate and her, for filling up their blanks.
For future virtuous deeds are legacies,
Which from the gift of her example rise;
And 'tis in heaven part of spiritual mirth,
To see how well the good play her on earth.

THE SECOND ANNIVERSARY

The Harbinger to the Progress

Two souls move here, and mine (a third) must move
Paces of admiration, and of love.
Thy soul (dear virgin) whose this tribute is,
Moved from this mortal sphere to lively bliss;
And yet moves still, and still aspires to see
The world's last day, thy glory's full degree;
Like as those stars, which thou o'erlookest far,
Are in their place, and yet still moved are:
No soul (whilst with the luggage of this clay
It clogged is) can follow thee half way,
Or see thy flight, which doth our thoughts outgo
So fast, as now the lightning moves but slow.
But now thou art as high in heaven flown,
As heaven 's from us; what soul beside thine own

Can tell thy joys, or say, he can relate
Thy glorious journals in that blessed state?
I envy thee (rich soul) I envy thee,
Although I cannot yet thy glory see:
And thou (great spirit) which hers followed hast
So fast, as none can follow thine so fast,
So far, as none can follow thine so far,
(And if this flesh did not the passage bar,
Hadst caught her) let me wonder at thy flight,
Which long agone hadst lost the vulgar sight,
And now mak'st proud the better eyes, that they
Can see thee lessened in thine airy way;
So while thou mak'st her soul by progress known,
Thou mak'st a noble progress of thine own,
From this world's carcass having mounted high
To that pure life of immortality;
Since thine aspiring thoughts themselves so raise,
That more may not beseem a creature's praise,
Yet still thou vow'st her more, and every year
Mak'st a new progress, whilst thou wander'st here;
Still upward mount; and let thy Maker's praise
Honor thy Laura, and adorn thy lays:
And since thy Muse her head in heaven shrouds,
Oh, let her never stoop below the clouds!
And if those glorious sainted souls may know
Or what we do, or what we sing below,
Those acts, those songs shall still content them best,
Which praise those awful Powers, that make them blest.

Nothing could make me sooner to confess,
That this world had an everlastingness,
Than to consider that a year is run,

Since both this lower world's and the sun's sun,
The luster and the vigor of this All,
Did set, 'twere blasphemy to say, did fall.
But, as a ship which hath struck sail, doth run
By force of that force which before it won;
Or as sometimes in a beheaded man,
Though at those two Red Seas, which freely ran,
One from the trunk, another from the head,
His soul be sailed to her eternal bed,
His eyes will twinkle, and his tongue will roll,
As though he beckoned and called back his soul,
He grasps his hands, and he pulls up his feet,
And seems to reach, and to step forth to meet
His soul, when all these motions which we saw,
Are but as ice which crackles at a thaw;
Or as a lute, which in moist weather rings
Her knell alone, by cracking of her strings;
So struggles this dead world, now she is gone:
For there is motion in corruption.
As some days are at the creation named,
Before the sun, the which framed days, was framed,
So after this sun's set some show appears,
And orderly vicissitude of years;
Yet a new deluge, and of Lethe flood,
Hath drowned us all; all have forgot all good,
Forgetting her, the main reserve of all;
Yet in this deluge, gross and general,
Thou seest me strive for life; my life shall be
To be hereafter praised for praising thee,
Immortal maid, who though thou would'st refuse
The name of mother, be unto my Muse
A father, since her chaste ambition is

Yearly to bring forth such a child as this.
These hymns may work on future wits, and so
May great grand-children of thy praises grow,
And so, though not revive, embalm and spice
The world, which else would putrefy with vice.
For thus man may extend thy progeny,
Until man do but vanish, and not die.
These hymns thy issue may increase so long
As till God's great *Venite* change the song.
Thirst for that time, O my insatiate soul,
And serve thy thirst with God's safe-sealing bowl.
Be thirsty still, and drink still, till thou go
To the only health; to be hydroptic so,
Forget this rotten world; and unto thee
Let thine own times as an old story be;
Be not concerned; study not why, nor when;
Do not so much as not believe a man;
For though to err be worst, to try truths forth
Is far more business than this world is worth.
The world is but a carcass; thou art fed
By it but as a worm that carcass bred;
And why should'st thou, poor worm, consider more
When this world will grow better than before,
Than those thy fellow-worms do think upon
That carcass's last resurrection?
Forget this world and scarce think of it so
As of old clothes cast off a year ago.
To be thus stupid is alacrity;
Men thus lethargic have best memory.
Look upward, that's towards her whose happy state
We now lament not, but congratulate.
She, to whom all this world was but a stage,

Where all sat hearkening how her youthful age
Should be employed, because in all she did
Some figure of the golden times was hid;
Who could not lack whate'er this world could give,
Because she was the form that made it live;
Nor could complain that this world was unfit
To be stayed in then, when she was in it;
She, that first tried indifferent desires
By virtue, and virtue by religious fires;
She, to whose person paradise adhered,
As Courts to princes; she, whose eyes ensphered
Star-light enough, to have made the south control
(Had she been there) the starful northern pole;
She, she is gone; she's gone: when thou know'st this,
What fragmentary rubbish this world is
Thou know'st, and that it is not worth a thought;
He honors it too much, that thinks it naught.
Think then, my soul, that death is but a groom,
Which brings a taper to the outward room,
Whence thou spy'st first a little glimmering light,
And after brings it nearer to thy sight;
For such approaches doth heaven make in death:
Think thyself laboring now with broken breath,
And think those broken and soft notes to be
Division, and thy happiest harmony;
Think thee laid on thy death-bed, loose and slack;
And think that but unbinding of a pack,
To take one precious thing, thy soul, from thence;
Think thyself parched with fever's violence;
Anger thine ague more, by calling it
Thy physic; chide the slackness of the fit.
Think that thou hear'st thy knell, and think no more,

But that, as bells called thee to church before,
So this to the triumphant church calls thee;
Think Satan's sergeants round about thee be,
And think that but for legacies they thrust;
Give one thy pride, to another give thy lust;
Give them those sins, which they gave thee before,
And trust the immaculate blood to wash thy score;
Think thy friends weeping round, and think that they
Weep but because they go not yet thy way;
Think that they close thine eyes, and think in this,
That they confess much in the world amiss,
Who dare not trust a dead man's eye with that,
Which they from God and angels cover not;
Think that they shroud thee up, and think from thence,
They re-invest thee in white innocence;
Think that thy body rots, and (if so low,
Thy soul exalted so, thy thoughts can go)
Think thee a prince, who of themselves create
Worms which insensibly devour their state;
Think that they bury thee, and think that rite
Lays thee to sleep but a saint Lucie's night;
Think these things cheerfully, and if thou be
Drowsy or slack, remember then that she,
She, whose complexion was so even made,
That which of her ingredients should invade
The other three, no fear, no art could guess,
So far were all removed from more or less;
But as in mithridate, or just perfumes,
Where all good things being met, no one presumes
To govern, or to triumph on the rest,
Only because all were, no part was, best;
And as, though all do know, that quantities

Are made of lines, and lines from points arise,
None can these lines or quantities unjoint,
And say, this is a line, or this a point;
So, though the elements and humors were
In her, one could not say, this governs there;
Whose even constitution might have won
Any disease to venture on the sun,
Rather than her; and make a spirit fear,
That he to disuniting subject were;
To whose proportions if we would compare
Cubes, they're unstable; circles, angular;
She, who was such a chain as fate employs
To bring mankind all fortunes it enjoys,
So fast, so even wrought, as one would think
No accident could threaten any link;
She, she embraced a sickness, gave it meat,
The purest blood and breath that e'er it eat;
And hath taught us, that though a good man hath
Title to heaven, and plead it by his faith,
And though he may pretend a conquest, since
Heaven was content to suffer violence;
Yea, though he plead a long possession, too,
(For they're in heaven on earth, who heaven's works do)
Though he had right, and power, and place before,
Yet death must usher and unlock the door;
Think further on thyself, my soul, and think
How thou at first wast made but in a sink;
Think, that it argued some infirmity,
That those two souls, which then thou found'st in me,
Thou fed'st upon, and drew'st into thee both
My second soul of sense, and first of growth;
Think but how poor thou wast, how obnoxious,

When a small lump of flesh could poison thus:
This curdled milk, this poor unlittered whelp,
My body, could, beyond escape or help,
Infect thee with original sin, and thou
Could'st neither then refuse, nor leave it now;
Think, that no stubborn sullen anchorite,
Which fixed to a pillar, or a grave, doth sit
Bedded, and bathed in all his ordures, dwells
So foully as our souls in their first-built cells;
Think in how poor a prison thou dost lie,
After enabled but to suck, and cry;
Think, when 'twas grown to most, 'twas a poor inn,
A province packed up in two yards of skin,
And that usurped, or threatened with a rage
Of sicknesses, or their true mother, Age;
But think that death hath now enfranchised thee,
Thou hast thy expansion now, and liberty;
Think, that a rusty piece discharged is flown
In pieces, and the bullet is his own,
And freely flies; this to thy soul allow;
Think thy shell broke, think thy soul hatched but now;
And think this slow-paced soul, which late did cleave
To a body, and went but by the body's leave,
Twenty perchance or thirty mile a day,
Dispatches in a minute all the way
'Twixt heaven and earth; she stays not in the air,
To look what meteors there themselves prepare;
She carries no desire to know, nor sense,
Whether the air's middle region be intense;
For the clement of fire, she doth not know,
Whether she passed by such a place or no;
She baits not at the moon, nor cares to try

Whether in that new world men live and die;
Venus retards her not, to inquire how she
Can (being one star) Hesper and Vesper be;
He, that charmed Argus' eyes, sweet Mercury,
Works not on her, who now is grown all eye;
Who, if she meet the body of the sun,
Goes through, not staying till his course be run;
Who finds in Mars's camp no corps of guard,
Nor is by Jove, nor by his father, barred,
But ere she can consider how she went,
At once is at and through the firmament.
And, as these stars were but so many beads
Strung on one string, speed undistinguished leads
Her through those spheres, as through the beads a string,
Whose quick succession makes it still one thing:
As doth the pith, which, lest our bodies slack,
Strings fast the little bones of neck and back,
So by the soul doth death string heaven and earth;
For when our soul enjoys this her third birth,
(Creation gave her one, a second Grace)
Heaven is as near and present to her face,
As colors are and objects in a room,
Where darkness was before, when tapers come.
This must, my soul, thy long-short progress be
To advance these thoughts; remember then that she,
She, whose fair body no such prison was,
But that a soul might well be pleased to pass
An age in her; she, whose rich beauty lent
Mintage to other beauties, for they went
But for so much as they were like to her;
She, in whose body (if we dare prefer
This low world to so high a mark as she)

The western treasure, eastern spicery,
Europe and Afric, and the unknown rest
Were easily found, or what in them was best;
(And when we've made this large discovery
Of all, in her some one part then will be
Twenty such parts, whose plenty and riches is
Enough to make twenty such worlds as this)
She, whom had they known, who did first betroth
The tutelar angels, and assigned one both
To nations, cities, and to companies,
To functions, offices, and dignities,
And to each several man, to him, and him,
They would have given her one for every limb;
She, of whose soul if we may say, 'twas gold,
Her body was the electrum, and did hold
Many degrees of that; we understood
Her by her sight; her pure and eloquent blood
Spoke in her cheeks, and so distinctly wrought,
That one might almost say her body thought;
She, she thus richly and largely housed, is gone,
And chides us, slow-paced snails, who crawl upon
Our prison's prison, earth, nor think us well,
Longer than whilst we bear our brittle shell.
But 'twere but little to have changed our room,
If, as we were in this our living tomb
Oppressed with ignorance, we still were so.
Poor soul, in this thy flesh what dost thou know?
Thou know'st thyself so little, as thou know'st not
How thou didst die, nor how thou wast begot;
Thou neither know'st, how thou at first cam'st in,
Nor how thou took'st the poison of man's sin;
Nor dost thou, (though thou know'st that thou art so)

By what way thou art made immortal, know.
Thou art too narrow, wretch, to comprehend
Even thyself, yea, though thou would'st but bend
To know thy body. Have not all souls thought
For many ages, that our body is wrought
Of air and fire, and other elements?
And now they think of new ingredients;
And one soul thinks one, and another way
Another thinks, and 'tis an even lay.
Know'st thou but how the stone doth enter in
The bladder's cave, and never break the skin?
Know'st thou how blood, which to the heart doth flow,
Doth from one ventricle to the other go?
And for the putrid stuff, which thou dost spit,
Know'st thou how thy lungs have attracted it?
There are no passages; so that there is
(For ought thou know'st) piercing of substances.
And of those many opinions, which men raise
Of nails and hairs, dost thou know which to praise?
What hope have we to know ourselves, when we
Know not the least things which for our use be?
We see in authors, too stiff to recant,
A hundred controversies of an ant;
And yet one watches, starves, freezes, and sweats,
To know but catechisms and alphabets
Of unconcerning things, matters of fact,
How others on our stage their parts did act,
What Caesar did, yea, and what Cicero said;
Why grass is green, or why our blood is red,
Are mysteries which none have reached unto;
In this low form, poor soul, what wilt thou do?
Oh! when will thou shake off this pedantry,

Of being taught by sense and fantasy?
Thou look'st through spectacles; small things seem great
Below; but up unto the watch-tower get,
And see all things despoiled of fallacies:
Thou shalt not peep through lattices of eyes,
Nor hear through labyrinths of ears, nor learn
By circuit or collections to discern;
In heaven thou straight know'st all concerning it,
And what concerns it not shalt straight forget.
There thou (but in no other school) may'st be
Perchance as learned and as full as she;
She, who all libraries had thoroughly read
At home in her own thoughts, and practiced
So much good, as would make as many more;
She, whose example they must all implore,
Who would or do, or think well, and confess
That all the virtuous actions they express,
Are but a new and worse edition
Of her some one thought, or one action;
She who in the art of knowing Heaven was grown
Here upon earth to such perfection,
That she hath, ever since to heaven she came,
In a far fairer print but read the same;
She, she not satisfied with all this weight,
(For so much knowledge as would overfreight
Another, did but ballast her) is gone.
As well to enjoy, as get, perfection,
And calls us after her, in that she took
(Taking herself) our best and worthiest book.
Return not, my soul, from this ecstasy,
And meditation of what thou shalt be,
To earthly thoughts, till it to thee appear,

With whom thy conversation must be there.
With whom wilt thou converse? what station
Canst thou choose out free from infection,
That will not give thee theirs, nor drink in thine?
Shalt thou not find a spongy slack divine
Drink and suck in the instructions of great men,
And for the word of God vent them again?
Are there not some courts (and then no things be
So like as courts) which in this let us see,
That wits and tongues of libellers are weak,
Because they do more ill, than these can speak?
The poison's gone through all; poisons affect
Chiefly the chiefest parts; but some effect
In nails, and hairs, yea excrements, will show;
So lies the poison of sin in the most low.
Up, up, my drowsy soul, where thy new ear
Shall in the angels' songs no discord hear;
Where thou shalt see the blessed Mother-maid
Joy in not being that, which men have said;
Where she's exalted more for being good,
Than for her interest of motherhood;
Up to those Patriarchs, which did longer sit
Expecting Christ, than they've enjoyed him yet;
Up to those Prophets, which now gladly see
Their prophesies grown to be history;
Up to the Apostles, who did bravely run
All the sun's course, with more light than the sun;
Up to those Martyrs, who did calmly bleed
Oil to the Apostle's lamps, dew to their seed;
Up to those Virgins, who thought that almost
They made joint-tenants with the Holy Ghost,
If they to any should his temple give;

Up, up, for in that squadron there doth live
She, who hath carried thither new degrees
(As to their number) to their dignities;
She, who being to herself a state, enjoyed
All royalties, which any state employed;
For she made wars, and triumphed; reason still
Did not o'erthrow, but rectify her will;
And she made peace; for no peace is like this,
That beauty and chastity together kiss;
She did high justice; for she crucified
Every first motion of rebellious pride;
And she gave pardons, and was liberal,
For, only herself except, she pardoned all;
She coined; in this, that her impression gave
To all our actions all the worth they have;
She gave protections; the thoughts of her breast
Satan's rude officers could ne'er arrest.
As these prerogatives being met in one,
Made her a sovereign state, Religion
Made her a church; and these two made her all.
She, who was all this all, and could not fall
To worse, by company, (for she was still
More antidote, than all the world was ill)
She, she doth leave it, and by death survive
All this in heaven; whither who doth not strive
The more because she's there, he doth not know
That accidental joys in heaven do grow.
But pause, my soul, and study, ere thou fall
On accidental joys, the essential;
Still before accessories do abide
A trial, must the principal be tried;
And what essential joy canst thou expect

Here upon earth? what permanent effect
Of transitory causes? Dost thou love
Beauty? (and beauty worthiest is to move)
Poor cozened cozener, *that* she, and *that* thou,
Which did begin to love, are neither now;
You are both fluid, changed since yesterday;
Next day repairs (but ill) last day's decay;
Nor are (although the river keep the name)
Yesterday's waters and today's the same,
So flows her face, and thine eyes; neither now,
That saint nor pilgrim which your loving vow
Concerned, remains; but whilst you think you be
Constant, you are hourly in inconstancy.
Honor may have pretense unto our love,
Because that God did live so long above
Without this honor, and then loved it so,
That he at last made creatures to bestow
Honor on him; not that he needed it,
But that to his hands man might grow more fit.
But since all honors from inferiors flow,
(For they do give it; princes do but show
Whom they would have so honored) and that this
On such opinions and capacities
Is built, as rise and fall, to more and less,
Alas! 'tis but a casual happiness.
Hath ever any man to himself assigned
This or that happiness to arrest his mind,
But that another man, which takes a worse,
Thinks him a fool for having ta'en that course?
They who did labor Babel's tower to erect,
Might have considered that for that effect
All this whole solid earth could not allow,

Nor furnish forth materials enow,
And that his center, to raise such a place,
Was far too little to have been the base;
No more affords this world foundation
To erect true joy, were all the means in one.
But as the heathen made them several gods
Of all God's benefits, and all his rods,
(For as the wine and corn and onions are
Gods unto them, so agues be, and war)
And as by changing that whole precious gold
To such small copper coins, they lost the old,
And lost their only God, who ever must
Be sought alone, and not in such a thrust;
So much mankind true happiness mistakes;
No joy enjoys that man, that many makes.
Then, soul, to thy first pitch work up again;
Know that all lines which circles do contain,
For once that they the center touch, do touch
Twice the circumference; and be thou such;
Double on heaven thy thoughts; on earth employed,
All will not serve; only who have enjoyed
The sight of God in fulness, can think it;
For it is both the object and the wit;
This is essential joy, where neither he
Can suffer diminution, nor we;
'Tis such a full and such a filling good,
Had the angels once looked on him, they had stood.
To fill the place of one of them, or more,
She, whom we celebrate, is gone before;
She, who had here so much essential joy,
As no chance could distract, much less destroy;
Who with God's presence was acquainted so,

(Hearing, and speaking to him) as to know
His face in any natural stone or tree,
Better than when in images they be;
Who kept by diligent devotion
God's image in such reparation
Within her heart, that what decay was grown,
Was her first parent's fault, and not her own;
Who, being solicited to any act,
Still heard God pleading his safe precontract;
Who by a faithful confidence was here
Betrothed to God, and now is married there;
Whose twilights were more clear than our mid-day;
Who dreamt devoutlier than most use to pray;
Who being here filled with grace, yet strove to be
Both where more grace, and more capacity
At once is given; she to heaven is gone,
Who made this world in some proportion
A heaven, and here became unto us all,
Joy (as our joys admit) essential.
But could this low world joys essential touch,
Heaven's accidental joys would pass them much.
How poor and lame must then our casual be?
If thy prince will his subjects to call thee
My Lord, and this do swell thee, thou art than,
By being greater, grown to be less man.
When no physician of redress can speak,
A joyful casual violence may break
A dangerous apostem in thy breast;
And whilst thou joy'st in this, the dangerous rest,
The bag may rise up, and so strangle thee.
Whate'er was casual, may ever be:
What should the nature change? or make the same

Certain, which was but casual when it came?
All casual joy doth loud and plainly say,
Only by coming, that it can away.
Only in heaven joy's strength is never spent,
And accidental things are permanent.
Joy of a soul's arrival ne'er decays,
(For that soul ever joys, and ever stays)
Joy, that their last great consummation
Approaches in the resurrection,
When earthly bodies more celestial
Shall be, than angels were, (for they could fall)
This kind of joy doth every day admit
Degrees of growth, but none of losing it.
In this fresh joy, 'tis no small part, that she,
She, in whose goodness he that names degree,
Doth injure her; ('tis loss to be called best,
There where the stuff is not such as the rest)
She, who left such a body, as even she
Only in heaven could learn, how it can be
Made better; for she rather was two souls,
Or like to full on-both-sides-written rolls,
Where eyes might read upon the outward skin
As strong records for God, as minds within;
She, who, by making full perfection grow,
Pieces a circle, and still keeps it so,
Longed for, and longing for 't, to heaven is gone,
Where she receives and gives addition.
Here, in a place, where misdevotion frames
A thousand prayers to saints, whose very names
The ancient church knew not, heaven knows not yet,
And where what laws of poetry admit,
Laws of religion have at least the same,

Immortal Maid, I might invoke thy name.
Could any saint provoke that appetite,
Thou here should'st make me a French convertite,
But thou would'st not; nor would'st thou be content
To take this, for my second year's true rent,
Did this coin bear any other stamp than his
That gave thee power to do, me, to say this:
Since his will is that to posterity
Thou should'st for life and death a pattern be,
And that the world should notice have of this,
The purpose and the authority is his;
Thou art the proclamation; and I am
The trumpet, at whose voice the people came.

FURTHER POEMS

THE ECSTASY

Where, like a pillow on a bed,
A pregnant bank swelled up, to rest
The violet's reclining head,
Sat we two, one another's best;
Our hands were firmly cemented
By a fast balm, which thence did spring,
Our eye-beams twisted, and did thread
Our eyes upon one double string;
So to engraft our hands as yet
Was all the means to make us one,
And pictures in our eyes to get
Was all our propagation.
As 'twixt two equal armies Fate
Suspends uncertain victory,
Our souls (which, to advance our state,
Were gone out) hung 'twixt her and me;
And whilst our souls negotiate there,
We like sepulchral statues lay,
All day the same our postures were,

And we said nothing all the day.
If any, so by love refined,
That he soul's language understood,
And by good love were grown all mind,
Within convenient distance stood,
He (though he knew not which soul spake,
Because both meant, both spake the same)
Might thence a new concoction take,
And part far purer than he came.
This ecstasy doth unperplex
(We said) and tell us what we love;
We see by this, it was not sex,
We see we saw not what did move:
But as all several souls contain
Mixture of things they know not what,
Love these mixt souls doth mix again,
And makes both one, each this and that,
A single violet transplant,
The strength, the color, and the size
(All which before was poor and scant)
Redoubles still and multiplies.
When love with one another so
Inter-animates two souls,
That abler soul, which thence doth flow,
Defects of loneliness controls.
We then, who are this new soul, know
Of what we are composed and made;
For the atomies, of which we grow,
Are soul, whom no change can invade.
But, O alas! so long, so far
Our bodies why do we forbear?
They are ours, though not we; we are

The intelligences, they the spheres,
We owe them thanks, because they thus
Did us to us at first convey,
Yielded their sense's force to us,
Nor are dross to us, but allay.
On man heaven's influence works not so,
But that it first imprints the air;
For soul into the soul may flow,
Though it to body first repair.
As our blood labors to beget
Spirits, as like souls as it can,
Because such fingers need to knit
That subtle knot which makes us man;
So must pure Lovers' souls descend
To affections and to faculties,
Which sense may reach and apprehend,
Else a great prince in prison lies;
To our bodies turn we then, that so
Weak men on love revealed may look;
Love's mysteries in souls do grow,
But yet the body is his book;
And if some lover, such as we,
Have heard this dialogue of one,
Let him still mark us, he shall see
Small change, when we're to bodies grown.

LOVE'S DEITY

I long to talk with some old lover's ghost,
Who died before the god of Love was born:
I cannot think that he, who then loved most,
Sunk so low, as to love one which did scorn.

But since this god produced a destiny,
And that vice-nature, custom, lets it be,
    I must love her that loves not me.

Sure they, which made him god, meant not so much,
    Nor he in his young godhead practiced it;
But when an even flame two hearts did touch,
    His office was indulgently to fit
Actives to passives, correspondency
Only his subject was; it cannot be
    Love, if I love who loves not me.

But every modern god will now extend
    His vast prerogative as far as Jove;
To rage, to lust, to write to, to commend,
    All is the purlieu of the god of Love.
Oh were we wakened by this tyranny
To ungod this child again, it could not be
    I should love her, who loves not me.

Rebel and atheist too, why murmur I
    As though I felt the worst that love could do?
Love may make me leave loving, or might try
    A deeper plague, to make her love me too,
Which, since she loves before, I'm loath to see;
Falsehood is worse than hate; and that must be,
    If she whom I love, should love me.

LOVE'S DIET

To what a cumbersome unwieldiness
And burdenous corpulence my love had grown,

But that I did, to make it less,
And keep it in proportion,
Give it a diet, made it feed upon,
That which love worst endures, discretion.

Above one sigh a day I allowed him not,
Of which my fortune and my faults had part;
And if sometimes by stealth he got
A she sigh from my mistress' heart,
And thought to feast on that, I let him see
'twas neither very sound, nor meant to me.

If he wrung from me a tear, I brined it so
With scorn or shame, that him it nourished not;
If he sucked hers, I let him know
'Twas not a tear, which he had got,
His drink was counterfeit, as was his meat;
For eyes, which roll towards all, weep not, but sweat.

Whatever he would dictate, I writ that,
But burnt her letters, when she writ to me;
And if that savor made him fat,
I said, if any title be
Conveyed by this, Ah! what doth it avail
To be the fortieth name in an entail?

Thus I reclaimed my buzzard love, to fly
At what, and when, and how, and where I choose;
Now negligent of sport I lie,
And now, as other falconers use,
I spring a mistress, swear, write, sigh, and weep,
And the game killed, or lost, go talk or sleep.

THE WILL

Before I sigh my last gasp, let me breathe,
Great Love, some legacies; here I bequeath
Mine eyes to Argus, if mine eyes can see;
If they be blind, then, Love, I give them thee;
My tongue to Fame; to ambassadors mine ears;
To women, or the sea, my tears;
Thou, Love, hast taught me heretofore
By making me serve her who had twenty more,
That I should give to none, but such as had too much before.

My constancy I to the planets give;
My truth to them who at the court do live;
Mine ingenuity and openness
To Jesuits; to buffoons my pensiveness;
My silence to any who abroad have been;
My money to a Capuchin.
Thou, Love, taught'st me, by appointing me
To love there, where no love received can be,
Only to give to such as have an incapacity.

My faith I give to Roman Catholics;
All my good works unto the schismatics
Of Amsterdam; my best civility
And courtship to a University;
My modesty I give to soldiers bare;
My patience let gamesters share;
Thou, Love, taught'st me, by making me
Love her, that holds my love disparity,
Only to give to those that count my gifts indignity.

I give my reputation to those
Which were my friends; mine industry to foes
To schoolmen I bequeath my doubtfulness;
My sickness to physicians, or excess;
To Nature all, that I in rhyme have writ;
And to my company my wit.
Thou, Love, by making me adore
Her, who begot this love in me before,
Taught'st me to make, as though I gave, when I do but restore.

To him, for whom the passing-bell next tolls,
I give my physic-books; my written rolls
Of moral counsels I to Bedlam give;
My brazen medals unto them which live
In want of bread; to them which pass among
All foreigners, mine English tongue;
Thou, Love, by making me love one
Who thinks her friendship a fit portion
For younger lovers, dost my gifts thus disproportion.

Therefore I'll give no more, but I'll undo
The world by dying; because love dies too.
Then all your beauties will be no more worth
Than gold in mines, where none doth draw it forth;
And all your graces no more use shall have,
Than a sundial in a grave.
Thou, Love, taught'st me, by making me
Love her, who doth neglect both me and thee,
To invent and practice this one way to annihilate all three.

THE FUNERAL

Whoever comes to shroud me, do not harm
Nor question much
That subtle wreath of hair which crowns mine arm;
The mystery, the sign you must not touch,
For 'tis my outward soul,
Viceroy to that, which unto heaven being gone,
Will leave this to control
And keep these limbs, her provinces, from dissolution.

For if the sinewy thread my brain lets fall
Through every part,
Can tie those parts, and make me one of all;
Those hairs, which upward grew, and strength and art
Have from a better brain,
Can better do't: except she meant that I
By this should know my pain,
As prisoners then are manacled, when they're condemned to die.

Whate'er she meant by't, bury it with me;
For since I am
Love's martyr, it might breed idolatry,
If into other hands these relics came.
As 'twas humility
To afford to it all that a soul can do,
So 'tis some bravery,
That, since you would have none of me,
I bury some of you.

THE BLOSSOM

Little think'st thou, poor flower,
Whom I have watched six or seven days,
And seen thy birth, and seen what every hour
Gave to thy growth, thee to this height to raise,
And now dost laugh and triumph on this bough,
Little think'st thou
That it will freeze anon, and that I shall
To-morrow find thee fallen, or not at all.

Little think'st thou poor heart,
That laborest yet to nestle thee,
And think'st by hovering here to get a part
In a forbidden or forbidding tree,
And hop'st her stiffness by long siege to bow,
Little think'st thou,
That thou to-morrow, ere the sun doth wake,
Must with this sun and me a journey take.

But thou which lov'st to be
Subtle to plague thyself, wilt say,
Alas! if you must go, what's that to me?
Here lies my business, and here I will stay:
You go to friends, whose love and means present
Various content.
To your eyes, ears, and taste, and every part;
If then your body go, what need your heart?

Well, then stay here: but know,
When thou hast stayed and done thy most,

A naked thinking heart, that makes no show,
Is to a woman but a kind of ghost;
How shall she know my heart, or, having none,
Know thee for one?
Practice may make her know some other part,
But take my word, she doth not know a heart.

Meet me at London, then,
Twenty days hence, and thou shalt see
Me fresher and more fat, by being with men,
Than if I had stayed still with her and thee.
For God's sake, if you can, be you so too;
I will give you
There to another friend, whom we shall find
As glad to have my body as my mind.

THE PRIMROSE

Being at Montgomery Castle, upon the hill, on which it is situate

Upon this primrose hill,
(Where if Heaven would distil
A shower of rain, each several drop might go
To his own primrose, and grow manna so,
And where their form and their infinity
Make a terrestrial galaxy,
As the small stars do in the sky)
I walk to find a true-love; and I see
That 'tis not a mere woman, that is she,
But must or more or less than woman be.

Yet know I not, which flower
I wish; a six, or four;
For should my true-love less than woman be,
She were scarce anything; and then, should she
Be more than woman, she would get above
All thought of sex, and think to move
My heart to study her, not to love;
Both these were monsters; since there must
reside Falsehood in woman, I could more abide,
She were by art, than nature falsified.

Live, primrose, then, and thrive
With thy true number five;
And women, whom this flower doth represent,
With this mysterious number be content;
Ten is the farthest number; if half ten
Belongs unto each woman, then
Each woman may take half us men:
Or if this will not serve their turn, since all
Numbers are odd or even, since they fall
First into five, women may take us all.

THE RELIC

When my grave is broke up again
Some second guest to entertain,
(For graves have learned that woman-head,
To be to more than one a bed)
And he, that digs it, spies
A bracelet of bright hair about the bone,
Will he not let us alone,
And think that there a loving couple lies,

Who thought that this device might be some way
To make their souls, at the last busy day,
Meet at this grave, and make a little stay?

If this fall in a time, or land,
Where mis-devotion doth command,
Then he, that digs us up, will bring
Us to the Bishop or the King,
To make us relics; then
Thou shalt be a Mary Magdalen, and I
A something else thereby;
All women shall adore us, and some men;
And since at such time miracles are sought,
I would have that age by this paper taught
What miracles we harmless lovers wrought.

First we loved well and faithfully,
Yet knew not what we loved, nor why;
Difference of sex we never knew,
No more than guardian angels do;
Coming and going we
Perchance might kiss, but yet between those meals
Our hands ne'er touched the seals,
Which nature, injured by late law, set free:
These miracles we did; but now, alas!
All measure and all language I should pass,
Should I tell what a miracle she was.

THE DAMP

When I am dead, and doctors know not why,
And my friends' curiosity

Will have me cut up, to survey each part,
When they shall find your picture in my heart,
You think a sudden damp of love
Will through all their senses move,
And work on them as me, and so prefer
Your murder to the name of massacre.

Poor victories! but if you dare be brave,
And pleasure in your conquest have,
First kill the enormous giant, your Disdain,
And let the enchantress Honor next be slain;
And like a Goth or Vandal rise,
Deface records and histories
Of your own arts and triumphs over men:
And without such advantage kill me then.

For I could muster up, as well as you,
My giants and my witches too,
Which are vast Constancy, and Secretness,
But these I neither look for nor profess.
Kill me as woman, let me die
As a mere man; do you but try
Your passive valor, and you shall find then,
Naked you've odds enough of any man.

THE DISSOLUTION

She's dead, and all which die,
To their first elements resolve;
And we were mutual elements to us,
And made of one another.
My body then doth hers involve,

And those things, whereof I consist, hereby
In me abundant grow and burdenous,
And nourish not, but smother.
My fire of passion, sighs of air,
Water of tears, and earthy sad despair,
Which my materials be,
(But near worn out by Love's security)
She, to my loss, doth by her death repair;
And I might live long wretched so,
But that my fire doth with my fuel grow.
Now as those active kings,
Whose foreign conquest treasure brings,
Receive more, and spend more, and soonest break;
This (which I am amazed that I can speak)
This death hath with my store
My use increased;
And so my soul, more earnestly released,
Will outstrip hers; as bullets flown before,
A later bullet may o'ertake, the powder being more.

A JET RING SENT

Thou art not so black as my heart,
Nor half so brittle as her heart thou art;
What wouldst thou say? shall both our proper ties by thee be spoke?
Nothing more endless, nothing sooner broke.
Marriage rings are not of this stuff;
Oh! why should aught less precious, or less tough
Figure our loves? except in thy name thou have bid it say,
I'm cheap and naught but fashion, fling me away.
Yet stay with me, since thou art come,

Circle this finger's top, which didst her thumb:
Be justly proud, and gladly safe, that thou dost dwell with me;
She that, oh! broke her faith, would soon break thee.

NEGATIVE LOVE

I never stooped so low as they,
Which on an eye, cheek, lip, can prey;
Seldom to them, which soar no higher
Than virtue or the mind to admire
For sense and understanding may
Know what gives fuel to their fire:
My Love, though silly, is more brave,
For may I miss, whene'er I crave,
If I know yet what I would have.

If that be simply perfectest,
Which can by no way be exprest
But negatives, my love is so.
To all, which all love, I say no.
If any, who deciphers best,
What we know not (ourselves) can know,
Let him teach me that nothing. This
As yet my ease and comfort is,
Though I speed not, I cannot miss.

THE PROHIBITION

Take heed of loving me,
At least remember, I forbad it thee;
Not that I shall repair my unthrifty waste

Of breath and blood, upon thy sighs and tears,
By being to thee then what to me thou wast;
But so great joy our life at once outwears:
Then lest thy love by my death frustrate be
If thou love me, take heed of loving me.

Take heed of hating me,
Or too much triumph in the victory;
Not that I shall be mine own officer,
And hate with hate again retaliate;
But thou wilt lose the style of conqueror,
If I, thy conquest, perish by thy hate:
Then, lest my being nothing lessen thee,
If thou hate me, take heed of hating me.

Yet love and hate me too,
So these extremes shall ne'er their office do;
Love me, that I may die the gentler way:
Hate me, because thy love's too great for me:
Or let these two themselves, not me, decay;
So shall I live thy stage, not triumph be:
Then lest thy love thou hate, and me undo,
O let me live, yet love and hate me too.

THE EXPIRATION

So, so, break off this last lamenting kiss,
Which sucks two souls, and vapors both away:
Turn thou, ghost, that way, and let me turn this,
And let ourselves benight our happiest day;
We ask none leave to love; nor will we owe
Any so cheap a death, as saying, go.

Go; and if that word have not quite killed thee,
    Ease me with death, by bidding me go too;
Or if it have, let my word work on me,
    And a just office on a murderer do;
Except it be too late to kill me so,
    Being double dead, going, and bidding go.

THE COMPUTATION

For my first twenty years, since yesterday,
        I scarce believed thou could'st be gone away;
For forty more I fed on favors past,
    And forty on hopes, that thou would'st they might last.
Tears drowned one hundred, and sighs blew out two;
    A thousand I did neither think, nor do,
    Or not divide, all being one thought of you:
    Or in a thousand more forgot that too.
Yet call not this long life; but think, that I
Am, by being dead, immortal; can ghosts die?

ELEGY XI: DEATH

Language, thou art too narrow and too weak
    To ease us now; great sorrows cannot speak;
If we could sigh out accents, and weep words!
    Grief wears and lessens, that tears breath affords;
Sad hearts, the less they seem, the more they are,
    (So guiltiest men stand mutest at the bar)
Not that they know not, feel not their estate,
    But extreme sense hath made them desperate;
Sorrow, to whom we owe all that we be,

Tyrant in the fifth and greatest monarchy,
Was't that she did possess all hearts before,
Thou hast killed her, to make thy empire more?
Knew'st thou some would, that knew her not, lament,
As in a deluge perish the innocent?
Was't not enough to have that palace won,
But thou must raze it too, that was undone?
Hadst thou stayed there, and looked out at her eyes,
All had adored thee, that now from thee flies;
For they let out more light than they took in,
They told not when, but did the day begin;
She was too sapphirine and clear for thee;
Clay, flint, and jet now thy fit dwellings be:
Alas! she was too pure, but not too weak;
Whoe'er saw crystal ordnance but would break?
And if we be thy conquest, by her fall
Thou hast lost thy end, in her we perish all:
Or if we live, we live but to rebel,
That know her better now, who knew her well.
If we should vapor out, and pine and die;
Since she first went, that were not misery:
She changed our world with hers: now she is gone,
Mirth and prosperity is oppression:
For of all moral virtues she was all
That Ethics speak of virtues cardinal.
Her soul was paradise; the Cherubin
Set to keep it was Grace, that kept out Sin:
She had no more than let in death, for we
All reap consumption from one fruitful tree:
God took her hence, lest some of us should love
Her, like that plant, him and his laws above:
And when we tears, he mercy shed in this,

To raise our minds to heaven, where now she is:
Who if her virtues would have let her stay,
We had had a saint, have now a holiday.
Her heart was that strange bush, where sacred fire,
Religion, did not consume, but inspire
Such piety, so chaste use of God's day,
That what we turn to feast, she turned to pray,
And did prefigure here in devout taste
The rest of her high sabbath which shall last.
Angels did hand her up, who next God dwell,
(For she was of that Order whence most fell)
Her body is left with us, lest some had said,
She could not die, except they saw her dead;
For from less virtue and less beauteousness
The gentiles framed them gods and goddesses;
The ravenous earth, that now woos her to be
Earth too, will be a Lemnia; and the tree,
That wraps that crystal in a wooden tomb,
Shall be took up spruee, filled with diamond:
And we her sad glad friends all bear a part
Of grief, for all would break a stoic's heart.

ELEGY TO THE LADY BEDFORD

You that are she and you, that's double she,
In her dead face half of yourself shall see;
She was the other part; for so they do,
Which build them friendships, become one of two;
So two, that but themselves no third can fit,
Which were to be so, when they were not yet
Twins, though their birth Cuzco and Moscow take,
As divers stars one constellation make,

Paired like two eyes, have equal motion, so
    Both but one means to see, one way to go.
Had you died first, a carcass she had been,
    And we your rich tomb in her face had seen.
She like the soul is gone, and you here stay,
    Not a live friend, but the other half of clay;
And since you act that part, as men say, here
    Lies such a prince, when but one part is there,
And do all honor and devotion due
    Unto the whole, so we all reverence you;
For such a friendship who would not adore
    In you, who are all what both were before?
Not all, as if some perished by this,
    But so, as all in you contracted is;
As of this all though many parts decay,
    The pure, which elemented them, shall stay.
And though diffused and spread in infinite,
    Shall recollect, and in one all unite:
So Madam, as her soul to heaven is filed,
    Her flesh rests in the earth, as in the bed;
Her virtues do, as to their proper sphere,
    Return to dwell with you, of whom they were;
As perfect motions are all circular,
    So they to you, their sea, whence less streams are.
She was all spices, you all metals; so
    In you two we did both rich Indias know.
And as no fire nor rust can spend or waste
    One dram of gold, but what was first shall last,
Though it be forced in water, earth, salt, air,
    Expansed in infinite, none will impair,
So to yourself you may additions take,
    But nothing can you less or changed make.

Seek not, in seeking new, to seem to doubt
    That you can match her, or not be without;
But let some faithful book in her room be,
    Yet but of Judith, no such book as she.

ELEGY XVI: THE EXPOSTULATION

To make the doubt clear, that no woman's true,
    Was it fate to prove it strong in you?
Thought I, but one had breathed purest air,
    And must she needs be false, because she's fair?
Is it your beauty's mark, or of your youth,
    Or your perfection not to study truth?
Or think you heaven is deaf, or hath no eyes,
    Or those it hath smile at your perjuries?
Are vows so cheap with women, or the matter
    Whereof they're made, that they are writ in water,
And blown away with wind? Or doth their breath
    (Both hot and cold) at once make life and death?
Who could have thought so many accents sweet
    Formed into words, so many sighs should meet,
As from our hearts, so many oaths, and tears
    Sprinkled among all sweetened by our fears)
And the divine impression of stolen kisses,
    That sealed the rest, should now prove empty blisses?
Did you draw bonds to forfeit? sign to break?
    Or must we read you quite from what you speak,
And find the truth out the wrong way? or must
    He first desire you false, who'd wish you just?
O, I profane: though most of women be
    This kind of beast, my thoughts shall except thee,
My dearest Love; though froward jealousy

With circumstance might urge thy inconstancy,
Sooner I'll think the sun will cease to cheer
The teeming earth, and that forget to bear:
Sooner that rivers will run back, or Thames
With ribs of ice in June will bind his streams;
Or Nature, by whose strength the world endures,
Would change her course, before you alter yours.
But oh! that treacherous breast, to whom weak you
Did trust our counsels, (and we both may rue,
Having his falsehood found too late) 'twas he
That made me cast you guilty, and you me;
Whilst he (black wretch) betrayed each simple word
We spake, unto the cunning of a third;
Curst may he be, that so our love hath slain,
And wander on the earth, wretched as Cain,
Wretched as he, and not deserve least pity;
In plaguing him let misery be witty.
Let all eyes shun him, and he shun each eye,
Till he be noisome as his infamy;
May he without remorse deny God thrice,
And not be trusted more on his soul's price;
And after all self-torment when he dies,
May wolves tear out his heart, vultures his eyes;
Swine eat his bowels; and his falser tongue,
That uttered all, be to some raven flung;
And let his carrion corse be a longer feast
To the King's dogs, than any other beast.
Now I have curst, let us our love revive;
In me the flame was never more alive;
I could begin again to court and praise,
And in that pleasure lengthen the short days
Of my life's lease; like painters, that do take

Delight, not in made works, but whilst they make.
I could renew those times, when first I saw
Love in your eyes, that gave my tongue the law
To like what you liked; and at masks and plays
Commend the self-same actors, the same ways;
Ask how you did, and often, with intent
Of being officious, be impertinent;
All which were such soft pastimes, as in these
Love was as subtly catched, as a disease;
But, being got, it is a treasure sweet,
Which to defend is harder than to get:
And ought not to be profaned on either part,
For though 'tis got by chance, 'tis kept by art.

THE PARADOX

No lover saith, I love, nor any other
Can judge a perfect lover;
He thinks that else none can or will agree,
That any loves but he:
I cannot say I loved, for who can say
He was killed yesterday?
Love, with excess of heat, more young than old;
Death kills with too much cold;
We die but once, and who loved last did die,
He that saith twice, doth lie:
For though he seem to move, and stir awhile,
It doth the sense beguile.
Such life is like the light, which bideth yet,
When the life's light is set,
Or like the heat, which fire in solid matter
Leaves behind two hours after.

Once I love and died; and am now become
    Mine epitaph and tomb.
Here dead men speak their last, and so do I;
    Love-slain, lo, here I die.

A HYMN TO CHRIST

At the Author's last going into Germany

In what torn ship soever I embark,
That ship shall be my emblem of thy Ark;
What sea soever swallow me, that flood
Shall be to me an emblem of thy blood.
Though thou with clouds of anger do disguise
Thy face, yet through that mask I know those eyes,
  Which, though they turn away sometimes,
    They never will despise.

I sacrifice this island unto thee,
And all whom I love here, and who love me;
When I have put this flood 'twixt them and me,
Put thou thy blood betwixt my sins and thee.
As the tree's sap doth seek the root below
In winter, in my winter now I go
  Where none but thee, the eternal root
    Of true love, I may know.

Nor thou, nor thy religion, dost control
The amorousness of a harmonious soul;
But thou would'st have that love thyself: as thou
Art jealous, Lord, so I am jealous now.
Thou lov'st not, till from loving more thou free
My soul: whoever gives, takes liberty:

Oh, if thou car'st not whom I love,
Alas, thou lov'st not me.

Seal then this bill of my divorce to all
On whom those fainter beams of love did fall;
Marry those lores, which in youth scattered be
On face, wit, hopes (false mistresses) to thee.
Churches are best for prayer that have least light;
To see God only, I go out of sight:
And to 'scape stormy days, I choose
An everlasting night.

THE LAMENTATIONS OF JEREMY

For the most part according to Tremellius

CHAP. I

How sits this city, late most populous,
Thus solitary, and like a widow thus?
Amplest of nations, queen of provinces
She was, who now thus tributary is.

2. Still in the night she weeps, and her tears fall
Down by her cheeks along, and none of all
Her lovers comfort her; perfidiously
Her friends have dealt, and now are enemy.

3. Unto great bondage and afflictions
Juda is captive led; those nations,
With whom she dwells, no place of rest afford;
In straits she meets her persecutor's sword.
4. Empty are the gates of Sion, and her ways
Mourn, because none come to her solemn days:

Her priests do groan, her maids are comfortless;
And she's unto herself a bitterness.

5. Her foes are grown her head, and live at peace;
Because, when her transgressions did increase,
The Lord strook her with sadness: the enemy
Doth drive her children to captivity.

6. From Sion's daughter is all beauty gone;
Like harts, which seek for pasture and find none,
Her princes are: and now before the foe,
Which still pursues them, without strength they go.

7. Now in their days of tears, Jerusalem
(Her men slain by the foe, none succoring them)
Remembers what of old she esteemed most,
Whilst her foes laugh at her, for which she hath lost.

8. Jerusalem hath sinned, therefore is she
Removed, as women in uncleanness be:
Who honored, scorn her; for her foulness they
Have seen; herself doth groan, and turn away.

9. Her foulness in her skirts was seen, yet she
Remembered not her end; miraculously
Therefore she fell, none comforting: behold,
O Lord, my affliction, for the foe grows bold.

10. Upon all things, where her delight hath been,
The foe hath stretched his hand; for she hath seen
Heathen, whom thou command'st should not do so,
Into her holy sanctuary go.

11. And all her people groan and seek for bread;
And they have given, only to be fed,
All precious things, wherein their pleasure lay:
How cheap I am grown, O Lord, behold, and weigh.

12. All this concerns not you, who pass by me;
O see, and mark if any sorrow be
Like to my sorrow, which Jehovah hath
Done to me in the day of his fierce wrath?

13. That fire, which by himself is governed,
He hath cast from heaven on my bones, and spread
A net before my feet, and me o'erthrown;
And made me languish all the day alone.

14. His hand hath of my sins framed a yoke,
Which wreathed, and cast upon my neck, hath broke
My strength: the lord unto those enemies
Hath given me, from whom I cannot rise.

15. He under foot hath trodden in my sight
My strong men, he did company invite
To break my young men; he the wine-press hath
Trod upon Juda's daughter in his wrath.

16. For these things do I weep; mine eye, mine eye
Casts water out; for he which should be nigh
To comfort me, is now departed far;
The foe prevails, forlorn my children are.

17. There's none, though Sion do stretch out her hand,
To comfort her; it is the Lord's command,

That Jacob's foes girt him: Jerusalem
  Is as an unclean woman amongst them.

18. But yet the Lord is just, and righteous still,
  I have rebelled against his holy will:
O hear, all people, and my sorrow see,
  My maids, my young men in captivity.

19. I called for my lovers then, but they
  Deceived me, and my priests and elders lay
Dead in the city; for they sought for meat,
  Which should refresh their souls, they could not get.

20. Because I am in straits, Jehovah, see
  My heart o'erturned, my bowels muddy be;
Because I have rebelled so much, as fast
  The sword without, as death within doth waste.

21. Of all, which here I mourn, none comforts me;
  My foes have heard my grief, and glad they be,
That thou hast done it; but thy promised day
  Will come, when, as I suffer, so shall they.

22. Let all their wickedness appear to thee;
  Do unto them, as thou hast done to me
For all my sins: the sighs which I have had
  Are very many, and my heart is sad.

CHAP. II.

1. How over Sion's daughter hath God hung
  His wrath's thick cloud! and from heaven hath flung

To earth the beauty of Israel, and hath
  Forgot his footstool in the day of wrath!

2. The Lord unsparingly hath swallowed
  All Jacob's dwellings, and demolished
To ground the strength of Juda, and profaned
  The princes of the kingdom and the land.

3. In heat of wrath the horn of Israel he
  Hath clean cut off, and, lest the enemy
Be hindered, his right hand he doth retire;
  But is towards Jacob all-devouring fire.

4. Like to an enemy he bent his bow,
  His right hand was in posture of a foe,
To kill what Sion's daughter did desire,
  'Gainst whom his wrath he poured forth like fire.

5. For like an enemy Jehovah is,
  Devouring Israel, and his palaces;
Destroying holds, giving additions
  To Juda's daughter's lamentations.

6. Like to a garden-hedge, he hath cast down
  The place, where was his congregation,
And Sion's feasts and sabbaths are forgot;
  Her king, her priest, his wrath regarded not.

7. The Lord forsakes his altar, and detests
  His sanctuary; and in the foe's hands rests
His palace, and the walls, in which their cries
  Are heard, as in the true solemnities.

8. The Lord hath cast a line, so to confound
    And levei Sion's walls unto the ground;
He draws not back his hand, which doth o'erturn
    The wall and rampart, which together mourn.

9. The gates are sunk into the ground, and he
    Hath broke the bar; their kings and princes be
Amongst the heathen, without law; nor there
    Unto the prophets doth the Lord appear.

10. There Sion's elders on the ground are placed,
    And silence keep; dust on their heads they cast;
In sackcloth have they girt themselves, and low
    The virgins towards ground their heads do throw.

11. My bowels are grown muddy, and mine eyes
    Are faint with weeping: and my liver lies
Poured out upon the ground, for misery,
    That sucking children in the streets do die.

12. When they had cried unto their mothers, where
    Shall we have bread and drink? they fainted there;
And in the street like wounded persons lay,
    Till 'twixt their mother's breasts they went away.

13. Daughter Jerusalem, oh! what may be
    A witness, or comparison for thee?
Sion, to ease thee, what shall I name like thee?
    Thy breach is like the sea; what help can be?

14. For thee vain foolish things thy prophets sought,
    Thee thine iniquities they have not taught,

Which might disturn thy bondage: but for thee
    False burthens and false causes they would see.

15. The passengers do clap their hands, and hiss,
    And wag their head at thee, and say, is this
That city which so many men did call
    Joy of the earth, and perfectest of all?

16. Thy foes do gape upon thee, and they hiss,
    And gnash their teeth, and say, devour we this;
For this is certainly the day which we
    Expected, and which now we find and see.

17. The Lord hath done that which he purposed;
    Fulfilled his word, of old determined;
He hath thrown down, and not spared, and thy foe
    Made glad above thee, and advanced him so.

18. But now their hearts unto the Lord do call,
    Therefore, O walls of Sion, let tears fall
Down like a river, day and night; take thee
    No rest, but let thine eye incessant be.

19. Arise, cry in the night, pour out thy sins,
    Thy heart, like water, when the watch begins;
Lift up thy hands to God, lest children die,
    Which, faint for hunger, in the streets do lie.

20. Behold, O Lord, consider unto whom
    Thou hast done this; what, shall the women come
To eat their children of a span? shall thy
    Prophet and priest be slain in sanctuary?

21. On ground in streets the young and old do lie,
My virgins and young men by sword do die;
Them in the day of thy wrath thou hast slain,
Nothing did thee from killing them contain.

22. As to a solemn feast, all whom I feared
Thou call'st about me: when thy wrath appeared,
None did remain or 'scape; for those which I
Brought up, did perish by mine enemy.

CHAP. III.

1. I am the man which have affliction seen,
Under the rod of God's wrath having been.
2. He hath led me to darkness, not to light:
3. And against me all day his hand doth fight.

4. He hath broke my bones, worn out my flesh and skin;
5. Built up against me; and hath girt me in
With hemlock, and with labor; 6. and set me
In dark, as they who dead forever be.

7. He hath hedged me, lest I scape, and added more
To my steel fetters, heavier than before.
8. When I cry out, he outshuts my prayer; 9. and hath
Stopped with hewn stone my way, and turned my path.

10. And like a lion hid in secrecy,
Or bear which lies in wait, he was to me.
11. He stops my way, tears me, made desolate;
12. And he makes me the mark he shooteth at.

13. He made the children of his quiver pass
  Into my reins. 14. I with my people was
All the day long a song and mockery.
  15. He hath filled me with bitterness, and he

Hath made me drunk with wormwood. 16. He hath burst
  My teeth with stones, and covered me with dust.
17. And thus my soul far off from peace was set,
  And my prosperity I did forget.

18. My strength, my hope, (unto myself I said)
  Which from the Lord should come, is perished.
19. But when my mournings I do think upon,
  My wormwood, hemlock, and affliction;

20. My soul is humbled in remembering this;
  21. My heart considers; therefore hope there is,
22. 'Tis God's great mercy we are not utterly
  Consumed, for his compassions do not die;

23. For every morning they renewed be;
  For great, O Lord, is thy fidelity.
24. The Lord is, saith my soul, my portion,
  And therefore in him will I hope alone.

25. The Lord is good to them who on him rely,
  And to the soul that seeks him earnestly.
26. It is both good to trust, and to attend
  The Lord's salvation unto the end.

27. 'Tis good for one his yoke in youth to bear.
  28. He sits alone, and doth all speech forbear,

Because he hath borne it: 29. and his mouth he lays
Deep in the dust, yet then in hope he stays.

30. He gives his cheeks to whosoever will
Strike him, and so he is reproached still.
31. For not forever doth the Lord forsake;
32. But when he hath struck with sadness, he doth take

Compassion, as his mercy is infinite.
33. Nor is it with his heart, that he doth smite,
34. That under foot the prisoners stamped be;
35. That a man's right the judge himself doth see

36. To be wrung from him; that he subverted is
In his just cause, the Lord allows not this.
37. Who then will say, that ought doth come to pass,
But that which by the Lord commanded was?

38. Both good and evil from his mouth proceeds;
39. Why then grieves any man for his misdeeds?
40. Turn we to God, by trying out our ways;
41. To him in heaven our hands with hearts upraise.

42. We have rebelled, and fallen away from thee;
Thou pardon'st not; 43. usest no clemency;
Pursu'st us, kill'st us, cover'st us with wrath;
44. Cover'st thyself with clouds, that our prayer hath

No power to pass: 45. And thou hast made us fall,
As refuse and off-scouring to them all.
46. All our foes gape at us. 47. Fear and a snare,
With ruin and with waste, upon us are.

48. With watery rivers doth mine eye o'erflow,
For ruin of my people's daughters so;
49. Mine eye doth drop down tears incessantly;
50. Until the Lord look down from heaven to see.

51. And for my city-daughter's sake, mine eye
Doth break mine heart. 52. Causeless mine enemy
Like a bird chased me. 53. In a dungeon
They've shut my life, and cast me on a stone.

54. Waters flowed o'er my head; then thought I, I am
Destroyed: 55. I called, Lord, upon thy name,
Out of the pit; 56. And thou my voice didst hear:
Oh! from my sight and cry stop not thine ear.

57. Then when I called upon thee, thou drew'st near
Unto me, and saidst unto me, Do not fear.
58. Thou, Lord, my soul's cause handled hast, and thou
Rescu'st my life. 59. O Lord, do thou judge now.

Thou heard'st my wrong. 60. Their vengeance all they've wrought;
61. How they reproached, thou 'st heard, and what they thought;
62. What their lips uttered, which against me rose,
And what was ever whispered by my foes.

63. I am their song, whether they rise or sit.
64. Give them rewards, Lord, for their working fit,
65. Sorrow of heart, thy curse: 66. And with thy might
Follow, and from under heaven destroy them quite.

CHAP. IV.

1. How is the gold become so dim! How is
   Purest and finest gold thus changed to this!
The stones, which were stones of the sanctuary,
   Scattered in corners of each street do lie.

2. The precious sons of Sion, which should be
   Valued as purest gold, how do we see
Low-rated now, as earthern pitchers, stand,
   Which are the work of a poor potter's hand!

3. Even the sea-calfs draw their breasts, and give
   Suck to their young: my people's daughters live,
By reason of the foe's great cruelness,
   As do the owls in the vast wilderness.

4. And when the sucking child doth strive to draw,
   His tongue for thirst cleaves to his upper jaw:
And when for bread the little children cry,
   There is no man that doth them satisfy.

5. They, which before were delicately fed,
   Now in the streets forlorn have perished:
And they, which ever were in scarlet clothed,
   Sit and embrace the dunghills, which they loathed.

6. The daughters of my people have sinned more,
   Than did the town of Sodom sin before;
Which being at once destroyed, there did remain
   No hands amongst them to vex them again.

7. But heretofore purer her Nazarite
   Was than the snow, and milk was not so white:
As carbuncles, did their pure bodies shine;
   And all their polishedness was sapphirine.

8. They're darker now than blackness; none can know
   Them by the face, as through the street they go:
For now their skin doth cleave unto their bone,
   And withered is like to dry wood grown.

9. Better by sword than famine 'tis to die;
   And better through-pierced, than through penury.
10. Women, by nature pitiful, have eat
   Their children (dressed with their own hand) for meat.

11. Jehovah here fully accomplished hath
   His indignation, and poured forth his wrath;
Kindled a fire in Sion, which hath power
   To eat, and her foundations to devour.

12. Nor would the kings of the earth, nor all, which live
   In the inhabitable world, believe,
That any adversary, any foe
   Into Jerusalem should enter so.

13. For the priest's sins, and prophet's, which have shed
   Blood in the streets, and the just murthered:
14. Which, when those men, whom they made blind, did stray
   Thorough the streets, defiled by the way

With blood, the which impossible it was
   Their garment should 'scape touching, as they pass;

15. Would cry aloud, Depart, defiled men!
    Depart, depart, and touch us not! and then

They fled, and strayed, and with the Gentiles were,
    Yet told their friends, they should not long dwell there.
16. For this they're scattered by Jehovah's face,
    Who never will regard them more; no grace

Unto the old men shall their foe afford;
    Nor, that they're priests, redeem them from the sword:
17. And we as yet, for all these miseries
    Desiring our vain help, consume our eyes:

18. And such a nation, as cannot save,
    We in desire and speculation have.
They hunt our steps, that in the streets we fear
    To go; our end is now approached near.

Our days accomplished are, this the last day;
    Eagles of heaven are not so swift as they
19. Which follow us; o'er mountain's tops they fly
    At us, and for us in the desert lie.

20. The anointed Lord, breath of our nostrils, he
    Of whom we said, under his shadow we
Shall with more ease under the heathen dwell,
    Into the pit, which these men digged, fell.

21. Rejoice, O Edom's daughter; joyful be,
    Thou that inhabit'st Uz; for unto thee
This cup shall pass, and thou with drunkenness
    Shalt fill thyself, and show thy nakedness.

22. And then thy sins, O Sion, shall be spent;
The Lord will not leave thee in banishment:
Thy sins, O Edom's daughter, he will see,
And for them pay thee with captivity.

CHAP. V.

1. Remember, O Lord, what is fallen on us;
See and mark how we are reproached thus.
2. For unto strangers our possession
Is turned, our houses unto aliens gone.

3. Our mothers are become as widows, we
As orphans all, and without fathers be.
4. Waters, which are our own, we drink, and pay;
And upon our own wood a price they lay.

5. Our persecutors on our necks do sit,
They make us travail, and not intermit.
6. We stretch our hands unto the Egyptians
To get us bread; and to the Assyrians.

7. Our fathers did these sins, and are no more;
But we do bear the sins they did before.
8. They are but servants, which do rule us thus;
Yet from their hands none would deliver us.

9. With danger of our life our bread we gat;
For in the wilderness the sword did wait.
10. The tempests of this famine we lived in
Black as an oven colored had our skin.

11. In Juda's cities they the maids abused
By force, and so women in Sion used.
12. The princes with their hands they hung; no grace
Nor honor gave they to the elder's face.

13. Unto the mill our young men carried are,
And children fell under the wood they bare:
14. Elders the gates, youth did their songs forbear;
Gone was our joy; our dancings mournings were.

15. Now is the crown fallen from our head; and woe
Be unto us, because we've sinned so.
16. For this our hearts do languish, and for this,
Over our eyes a cloudy dimness is;

17. Because Mount Sion desolate doth lie,
And foxes there do go at liberty.
18. But thou, O Lord, art ever; and thy throne
From generation to generation.

19. Why shouldst thou forget us eternally;
Or leave us thus long in this misery?
20. Restore us, Lord, to thee; that so we may
Return, and, as of old, renew our day.

21. For oughtest thou, O Lord, despise us thus,
22. And to be utterly enraged at us?

SATIRES

SATIRE I

Away, thou changeling motley humorist,
Leave me, and in this standing wooden chest,
Consorted with these few books, let me lie
In prison, and here be coffined, when I die.
Here are God's conduits, grave divines; and here
Is nature's secretary, the philosopher;
And wily statesmen, which teach how to tie
The sinews of a city's mystic body;
Here gathering chroniclers, and by them stand
Giddy fantastic poets of each land.
Shall I leave all this constant company,
And follow headlong wild uncertain thee?
First swear by thy best love here, in earnest,
(If thou, which lov'st all, canst love any best)
Thou wilt not leave me in the middle street,
Though some more spruce companion thou dost meet;
Not though a captain do come in thy way,
Bright parcel-gilt, with forty dead men's pay;
Not though a brisk, perfumed, pert courtier

Deign with a nod thy courtesy to answer;
Nor come a velvet justice with a long
Great train of blue coats, twelve or fourteen strong,
Wilt thou grin or fawn on him, or prepare
A speech to court his beauteous son and heir.
For better or worse take me, or leave me:
To take and leave me is adultery.
O monstrous, superstitious Puritan,
Of refined manners, yet ceremonial man,
That, when thou meet'st one, with inquiring eyes,
Doth search, and like a needy broker prize
The silk and gold he wears, and to that rate,
So high or low, dost raise thy formal hat:
That wilt consort none, till thou have known
What lands he hath in hope, or of his own;
As though all thy companions should make thee
Jointures, and marry thy dear company.
Why should'st thou (that dost not only approve,
But in rank itchy lust, desire and love,
The nakedness and barrenness to enjoy
Of thy plump muddy whore, or prostitute boy)
Hate Virtue, though she naked be and bare?
At birth and death our bodies naked are;
And, till our souls be unapparelled
Of bodies, they from bliss are banished:
Man's first blest state was naked; when by sin
He lost that, he was clothed but in beast's skin,
And in this coarse attire which I now wear,
With God and with the Muses I confer.
But since thou, like a contrite penitent,
Charitably warned of thy sins, dost repent
These vanities and giddinesses, lo

I shut my chamber door, and come, let's go.
But sooner may a cheap whore, who hath been
Worn out by as many several men in sin,
As are black feathers, or musk-colored hose,
Name her child's right true father 'mongst all those;
Sooner may one guess, who shall bear away
The infantry of London hence to India;
And sooner may a gulling weather-spy,
By drawing forth heaven's scheme, tell certainly
What fashioned hats or ruffs, or suits, next year
Our giddy-headed antic youth will wear;
Than thou, when thou depart'st from me, can show
Whither, why, when, or with whom thou would'st go.
But how shall I be pardoned my offence,
That thus have sinned against my conscience?
Now we are in the street; he first of all,
Improvidently proud, creeps to the wall;
And so imprisoned and hemmed in by me,
Sells for a little state his liberty.
Yet though he cannot skip forth now to greet
Every fine silken painted fool we meet,
He them to him with amorous smiles allures,
And grins, smacks, shrugs, and such an itch endures,
As 'prentices or school-boys, which do know
Of some gay sport abroad, yet dare not go;
And as fiddlers stop lowest at highest sound,
So to the most brave stoops he nigh'st the ground;
But to a grave man he doth move no more
Than the wise politic horse would heretofore,
Now leaps he upright, jogs me, and cries, "Do you see
Yonder well-favored youth?" "Which?" "Oh! 'tis he
That dances so divinely." "Oh," said I,

"Stand still, must you dance here for company?"
He drooped; we went, till one (which did excel
The Indians in drinking his tobacco well)
Met us: they talked; I whispered, "Let us go;
'T may be you smell him not, truly I do."
He hears not me, but on the other side
A many-colored peacock having spied,
Leaves him and me; I for my lost sheep stray;
He follows, overtakes, goes on the way,
Saying, "Him, whom I last left, all repute
For his device, in handsoming a suit,
To judge of lace, pink, panes, print, cut, and plight,
Of all the court to have the best conceit."
"Our dull comedians want him, let him go;
But oh! God strengthen thee, why stoop'st thou so?"
Why, he hath travelled long; no, but to me
Which understood none, he doth seem to be
Perfect French and Italian." I replied
So is the pox." He answered not, but spied
More men of sort, of parts and qualities;
At last his love he in a window spies,
And, like light dew exhaled, he flings from me
Violently ravished to his liberty.
Many there were, he could command no more;
He quarreled, fought, bled; and, turned out of door,
Directly came to me, hanging the head,
And constantly awhile must keep his bed.

SATIRE II

Sir, though (I thank God for it) I do hate
Perfectly all this town, yet there's one state

In all ill things so excellently best,
That hate towards them breeds pity towards the rest;
Though poetry indeed be such a sin,
As I think that brings dearth and Spaniards in;
Though, like the pestilence and old fashioned love,
Riddlingly it catch men, and doth remove
Never, till it be starved out, yet their state
Is poor, disarmed, like Papists, not worth hate.
One (like a wretch, which at bar judged as dead,
Yet prompts him, which stands next, and cannot read,
And saves his life) gives idiot actors means,
(Starving himself) to live by 's labored scenes.
As in some organ puppets dance above,
And bellows pant below which them do move,
One would move love by rhymes; but witchcraft's charms,
Bring not now their old fears, nor their old harms;
Rams and slings now are silly battery,
Pistollers are the best artillery.
And they who write to lords, rewards to get,
Are they not like singers at doors for meat?
And they who write, because all write, have still
The excuse for writing, and for writing ill.
But he is worst, who (beggarly) doth chaw
Others' wit's fruits, and in his ravenous maw,
Rankly digested, doth those things outspew,
As his own things; and they're his own, 'tis true;
For if one eat my meat, though it be known
The meat was mine, the excrement is his own.
But these do me no harm, nor they which use
To outdo dildoes, and out-usure Jews,
To outdrink the sea, to outswear the litany,
Who with sin's all kinds as familiar be

As confessors, and for whose sinful sake
Schoolmen new tenements in hell must make;
Whose strange sins canonists could hardly tell
In which commandment's large receipt they dwell.
But these punish themselves. The insolence
Of Coscus only breeds my just offence,
Whom time (which rots all, and makes botches pox,
And plodding on must make a calf an ox,
Hath made a lawyer; which (alas) of late
But scarce a poet, jollier of this state
Than are new beneficed ministers, he throws
Like nets or lime-twigs, wheresoe'er he goes,
His title of barrister on every wench,
And wooes in language of the pleas and bench.
"A motion, Lady:" " Speak, Coscus." "I have been
In love e'er since *tricesimo* of the queen.
Continual claims I've made, injunctions got
To stay my rival's suit, that he should not
Proceed; spare me, in Hilary term I went;
You said, if I returned next 'size in Lent,
I should be in remitter of your grace;
In the interim my letters should take place
Of affidavits." Words, words, which would tear
The tender labyrinth of a maid's soft ear
More, more than ten Slavonians' scoldings, more
Than when winds in our ruined abbeys roar.
When sick with poetry and possesed with muse
Thou wast, and mad, I hoped; but men which choose
choose Law practice for mere gain, bold souls repute
Worse than imbrotheled strumpets prostitute.
Now, like an owl-like watchman, he must walk
His hand still at a bill; now he must talk

Idly, like prisoners, which whole months will swear,
That only suretyship hath brought them there,
And to every suitor lie in every thing,
Like a king's favorite, or like a king:
Like a wedge in a block, wring to the bar,
Bearing like asses, and more shameless far
Than carted whores, lie to the grave judge; for
Bastardy abounds not in kings' titles, nor
Simony and sodomy in churchmen's lives,
As these things do in him; by these he thrives.
Shortly, as th' sea, he'll compass all the land,
From Scots to Wight, from Mount to Dover-strand,
And spying heirs melting with luxury,
Satan will not joy at their sins, as he.
For (as a thrifty wench scrapes kitchen stuff,
And barreling the droppings, and the snuff
Of wasting candles, which in thirty year,
Relicly kept, perchance buys wedding-gear)
Piecemeal he gets lands, and spends as much time
Wringing each acre, as maids pulling prime.
In parchment then, large as the fields, he draws
Assurances; big as glossed civil laws,
So huge, that men (in our time's forwardness)
Are fathers of the Church for writing less.
These he writes not; nor for these written pays,
Therefore spares no length, (as in those first days,
When Luther was professed, he did desire
Short paternosters, saying as a friar
Each day his beads; but having left those laws,
Adds to Christ's prayer the power and glory clause.)
But when he sells or changes land, he impairs
His writings, and (unwatched) leaves out *ses heires*,

And slily as any commenter goes by
Hard words or sense; or in divinity
As controverters in vouched texts leave out
Shrewd words, which might against them clear the doubt.
Where are those spread woods, which clothed heretofore
Those bought lands? not built, nor burnt within door.
Where the old landlord's troops and alms, great halls?
Carthusian fasts and fulsome bacchanals
Equally I hate. Mean's blest. In rich men's
homes I bid kill some beasts, but no hecatombs;
None starve, none surfeit so. But O we allow
Good works as good, but out of fashion now,
Like old rich wardrobes. But my words none draws
Within the vast reach of th' huge statute laws.

SATIRE III

Kind pity checks my spleen; brave scorn forbids
Those tears to issue, which swell my eyelids.
I must not laugh, nor weep sins, but be wise;
Can railing then cure these worn maladies?
Is not our mistress, fair Religion,
As worthy of our soul's devotion,
As virtue was to the first blinded age
Are not Heaven's joys as valiant to assuage
Lusts, as earth's honor was to them? Alas,
As we do them in means, shall they surpass
Us in the end? and shall thy father's spirit
Meet blind philosophers in heaven, whose merit
Of strict life may be imputed faith, and hear
Thee, whom he taught so easy ways and near
To follow, damned? Oh, if thou dar'st, fear this:

This fear great courage, and high valor is.
Dar'st thou aid mutinous Dutch? and dar'st thou lay
Thee in ship's wooden sepulchers, a prey
To leader's rage, to storms, to shot, to dearth?
Dar'st thou dive seas, and dungeons of the earth?
Hast thou courageous fire to thaw the ice
Of frozen North discoveries, and thrice
Colder than salamanders? Like divine
Children in the oven, fires of Spain and the line,
Whose countries limbecs to our bodies be,
Canst thou for gain bear? and must every he
Which cries not *goddess* to thy mistress, draw,
Or eat thy poisonous words? Courage of straw!
O desperate coward, wilt thou seem bold, and
To thy foes and his (who made thee to stand
Sentinel in this world's garrison) thus yield,
And for forbid wars leave the appointed field?
Know thy foes: the foul devil (he, whom thou
Striv'st to please) for hate, not love, would allow
Thee fain his whole realm to be quit; and as
The world's all parts wither away and pass,
So the world's self, thy other loved foe, is
In her decrepit wane, and thou, loving this,
Dost love a withered and worn strumpet; last,
Flesh (itself's death) and joys, which flesh can taste,
Thou lov'st; and thy fair goodly soul, which doth
Give this flesh power to taste joy, thou dost loath.
Seek true religion: O where? Mirreus,
Thinking her unhoused here, and fled from us,
Seeks her at Rome, there, because he doth know
That she was there a thousand years ago;
He loves the rags so, as we here obey

The state-cloth where the prince sate yesterday.
Crantz to such brave loves will not be enthralled,
But loves her only, who at Geneva is called
Religion—plain, simple, sullen, young,
Contemptuous, yet unhandsome; as among
Lecherous humors, there is one that judges
No wenches wholesome but coarse country drudges.
Graius stays still at home here, and because
Some preachers, vile ambitious bawds, and laws
Still new, like fashions, bid him think that she
Which dwells with us, is only perfect, he
Embraceth her, whom his godfathers will
Tender to him, being tender; as wards still
Take such wives as their guardians offer, or
Pay values. Careless Phrygius, doth abhor
All, because all cannot be good; as one,
Knowing some women whores, dares marry none.
Gracchus loves all as one, and thinks that so
As women do in divers countries go
In divers habits, yet are still one kind,
So doth, so is, Religion; and this blind
Ness too much light breeds. But unmoved thou
Of force must one, and forced but one allow,
And the right. Ask thy father which is she;
Let him ask his. Though truth and falsehood be
Near twins, yet truth a little elder is.
Be busy to seek her; believe me this,
He's not of none, nor worst, that seeks the best:
To adore, or scorn an image, or protest,
May all be bad. Doubt wisely, in strange way
To stand inquiring right, is not to stray;
To sleep or run wrong, is. On a huge hill,

Cragged and steep, Truth stands; and he, that will
Reach her, about must and about it go,
And what the hill's suddenness resists, win so.
Yet strive so, that before age, death's twilight,
Thy soul rest, for none can work in that night.
To will implies delay, therefore now do:
Hard deeds the body's pains; hard knowledge to
The mind's endeavors reach; and mysteries
Are like the sun, dazzling, yet plain to all eyes.
Keep the truth which thou hast found; men do not stand
In so ill case, that God hath with his hand
Signed kings' blank-charters to kill whom they hate,
Nor are they vicars, but hangmen to fate.
Fool and wretch, wilt thou let thy soul be tied
To man's laws, by which she shall not be tried
At the last day? Or will it then boot thee
To say a Philip or a Gregory,
A Harry or a Martin, taught me this?
Is not this excuse for mere contraries,
Equally strong? Cannot both sides say so?
That thou mayst rightly obey power, her bounds know;
Those past, her nature and name's changed; to be
Then humble to her is idolatry.
As streams are, power is; those blest flowers, that dwell
At the rough stream's calm head, thrive and do well;
But having left their roots, and themselves given
To the stream's tyrannous rage, alas! are driven
Through mills, rocks, and woods, and at last, almost
Consumed in going, in the sea are lost:
So perish souls, which more choose men's unjust
Power, from God claimed, than God himself to trust.

SATIRE IV

Well; I may now receive, and die. My sin
Indeed is great, but yet I have been in
A purgatory, such as feared hell is
A recreation, and scant map of this.
My mind, neither with pride's itch, nor yet hath been
Poisoned with love to see, or to be seen;
I had no suit there, nor new suit show,
Yet went to court. But as Glare, which did go
To mass in jest, catched, was fain to disburse
The hundred marks, which is the statute's curse,
Before he 'scaped; so't pleased my destiny
(Guilty of my sin of going) to think me
As prone to all ill, and of good as forget
full, as proud, lustful, and as much in debt,
As vain, as witless, and as false as they
Which dwell in court, for once going that way.
Therefore I suffered this. Towards me did run
A thing more strange, than on Nile's slime the sun
E'er bred, or all which into Noah's ark came:
A thing which would have posed Adam to name:
Stranger than seven antiquaries' studies,
Than Afric's monsters, Guiana's rarities,
Stranger than strangers: one, who for a Dane
In the Dane's massacre had sure been slain,
If he had lived then; and without help dies,
When next the 'prentices 'gainst strangers rise:
One, whom the watch at noon lets scarce go by:
One, t' whom th' examining justice sure would cry,
"Sir, by your priesthood, tell me what you are."

His clothes were strange, though coarse, and black, though bare;
Sleeveless his jerkin was, and it had been
Velvet, but 'twas now (so much ground was seen)
Become tufftaffaty; and our children shall
See it plain rash a while, then naught at all.
The thing hath travelled, and faith, speaks all tongues,
And only knoweth what to all states belongs.
Made of the accents, and best phrase of all these,
He speaks one language. If strange meats displease,
Art can deceive, or hunger force my taste:
But pedant's motley tongue, soldier's bombast,
Mountebank's drug-tongue, nor the terms of law,
Are strong enough preparatives to draw
Me to hear this, yet I must be content
With his tongue, in his tongue called compliment:
In which he can win widows, and pay scores,
Make men speak treason, cozen subtlest whores,
Out-flatter favorites, or outlie either
Jovius or Surius, or both together.
He names me, and comes to me; I whisper, "God!
How have I sinned, that thy wrath's furious rod,
This fellow, chooseth me"? He saith, "Sir,
I love your judgment; whom do you prefer,
For the best linguist?" and I sillily
Said that I thought Calepine's dictionary.
"Nay, but of men, most sweet Sir?" Beza, then,
Some Jesuits, and two reverend men
Of our two academies I named; here
He stopped me, and said: "Nay, your apostles were
Good pretty linguists; so Panurgus was,
Yet a poor gentleman; all these may pass
By travail;" then, as if he would have sold

His tongue, he praised it, and such wonders told,
That I was fain to say, "If you had lived, Sir,
Time enough to have been interpreter
To Babel's bricklayers, sure the tower had stood."
He adds, "If of court-life you knew the good,
You would leave loneness." I said, "Not alone
My loneness is; but Spartan's fashion,
To teach by painting drunkards, doth not last
Now; Aretine's pictures have made few chaste;
No more can princes' courts, though there be few
Better pictures of vice, teach me virtue."
He, like to a high-stretched lute-string, squeaked, "O Sir,
'Tis sweet to talk of kings." "At Westminster,"
Said I, "the man that keeps the abbey tombs,
And for his price doth, with whoever comes,
Of all our Harrys, and our Edwards talk,
From king to king, and all their kin can walk:
Your ears shall hear naught but kings; your eyes meet
Kings only; the way to it is King's-street."
He smacked, and cried, "He's base, mechanic, coarse;
So 're all your Englishmen in their discourse.
Are not your Frenchmen neat? Fine, as you see
I have but one, Frenchman, sir, look, he follows me."
"*Certes* they're neatly clothed. I of this mind am,
Your only wearing is your grogaram."
"Not so, Sir, I have more." Under this pitch
He would not fly; I chafed him: but, as itch
Scratched into smart, and as blunt iron ground
Into an edge, hurts worse, so I (fool) found,
Crossing hurt me. To fit my sullenness,
He to another key his style doth dress,
And asks, What news? I tell him of new plays;

He takes my hand, and as a still which stays
A semibrief, 'twixt each drop, he niggardly,
As loath to enrich me, so tells many a lie,
More than ten Hollinsheds, or Halls, or Stows,
Of trivial household trash he knows: he knows
When the queen frowned or smiled, and he knows what
A subtle statesman may gather of that;
He knows who loves whom; and who by poison
Hastes to an office's reversion;
He knows who hath sold his land, and now doth beg
A license old iron, boots, shoes, and egg
shells to transport; shortly boys shall not play
At span-counter or blow-point, but shall pay
Toll to some courtier; and, wiser than all us,
He knows what lady is not painted. Thus
He with home-meats cloys me. I belch, spew, spit,
Look pale and sickly, like a patient, yet
He thrusts on more; and as he had undertook
To say Gallo-Belgicus without book,
Speaks of all states and deeds, that have been since
The Spaniards came to th' loss of Amiens.
Like a big wife, at sight of loathed meat,
Ready to travail, so I sigh, and sweat
To hear this macaron talk in vain; for yet,
Either my humor or his own to fit,
He like a privileged spy, whom nothing can
Discredit, libels now 'gainst each great man.
He names a price for every office paid;
He saith, our wars thrive ill because delayed;
That offices are entailed, and that there are
Perpetuities of them, lasting as far
As the last day; and that great officers

Do with the pirates share and Dunkirkers.
Who wastes in meat, in clothes, in horse, he notes;
Who loves whores, who boys, and who goats.
I, more amazed than Circe's prisoners, when
They felt themselves turn beasts, felt myself then
Becoming traitor, and methought I saw
One of our giant statutes ope his jaw
To suck me in, for hearing him; I found
That as burnt venomous lechers do grow sound
And says, "By giving others their sores, I might grow
Guilty, and he free: therefore I did show
All signs of loathing; but since I am in,
I must pay mine and my forefathers' sin
To the last farthing. Therefore to my power
Toughly and stubbornly I bear this cross; but th' hour
Of mercy now was come. He tries to bring
Me to pay a fine to 'scape his torturing,
Sir, can you spare me?" I said, " Willingly;"
"Nay, Sir, can you spare me a crown?" Thankfully I
Gave it, as ransom; but as fiddlers still,
Though they be paid to be gone, yet needs will
Thrust one more jig upon you, so did he
With his long complimental thanks vex me.
But he is gone, thanks to his needy want,
And the prerogative of my crown. Scant
His thanks were ended, when I (which did see
All the court filled with such strange things as he)
Ran from thence with such or more haste than one,
Who fears more actions, doth haste from prison.
At home in wholesome solitariness
My piteous soul began the wretchedness
Of suitors at court to mourn, and a trance

Like his who dream't he saw hell, did advance
Itself o'er me: such men as he saw there,
I saw at court, and worse, and more. Low fear
Becomes the guilty, not the accuser: then
Shall I, none's slave, of high born or raised men,
Fear frowns, and my mistress, Truth, betray thee
To the huffing, braggart, puffed nobility?
No, no; thou, which since yesterday hast been
Almost about the whole world, hast thou seen,
O sun, in all thy journey, vanity
Such as swells the bladder of our court? I
Think, he which made your waxen garden, and
Transported it from Italy, to stand
With us at London, flouts our courtiers, for
Just such gay painted things, which no sap nor
Taste have in them, ours are; and natural
Some of the stocks are, their fruits bastard all.
'Tis ten o'clock and past; all whom the Mews,
Baloun, Tennis, Diet, or the stews
Had all the morning held, now the second
Time made ready, that day in flocks were found
In the presence, and I, (God pardon me)
As fresh and sweet their apparels be, as be
The fields they sold to buy them. "For a king
Those hose are," cry his flatterers; and bring
Them next week to the theatre to sell;
Wants reach all states. Meseems they do as well
At stage, as court; all are players; whoe'er looks
(For themselves dare not go) o'er Cheapside books,
Shall find their wardrobe's inventory. Now,
The ladies come. As pirates which do know
That there came weak ships fraught with cochineal,

The men board them; and praise (as they think), well
well Their beauties; they the men's wits; both are bought.
Why good wits ne'er wear scarlet gowns, I thought
This cause: these men men's wits for speeches buy,
And women buy all reds, which scarlets dye.
He called her beauty lime-twigs, her hair net;
She fears her drugs ill laid, her hair loose set.
Wouldn't Heraclitus laugh to see Macrine
From hat to shoe himself at door refine,
As if the presence were a Moschite; and lift
His skirts and hose, and call his clothes to shrift,
Making them confess not only mortal
Great stains and holes in them, but venial
Feathers and dust, wherewith they fornicate:
And then by Durer's rules survey the state
Of his each limb, and with strings the odds tries
Of his neck to his leg, and waist to thighs.
So in immaculate clothes and symmetry
Perfect as circles, with such nicety
As a young preacher at his first time goes
To preach, he enters; and a lady, which owes
Him not so much as good-will, he arrests,
And unto her protests, protests, protests;
So much as at Rome would serve to have thrown
Ten cardinals into the inquisition;
And whispers by Jesu so oft, that a
Pursuivant would have ravished him away,
For saying of our lady's psalter. But 'tis fit
That they each other plague, they merit it.
But here comes Glorius, that will plague them both,
Who in the other extreme only doth
Call a rough carelessness good fashion;

Whose cloak his spurs tear, or whom he spits on,
He cares not, he. His ill words do no harm
To him, he rushes in, as if arm, arm,
He meant to cry; and though his face be as ill
As theirs, which in old hangings whip Christ, still
He strives to look worse, he keeps all in awe,
Jests like a licensed fool, commands like law.
Tired now I leave this place, and but pleased so
As men from jails to execution go,
Go through the great chamber (why is it hung
With the seven deadly sins?) Being among
Those Ascaparts, men big enough to throw
Charing-Cross for a bar, men that do know
No token of worth, but queen's man, and fine
Living, barrels of beef, and flagons of wine,
I shook like a spied spy. Preachers, which are
Seas of wits and arts, you can, then dare
Drown the sins of this place, for, for me,
Which am but a scant brook, it enough shall be
To wash the stains away: although I yet
(With Macabee's modesty) the known merit
Of my work lessen, yet some wise men shall,
I hope, esteem my writs canonical.

SATIRE V

Thou shalt not laugh in this leaf, Muse, nor they,
Whom any pity warms. He which did lay
Rules to make courtiers, (he being understood
May make good courtiers, but who courtiers good?)
Frees from the sting of jests, all who in extreme
Are wretched or wicked: of these two a theme

Charity and liberty give me. What is he
Who officer's rage, and suitor's misery
Can write in jest? If all things be in all,
As I think, (since all, which were, are, and shall
Be, be made of the same elements)
Each thing each thing implies or represents.
Then man is a world, in which officers
Are the vast ravishing seas, and suitors
Springs, now full, now shallow, now dry, which to
That which drowns them run: these self reasons do
Prove the world a man, in which officers
Are the devouring stomach, and suitors
Th' excrements which they void. All men are dust:
How much worse are suitors, who to men's lust
Are made preys? O worse than dust or worm's meat!
For they eat you now, whose selves worms shall eat.
They are the mills which grind you; yet you are
The wind which drives them; and a wasteful war
Is fought against you, and you fight it; they
Adulterate law, and you prepare the way,
Like wittols; the issue your own ruin is.
Greatest and fairest empress, know you this?
Alas! no more than Thames' calm head doth know,
Whose meads her arms drown, or whose corn o'er-flow.
You, Sir, whose righteousness she loves, whom I,
By having leave to serve, am most richly
For service paid authorized, now begin
To know and weed out this enormous sin.
O age of rusty iron! Some better wit
Call it some worse name, if aught equal it.
The iron age was, when justice was sold; now
Injustice is sold dearer far; allow

All claimed fees and duties, gamesters, anon
The money, which you sweat and swear for 's gone
Into other hands: so controverted lands
Scape, like Angelica, the striver's hands.
If law be in the judge's heart, and he
Have no heart to resist letter or fee,
Where wilt thou appeal? Power of the courts below
Flows from the first main head; and these can throw
Thee, if they suck thee in, to misery,
To fetters, halters. But if th' injury
Steel thee to dare complain, alas! thou go'st
Against the stream upwards, when thou art most
Heavy, and most faint; and in these labors they,
'Gainst whom thou shouldst complain, will in the way
Become great seas, o'er which when thou shalt be
Forced to make golden bridges, thou shalt see
That all thy gold was drowned in them before.
All things follow their like; only who have may have more.
Judges are gods; and he who made them so,
Meant not men should be forced to them to go
By means of angels. When supplications
We send to God, to dominations,
Powers, cherubins, and all heaven's courts, if we
Should pay fees, as here, daily bread would be
Scarce to kings; so 'tis. Would it not anger
A stoic, a coward, yea a martyr,
To see a pursuivant come in, and call
All his clothes, copes; books, primers; and all
His plate, chalices; and mistake them away,
And ask a fee for coming? Oh, ne'er may
Fair Law's white reverend name be strumpeted,
To warrant thefts: she is established

Recorder to Destiny on earth, and she
Speaks Fate's words, and tells who must be
Rich, who poor, who in chairs, and who in jails:
She is all fair, but yet hath foul long nails,
With which she scratcheth suitors. In bodies
Of men, so in law, nails are extremities;
So officers stretch to more than law can do,
As our nails reach what no else part comes to.
Why bar'st thou to yon officer? Fool, hath he
Got those goods, for which erst men bared to thee?
Fool, twice, thrice, thou hast bought wrong, and now hungerly
Begg'st right, but that dole comes not till these die.
Thou hadst much, and law's urim and thummim try
Thou wouldst, for more; and for all hast paper
Enough to clothe all the great Carrick's pepper.
Sell that, and by that thou much more shalt lease
Than Hammon, when he sold his antiquities.
O Wretch! that thy fortunes should moralize
Aesop's fables, and make tales prophesies.
Thou art the swimming dog whom shadows cozened,
Which div'st, near drowning, for what vanished.

A HYMN TO GOD THE FATHER

I.

Wilt thou forgive that sin where I begun,
Which was my sin, though it were done before?
Wilt thou forgive that sin, through which I run,
And do run still, though still I do deplore?
When thou hast done, thou hast not done;
For I have more.

II.

Wilt thou forgive that sin, which I have won
Others to sin, and made my sin their door?
Wilt thou forgive that sin, which I did shun
A year or two, but wallowed in a score?
When thou hast done, thou hast not done;
For I have more.

III.

I have a sin of fear, that when I've spun
My last thread, I shall perish on the shore;
But swear by thyself, that at my death thy Son
Shall shine, as he shines now and heretofore:

And having done that, thou hast done;
I fear no more.

LETTERS

TO SIR H. G.

I send not my Letters as tribute, nor interest, not recompense, nor for commerce, nor as testimonials of my love, nor provokers of yours, nor to justify my custom of writing, nor for a vent and utterance of my meditations; for my Letters are either above or under all such offices; yet I write very affectionately, and I chide and accuse my self of diminishing that affection which sends them, when I ask my self why: only I am sure that I desire that you might have in your hands Letters of mine of all kinds, as conveyances and deliverers of me to you, whether you accept me as a friend, or as a patient, or as a penitent, or as a beadsman, for I decline no jurisdiction, or refuse any tenure. I would not open any door upon you, but look in when you open it. Angels have not, nor affect not other knowledge of one another, then they list to reveal to one another. It is then in this only, that friends are Angels, that they are capable and fit for such revelations when they are offered. If at any time I seem to study you more inquisitively, it is for no other end but to know how to present you to God in my prayers, and what to ask of him for you; for even that holy exercise may not be done inopportunely, no nor importunely. I find little error in that Grecians counsel, who says, If thou ask any thing of God, offer no sacrifice, nor ask elegantly, nor vehemently, but remember that thou wouldst not give to such an asker: Nor in his other Countryman, who affirms sacrifice of blood to be so unproportionable to God, that perfumes, though much more spiritual, are too gross. Yea words which are our subtlest and delicatest outward creatures, being composed of thoughts and breath, are so muddy, so thick, that our thoughts themselves are so, because (except at the first rising) they are ever leavened with passions and affections: And that advantage of nearer familiarity with God, which the act of incarnation gave us, is grounded upon Gods assuming us, not our going to him. And, our accesses to his presence are but his descents into us; and when we get anything by prayer, he gave us beforehand the thing and the petition. For, I scarce think any ineffectual prayer free from both sin, and the punishment of sin: yet as God seposed a seventh of our time for his exterior worship, and as his Christian Church early presented him a type of the whole year in a Lent, and after imposed the obligation of canonical hours, constituting thereby moral Sabbaths every day; I am far from dehorting those fixed devotions: But I had rather it were bestowed upon thanksgiving then petition, upon praise then prayer; not that God is endeared by that, or wearied by this; all is one in the receiver, but not in the sender: and thanks doth both offices; for, nothing doth so innocently provoke new graces, as gratitude. I would also rather make short prayers then extend them, though God can neither be surprised, nor besieged: for, long prayers have more of the man, as ambition of eloquence, and a complacency in the work, and more of the Devil by often distractions: for, after in the beginning we have well intreated God to hearken, we speak no more to him. Even this Letter is some example of such infirmity, which being intended for a Letter, is extended and strayed into a Homily. And whatsoever is not what it was purposed, is worse; therefore it shall at last end like a Letter by assuring you I am &c.

TO SIR H. G. (2)

Sir,

Nature hath made all bodies alike, by mingling and kneading up the same elements in every one. And amongst men, the other nature, Custom, hath made every mind like some other; we are patterns, or copies, we inform, or imitate. But as he hath not presently attained to write a good hand, which hath equaled one excellent Master in his *A*, another in his *B*, much less he which hath sought all the excellent Masters, and employed all his time to exceed on one Letter, because not so much an excellency of any, nor every one, as an evenness and proportion, and respect to one another gives the perfection: so is no man virtuous by particular example. Not he that doth all actions to the pattern of the most valiant, or liberal, which Histories afford: nor he which chooses from every one their best actions, and thereupon doth something like those. Perchance such may be *in via perficiendorum*, which Divines allow to Monastic life, but not *perfectorum*, which by them is only due to Prelacy. For virtue is even, and continual, and the same, and can therefore break nowhere, nor admit ends, nor beginnings: it is not only not broken, but not tied together. He is not virtuous, out of whose actions you can pick an excellent one. Vice and her fruits may be seen, because they are thick bodies, but not virtue, which is all light, and vices have swellings and fits, and noise, because being extremes, they dwell far asunder, and they maintain both a foreign war against virtue, and a civil against one another, and affect Sovereignty, as virtue doth society. The later Physicians say, that when our natural inborn preservative is corrupted or wasted, and must be restored by a like extracted from other bodies; the chief care is that the Mummy have in it no excelling quality, but an equally digested temper: And such is true virtue. But men who have preferred money before all, think they deal honorably with virtue, if they compare her with money: And think that as money is not called base, till the allay exceed the pure; so they are virtuous enough, if they have enough to make their actions current, which is, if either they get praise, or (in a lower abasing) if they incur not infamy or penalty. But you know who said, *Angusta innocentia est ad legem bonum esse*: which rule being given for positive Laws, severe mistakers apply even to God's Law, and (perchance against his Commandment) bind themselves to his Counsels, beyond his Laws. But they are worse, that think that because some men formerly wasteful, live better with half their rents then they did with all, being now advantaged with discretion and experience, therefore our times need less moral virtue then the first, because we have Christianity, which is the use and application of all virtue: as though our religion were but an art of thrift, to make a little virtue go far. For as plentiful springs are fittest, and best become large Aqueducts, so doth much virtue such a steward and officer as a Christian. But I must not give you a Homily for a Letter. I said a great while since, that custom made men like; we who have been accustomed to one another are like in this, that we love not business: this therefore shall not be to you nor me a busy Letter. I end with a problem, whose errand is, to ask for his fellows. I pray before you engulf yourself in the progress, leave them for me, and such other of my papers as you will lend me till you return. And besides this Allegorical lending, send me truly your counsels, and love God and me, whilst I love him and you.

TO SIR H. G. (3)

Sir,

This Tuesday morning, which hath brought me to *London*, presents me with all your Letters. Me thought it was a rent day, I mean such as yours, and not as mine; and yet such too, when I considered how much I ought you for them, how good a mother, how fertile and abundant the understanding is, if she have a good father; and how well friendship performs that office. For that which is denied in other generations is done in this of yours: for here is superfetation, child upon child, and that which is more strange twins at a latter conception. If in my second religion, friendship, I had a conscience, either *errantem* to mistake good and bad and indifferent, or *opinantem* to be ravished by others opinions or examples, or *dubiam* to adhere to neither part, or *scrupulosam* to incline to one, but upon reasons light in themselves, or indiscussed in me, (which are almost all the diseases of conscience) I might mistake your often, long, and busy Letters, and fear you did but intreat me to have mercy upon you and spare you; for you know our Court took the resolution, that it was the best way to dispatch the French Prince back again quickly, to receive him solemnly, ceremoniously, and expensively, when he hoped a domestique and durable entertainment. I never meant to excel you in weight nor price, but in number and bulk I thought I might, because he may cast up a greater sum who hath but forty small monies, then he with twenty Portuguesses. The memory of friends, (I mean only for Letters) neither enters ordinarily into busied men, because they are never employed within, nor into men of pleasure, because they are never at home. For these wishes therefore which you won out of your pleasure and recreation, you were as excusable to me if you writ seldom, as Sir *H. Wotton* is, under the oppression of business, or the necessity of seeming so; or more than he, because I hope you have both pleasure and business: only to me, who have neither, this omission were sin; for though writing be not of the precepts of friendship, but of the counsels, yet, as in some cases to some men counsels become precepts, and though not immediately from God, yet very roundly and quickly from his Church, (as selling and dividing goods in the first time, continence in the Roman Church, and order and decency in ours) so to me who can do nothing else, it seems to bind my conscience to write; and it is sin to do against the conscience, though that err. Yet no man's Letters might be better wanted then mine, since my whole Letter is nothing else but a confession that I should and would write. I owed you a Letter in verse before by mine own promise, and now that you think that you have hedged in that debt by a greater by your Letter in verse, I think it now most seasonable and fashionable for me to break. At least, to write presently, were to accuse myself of not having read yours so often as such a Letter deserves from you to me. To make my debt greater (for such is the desire of all, who cannot or mean not to pay) I pray read these two problems: for such light flashes as these have been my hawkings in my sorry [Surrey?] journeys. I accompany them with another rag of verses, worthy of that name for the smallness, and age, for it hath long lien among my other papers, and laughs at them that have adventured to you: for I think till now you saw it not, and neither you, nor it should repent it. Sir, if I were any thing, my love to you might multiply it, and dignify it: But infinite nothings are but one such; yet since even Chimera's have some name and titles, I am also *Yours.*

TO SIR H. G. (4)

Sir,

In the History or style of friendship, which is best written both in deeds and words, a Letter, which is of a mixed nature, and hath something of both, is a mixed Parenthesis: It may be left out, yet it contributes, though not to the being, yet to the verdure, and freshness thereof. Letters have truly the same office, as oaths. As these amongst light and empty men, are but fillings, and pauses, and interjections; but with weightier, they are sad attestations: So are Letters to some complement, and obligation to others. For mine, as I never authorized my servant to lie in my behalf, (for if it were officious in him, it might be worse in me) so I allow my Letters much less that civil dishonest, both because they go from me more considerately, and because they are permanent; for in them I may speak to you in your chamber a year hence before I know not whom, and not hear myself. They shall therefore ever keep the sincerity and intemerateness of the fountain, whence they are derived. And as wheresoever these leaves fall, the root is in my heart, so shall they, as that sucks good affections towards you there, have ever true impressions thereof. This much information is in very leaves, that they can tell what the tree is, and these can tell you I am a friend, and an honest man. Of what general use, the fruit should speak, and I have none: and of what particular profit to you, your application and experimenting should tell you, and you can make none of such a nothing; yet even of barren Sycamores, such as I, there were use, if either any light flashings, or scorching vehemencies, or sudden showers made you need so shadowy an example or remembrancer. But (Sir) your fortune and mind do you this happy injury, that they make all kind of fruits useless unto you; Therefore I have placed my love wisely where I need communicate nothing. All this, though perchance you read it not till Michaelmas, was told you at *Micham, 15. August. 1607.*

TO SIR H. G. (5)

Sir,

It should be no interruption to your pleasures, to hear me often say that I love you, and that you are as much my meditation as myself: I often compare not you and me, but the sphere in which your resolutions are, and my wheel; both I hope concentric to God: for methinks the new Astronomy is thus appliable well, that we which are a little earth, should rather move towards God, then that he which is fulfilling, and can come no whither, should move towards us. To your life full of variety, nothing is old, nor new to mine; and as to that life, all stickings and hesitations seem stupid and stony, so to this, all fluid slipperinesses, and transitory migrations seem giddy and feathery. In that life one is ever in the porch or postern, going in or out, never within his house himself: It is a garment made of remnants, a life raveled out into ends, a line discontinued, and a number of small wretched points, useless, because they concur not: A life built of past and future, not proposing any constant present; they have more pleasures than we, but not more pleasure; they joy oftener, we longer; and no man but of so much understanding as may deliver him from being a fool, would change with a mad-man, which had a better proportion of wit in his often *Lucidis*. You know, they which dwell farthest from the Sun, if in any convenient distance, have longer days, better appetites, better digestion, better growth, and longer life: And all these advantages have their minds who are well removed from the scorchings, and dazzlings, and exhalings of the world's glory: but neither of our lives are in such extremes; for you living at Court without ambition, which would burn you, or envy, which would devest others, live in the Sun, not in the fire: And I which live in the Country without stupefying, am not in darkness, but in shadow which is not no light, but a pallid, waterish, and diluted one. As all shadows are of one color, if you respect the body from which they are cast (for our shadows upon clay will be dirty, and in a garden green, and flowery) so all retirings into a shadowy life are alike from all causes, and alike subject to the barbarousness and insipid dullness of the Country; only the employment, and that upon which you cast and bestow your pleasure, business, or books, gives it the tincture, and beauty. But truly wheresoever we are, if we can but tell ourselves truly what and where we would be, we may make any state and place such; for we are so composed, that if abundance, or glory scorch and melt us, we have an earthly cave, our bodies, to go into by consideration, and cool ourselves: and if we be frozen, and contracted with lower and dark fortunes, we have within us a torch, a soul, lighter and warmer than any without: we are therefore our own umbrella's, and our own suns. These, Sir, are the salads and onions of *Micham*, sent to you with as wholesome affection as your other friends send Melons and Quelque-choses from Court and *London*. If I present you not as good diet as they, I would yet say grace to theirs, and bid much good do it you. I send you, with this, a Letter which I sent to the Countess. It is not my use nor duty to doe so, but for your having of it, there were but two consents, and I am sure you have mine, and you are sure you have hers. I also writ to her Lap for the verses she shewed in the garden, which I did not only to extort them, nor only to keep my promise of writing, for that I had done in the other Letter, and perchance she hath forgotten the promise; nor only because I think my Letters just good enough for a progress, but because I would write apace to her, whilst it is possible to express that which I yet know of her, for by this growth I see how soon she will be ineffable.

TO THE COUNTESS OF BEDFORD

Happiest and worthiest Lady,
I do not remember that ever I have seen a petition in verse, I would not therefore be singular, nor add these to your other papers. I have yet adventured so near as to make a petition for verse, it is for those your Ladyship did me the honor to see in *Twicknam* garden, except you repent your making; and having mended your judgement by thinking worse, that is, better, because juster, of their subject. They must needs be an excellent exercise of your wit, which speaks so well of so ill: I humbly beg them of your Ladyship, with two such promises, as to any other of your compositions were threatenings: that I will not shew them, and that I will not believe them; and nothing should be so used that comes from your brain or heart. If I should confess a fault in the boldness of asking them, or make a fault by doing it in a longer Letter, your Ladyship might use your style and old fashion of the Court towards me, and pay me with a Pardon. Here therefore I humbly kiss your Ladyship's fair learned hands, and wish you good wishes and speedy grants.

Your Ladyship's servant
J. Donne.

TO SIR H. G. (6)

Sir,

Because I am in a place and season where I see everything bud forth, I must do so too, and vent some of my meditations to you; the rather because all other buds being yet without taste or virtue, my Letters may be like them. The pleasantness of the season displeases me. Everything refreshes, and I wither, and I grow older and not better, my strength diminishes, and my load grows, and being to passe more and more storms, I find that I have not only cast out all my ballast which nature and time gives, Reason and discretion, and so am as empty and light as Vanity can make me; but I have over fraught myself with Vice, and so am riddingly subject to two contrary wracks, Sinking and Oversetting, and under the iniquity of such a disease as enforces the patient when he is almost starved, not only to fast, but to purge. For I have much to take in, and much to cast out; sometimes I think it easier to discharge myself of vice then of vanity, as one may sooner carry the fire out of a room than the smoke: and then I see it was a new vanity to think so. And when I think sometimes that vanity, because it is thin and airy, may be expelled with virtue or business, or substantial vice; I find that I give entrance thereby to new vices. Certainly as the earth and water, one sad, the other fluid, make but one body: so to air and Vanity, there is but one *Centium morbi*. And that which later Physicians say of our bodies, is fitter for our minds: for that which they call Destruction, which is a corruption and want of those fundamental parts whereof we consist, is Vice: and that *Collectio stercorum*, which is but the excrement of that corruption, is our Vanity and indiscretion: both these have but one root in me, and must be pulled out at once, or never. But I am so far from digging to it, that I know not where it is, for it is not in mine eyes only, but in every sense, nor in my concupiscence only, but in every power and affection. Sir, I was willing to let you see how impotent a man you love, not to dishearten you from doing so still (for my vices are not infectious nor wandering, they came not yesterday, nor mean to go away to day: they Inn not, but dwell in me, and see themselves so welcome, and find in me so good bad company of one another, that they will not change, especially to one not apprehensive, nor easily accessible) but I do it, that your counsel might cure me, and if you deny that, your example shall, for I will as much strive to be like you as I will wish you to continue good.

TO SIR H. G. (7)

Sir,

I hope you are now well come to *London*, and well, and well comforted in your Father's health and love, and well contented that we ask you how you do, and tell you how we are, which yet I cannot of myself; If I knew that I were ill, I were well; for we consist of three parts, a Soul, and Body, and Mind: which I call those thoughts and affections and passions, which neither soul nor body hath alone, but have been begotten by their communication, as Musique results out of our breath and a Cornet. And of all these the diseases are cures, if they be known. Of our souls sicknesses, which are sins, the knowledge is, to acknowledge, and that is her Physique, in which we are not dieted by drams and scruples, for we cannot take too much. Of our bodies infirmities, though our knowledge be partly *ab extrinseco*, from the opinion of the Physician, and that the subject and matter be flexible, and various; yet their rules are certain, and if the matter be rightly applied to the rule, our knowledge thereof is also certain. But of the diseases of the mind, there is no *Criterium*, no Canon, no rule; for, our own taste and apprehension and interpretation should be the Judge, and that is the disease itself. Therefore sometimes when I find myself transported with jollity, and love of company, I hang Leads at my heels; and reduce to my thoughts my fortunes, my years, the duties of a man, of a friend, of a husband, of a Father, and all the incumbencies of a family: when sadness dejects me, either I countermine it with another sadness, or I kindle squibs about me again, and fly into sportfullness and company: and I find ever after all, that I am like an exorcist, which had long labored about one, which at last appears to have the Mother, that I still mistake my disease. And I still vex myself with this, because if I know it not, nobody can know it. And I comfort myself, because I see dispassioned men are subject to the like ignorances. For divers minds out of the same thing often draw contrary conclusions, as *Augustine* thought devout *Anthony* to be therefore full of the holy Ghost, because not being able to read, he could say the whole Bible, and interpret it; and *Thyreus* the Jesuit for the same reason doth think all the Anabaptists to be possessed. And as often out of contrary things men draw one conclusion: as to the *Roman* Church, magnificence and splendor hath ever been an argument of God's favor, and poverty & affliction, to the *Greek*. Out of this variety of minds it proceeds, that though all our souls would go to one end, Heaven, and all our bodies must go to one end, the earth: yet our third part the mind, which is our natural guide here, chooses to every man a several way: scarce any man likes what another doth, nor advisedly, that which himself. But Sir, I am beyond my purpose; I meant to write a Letter, and I am fallen into a discourse, and I do not only take you from some business, but I make you a new business by drawing you into these meditations. In which yet let my openness be an argument of such love as I would fain express in some worthier fashion.

POEMS IN MEMORY OF JOHN DONNE

TO THE MEMORY OF MY EVER DESIRED FRIEND DR. DONNE

To have liv'd eminent, in a degree
Beyond our loftiest flights, that is, like thee,
Or t' have had too much merit, is not safe;
For, such excesses find no epitaph.
At common graves we have poetic eyes
Can melt themselves in easy elegies,
Each quill can drop his tributary verse,
And pin it, like the hatchments, to the hearse:
But at thine, poem, or inscription
(Rich soul of wit, and language) we have none.
Indeed a silence does that tomb befit,
Where is no herald left to blazon it.
Widow'd invention justly doth forbear
To come abroad, knowing thou art not here,
Late her great patron; whose prerogative
Maintain'd, and cloth'd her so, as none alive

Must now presume, to keep her at thy rate,
Though he the Indies for her dower estate.
Or else that awful fire, which once did burn
In thy clear brain, now fallen into thy urn
Lives there, to fright rude empirics from thence,
Which might prophane thee by their ignorance.
Whoever writes of thee, and in a stile
Unworthy such a them, does but revile
Thy precious dust, and wake a learned spirit
Which may revenge his rapes upon thy merit.
For, all a low pitch't fancy can devise,
Will prove, at best, but hallow'd injuries.
Thou, like the dying swan, didst lately sing
Thy mournful dirge, in audience of the king;
When pale looks, and faint accents of thy breath,
Presented so, to life, that piece of death,
That it was fear'd, and prophesied by all,
Thou thither cam'st to preach thy funeral.
O! had'st thou in an elegiac knell
Rung out unto the world thine own farewell,
And in thy high victorious numbers beat
The solemn measure of thy griev'd retreat;
Thou might'st the poets service now have mist
As well, as then thou did'st prevent the priest;
And never to the world beholding be
So much, as for an epitaph for thee.
I do not like the office. Nor is't fit
Thou, who did'st lend our age such sums of wit,
Should'st now re-borrow from her bankrupt mine,
That ore to bury thee, which once was thine.
Rather still leave us in thy debt; And know
(Exalted soul) more glory 'tis to owe

Unto thy hearse, what we can never pay,
Then, with embased coin those rites defray.
Commit we then thee to thyself: Nor blame
Our drooping loves, which thus to thy own fame
Leave thee executor. Since, but thine own,
No pen could do thee justice, nor bays crown
Thy vast desert; save that, wee nothing can
Depute, to be thy ashes' guardian.
So jewelers no art, or metal trust
To form the diamond, but the diamond's dust,
~Henry King

TO THE DECEASED AUTHOR, UPON THE PROMISCUOUS PRINTING OF HIS POEMS, THE LOOSER SORT WITH THE RELIGIOUS

When thy loose raptures, Donne, shall meet with those
That do confine
Tuning, unto the duller line,
And sing not, but in sanctified prose;
How will they, with sharper eyes,
The foreskin of thy fancy circumcise?
And fear, thy wantonness should now, begin
Example, that hath ceased to be sin?

And that fear fans their heat; whilst knowing eyes
Will not admire
At this strange fire,
That here is mingled with thy sacrifice:

But dare read even thy wanton Story,
As thy confession, not thy glory.
And will so envy both to future times,
That they would buy thy goodness, with thy crimes.
~Thomas Browne

ON THE DEATH OF DR. DONNE

I cannot blame those men, that knew thee well,
Yet dare not help the world, to ring thy knell
In tuneful elegies; there's not language known
Fit for thy mention, but 'twas first thy own;
The epitaphs thou writest, have so bereft
Our tongue of wit, there is not fancy left
Enough to weep thee; what henceforth we see
Of art or nature, must result from thee.
There may perchance some busy gathering friend
Steal from thy own works, and that, varied, lend,
Which thou bestow'st on others, to thy hearse,
And so thou shalt live still in thine own verse;
He that shall venture farther, may commit
A pitied error, shew his zeal, not wit.
Fate hath done mankind wrong; virtue may aim
Reward of conscience, never can, of fame,
Since her great trumpet's broke, could only give
Faith to the world, command it to believe;
He then must write, that world define thy parts:
Here lies the best divinity, all the arts.
~Edward Hyde.

ON DOCTOR DONNE, BY DR. C. B. OF O.

He that would write an epitaph for thee,
And do it well, must first begin to be
Such as thou wert; for, none can truly know
Thy worth, thy life, but he that hath liv'd so;
He must have wit to spare and to hurl down:
Enough, to keep the gallants of the town.
He must have learning plenty; both the laws,
Civil, and common, to judge any cause;
Divinity great store, above the rest;
Not of the last edition, but the best.
He must have language, travail, all the arts;
Judgement to use; or else he wants thy parts.
He must have friends the highest, able to do;
Such as Mecoenas, and Augustus too.
He must have such a sickness, such a death;
Or else his vain descriptions come beneath;
Who then shall write an epitaph for thee.
He must be dead first, let it alone for me.
~Richard Corbet, Bishop of Oxford

AN ELEGY UPON THE INCOMPARABLE DR. DONNE

All is not well when such a one as I
Dare peep abroad, and write an elegy;
When smaller Stars appear, and give their light,
Phoebus is gone to bed: Were it not night,
And the world witless now that Donne is dead,

You sooner should have broke, then seen my head.
Dead did I say? Forgive this injury
I do him, and his worth's infinity,
To say he is but dead; I dare aver
It better may be term'd a massacre,
Then sleep or death; See how the Muses mourn
Upon their oaten reeds, and from his urn
Threaten the world with this calamity,
    They shall have ballads, but no poetry.

Language lies speechless; and divinity,
Lost such a trump as even to ecstasy
Could charm the soul, and had an influence
To teach best judgements, and please dullest sense.
The court, the church, the university,
Lost chaplain, dean, and doctor, all these, three.
    It was his merit, that his funeral
    Could cause a loss so great and general.

If there be any spirit can answer give
Of such as hence depart, to such as live:
Speak, doth his body there vermiculate,
Crumble to dust, and feel the laws of fate?
Methinks, corruption, worms, what else is foul
Should spare the Temple of so fair a soul.
I could believe they do; but that I know
What inconvenience might hereafter grow:
    Succeeding ages would idolatrize,
    And as his numbers, so his relics prize.

If that philosopher, which did avow
The world to be but mores, was living now:

He would affirm that th' atoms of his mold
Were they in several bodies blended, would
Produce new worlds of travelers, divines,
Of linguists, poets: sith these several lines
In him concentered were, and flowing thence
Might fill again the worlds circumference.
I could believe this too; and yet my faith
Not want a president: The phoenix hath
(And such was he) a power to animate
Her ashes, and herself perpetuate.
But, busy soul, thou dost not well to pry
Into these secrets; grief, and jealousy,
The more they know, the further still advance,
And find no way so safe as ignorance.
Let this suffice thee, that his soul which flew
A pitch of all admir'd, known but of few,
(Save those of purer mold) is now translated
From earth to heaven, and there constellated.
    For, if each priest of God shine as a star,
    His glory is as his gifts, 'bove others far.
~Henry Valentine

AN ELEGY UPON DR. DONNE

Is Donne, great Donne deceas'd? then England say
Thou hast lost a man where language chose to stay
And shew it's graceful power. I would not praise
That and his vast wit (which in these vain days
Make many proud) but as they serv'd to unlock
That cabinet, his mind: where such a stock
Of knowledge was repos'd, as all lament
(Or should) this general cause of discontent.

And I rejoice I am not so severe,
But (as I write a line) to weep a tear
For his decease; such sad extremities
May make such men as I write elegies.
And wonder not; for, when a general loss
Falls on a nation, and they slight the cross,
God hath rais'd prophets to awaken them
From stupefaction; witness my mild pen,
Not us'd to upbraid the world, though now it must
Freely and boldly, for, the cause is just.
Dull age, oh I would spare thee, but th' art worse,
Thou art not only dull, but hast a curse
Of black ingratitude; if not, couldst thou
Part with miraculous Donne, and make no vow
For thee and thine, successively to pay
A sad remembrance to his dying day?
    Did his youth scatter poetry, wherein
Was all philosophy? Was every sin,
Character'd in his satires? made so foul
That some have fear'd their shapes, and kept their soul
Freer by reading verse? Did he give days
Past marble monuments, to those, whose praise
He would perpetuate? Did he (I fear
The dull will doubt:) these at his twentieth year?
But, more matur'd: did his full soul conceive,
And in harmonious-holy-numbers weave
A crown of sacred sonnets, fit to adorn
A dying martyrs brow: or, to be worn
On that blest head of Mary Magdalen:
After she wip'd Christ's feet, but not till then?
Did he (fit for such penitents as she
And he to use) leave us a litany?

Which all devout men love, and sure, it shall,
As times grow better, grow more classical.
Did he write hymns, for piety and wit
Equal to those great grave Prudentius writ?
Spake he all languages? knew he all laws?
The grounds and use of physic; but because
'Twas mercenary weigh'd it? Went to see
That blessed place of Christ's nativity?
Did he return and preach him? preach him so
As none but he did, or could do? They know
(Such as were blest to hear him know) 'tis truth.
Did he confirm thy age? Convert thy youth?
Did he these wonders? And is this dear loss
Mourn'd by so few? (Few for so great a cross.)
    But sure the silent are ambitious all
To be close mourners at his funeral;
If not; in common pity they forbear
By repetitions to renew our care;
Or, knowing, grief conceiv'd, conceal'd, consumes
Man irreparably, (as poison'd fumes
Do waste the brain) make silence a safe way
To enlarge the soul from these walls, mud and clay,
(Materials of this body) to remain
With Donne in heaven, where no promiscuous pain
Lessens the joy we have, for, with him, all
Are satisfied with joys essential.
My thoughts, dwell on this joy, and do not call
Grief back, by thinking of his funeral;
Forget he lov'd me; waste not my sad years;
(Which haste to David's seventy) fill'd with fears
And sorrow for his death) forget his parts,
Which find a living grave in good men's hearts;

And, (for, my first is daily paid for sin)
Forget to pay my second sigh for him:
Forget his powerful preaching; and forget
I am his convert. Oh my frailty! let
My flesh be no more heard, it will obtrude
This lethargy: so should my gratitude,
My vows of gratitude should so be broke;
Which can no more be, then Donne's virtues spoke
By any but himself; for which cause, I
Write no encomium, but an elegy.
~Izaak Walton

AN ELEGY UPON THE DEATH OF THE DEAN OF PAUL'S, DR. JOHN DONNE

Can we not force from widowed poetry,
Now thou art dead (great Donne) one elegy
To crown thy hearse? Why yet dare we not trust
Though with unkneaded dough bak't prose thy dust,
Such as the uncisor'd churchman from the flower
Of fading rhetoric, short liv'd as his hour,
Dry as the sand that measures it, should lay
Upon thy ashes, on the funeral day?
Have we no voice, no tune? Did'st thou dispense
Through all our language, both the words and sense?
'Tis a sad truth; The pulpit may her plain,
And sober Christian precepts still retain,
Doctrines it may, and wholesome uses frame,
Grave homilies, and lectures, But the flame
Of thy brave soul, that shot such heat and light,

As burnt our earth, and made our darkness bright,
Committed holy rapes upon our will,
Did through the eye the melting heart distill;
And the deep knowledge of dark truths so teach,
As sense might judge, what fancy could not reach;
Must be desir'd forever. So the fire,
That fills with spirit and heat the delphic choir,
Which kindled first by thy Promethean breath,
Glow'd here a while, lies quencht now in thy death;
The Muses garden with pedantic weeds
O'erspread, was purg'd by thee; the lazy seeds
Of servile imitation thrown away;
And fresh invention planted, thou didst pay
The debts of our penurious bankrupt age;
Licentious thefts, that make poetic rage
A mimic fury, when our souls must be
Possessed, or with Anacreons ecstasy,
Or Pindars, not their own; The subtle cheat
Of sly exchanges, and the juggling feat
Of two-edg'd words, or whatsoever wrong
By ours was done the Greek, or Latin tongue,
Thou hast redeem'd, and open'd us a mine
Of rich and pregnant fancy, drawn a line
Of masculine expression, which had good
Old Orpheus seen, Or all the ancient brood
Our superstitious fools admire, and hold
Their lead more precious, then thy burnish't gold,
Thou hadst been their exchequer, and no more
They each in others dust, had rak'd for ore.
Thou shalt yield no precedence, but of time,
And the blind fate of language, whose tun'd chime
More charms the outward sense; Yet thou mayst claim

From so great disadvantage greater fame,
Since to the awe of thy imperious wit
Our stubborn language bends, made only fit
With her tough-thick-rib'd hoops to gird about
Thy giant fancy, which had prov'd too stout
For their soft melting phrases. As in time
They had the start, so did they cull the prime
Buds of invention many a hundred year,
And left the rifled fields, besides the fear
To touch their harvest, yet from those bare lands
Of what is purely thine, thy only hands
(And that thy smallest work) have gleaned more
Then all those times, and tongues could reap before;
But thou art gone, and thy strict laws will be
Too hard for libertines in poetry.
They will repeal the goodly exil'd train
Of gods and goddesses, which in thy just reign
Were banish'd nobler poems, now, with these
The silenc'd tales o' th' Metamorphoses
Shall stuff their lines, and swell the windy page,
Till verse refin'd by thee, in this last age,
Turn ballad rime, Or those old idols be
Ador'd again, with new apostasy;
Oh, pardon me, that break with untun'd verse
The reverend silence that attends thy hearse,
Whose awful solemn murmurs were to thee
More then these faint lines, A loud elegy,
That did proclaim in a dumb eloquence
The death of all the arts, whose influence
Grown feeble, in these panting numbers lies
Gasping short winded accents, and so dies:
So doth the swiftly turning wheel not stand

In th' instant we withdraw the moving hand,
But some small time maintain a faint weak course
By virtue of the first impulsive force:
And so whil'st I cast on thy funeral pile
Thy crown of bays, Oh, let it crack a while,
And spit disdain, till the devouring flashes
Suck all the moisture up, then turn to ashes.
I will not draw the envy to engross
All thy perfections, or weep all our loss;
Those are too numerous for an elegy,
And this too great, to be express'd by me.
Though every pen should share a distinct part,
Yet art thou them enough to tire all art;
Let others carve the rest, it shall suffice
I on thy tomb this epitaph incise.

Here lies a king, that rul'd as he thought fit
The universal monarchy of wit;
Here lie two flamens, and both those, the best,
Apollo's first, at last, the true God's priest.
~Mr. Thomas Carie

AN ELEGY ON DR. DONNE

Poets attend, the elegy I sing
Both of a doubly-named priest, and king:
Instead of coats, and pennons, bring your verse,
For you must be chief mourners at his hearse,
A tomb your Muse must to his fame supply,
No other monuments can never die;
And as he was a two-fold priest; in youth,
Apollo's; afterwards, the voice of truth,

God's conduit-pipe for grace, who chose him for
His extraordinary ambassador,
So let his liegiers with the poets join,
Both having shares, both must in grief combine:
Whil'st Johnson forceth with his elegy
Tears from a grief-unknowing Scythian's eye,
(Like Moses at whose stroke the waters gushed
From forth the rock, and like a torrent rushed.)
Let Laud his funeral sermon preach, and shew
Those virtues, dull eyes were not apt to know,
Nor leave that piercing theme, till it appears
To be Good Friday, by the church's tears;
Yet make not grief too long oppress our powers,
Least that his funeral sermon should prove ours.
Nor yet forget that heavenly eloquence,
With which he did the bread of life dispense,
Preacher and orator discharg'd both parts
With pleasure for our sense, health for our hearts,
And the first such (though a long studied art
Tell us our soul is all in every part)
None was so marble, but whil'st him he hears,
His soul so long dwelt only in his ears.
And from thence (with the fierceness of a flood
Bearing down vice) victual'd with that blest food
Their hearts; his seed in none could fail to grow,
Fertile he found them all, or made them so:
No druggist of the soul bestow'd on all
So catholicly a curing cordial.
Nor only in the pulpit dwelt his store,
His words work'd much, but his example more,
That preach't on worky days, his poetry
It self was oftentimes divinity,

Those anthems (almost second Psalms) he writ
To make us know the cross, and value it,
(Although we owe that reverence to that name
Wee should not need warmth from an under flame.)
Creates a fire in us, so near extreme
That we would die, for, and upon this theme.
Next, his so pious litany, which none can
But count divine, except a Puritan,
And that but for the name, nor this, nor those
Want anything of sermons, but the prose.
Experience makes us see, that many a one
Owes to his country his religion;
And in another, would as strongly grow,
Had but his nurse and mother taught him so,
Not he the ballast on his judgment hung;
Nor did his preconceit do either wrong;
He labor'd to exclude whatever sin
By time or carelessness had entered in;
Winnow'd the chafe from wheat, but yet was loath
A too hot zeal should force him, burn them both;
Nor would allow of that so ignorant gall,
Which to save blotting often would blot all;
Nor did those barbarous opinions own,
To think the organ's sin, and faction, none;
Nor was there expectation to gain grace
From forth his sermons only, but his face;
So primitive a look, such gravity
With humbleness, and both with piety;
So mild was Moses's countenance, when he pray'd
For them whose Satanism his power gainsaid;
And such his gravity, when all God's band
Receive his word (through him) at second hand;

Which join'd, did flames of more devotion move
Then ever Argive Helen's could of love.
Now to conclude, I must my reason bring,
Where fore I call'd him in his title king,
That kingdom the philosophers believ'd
To excel Alexanders, nor were griev'd
By fear of loss (that being such a prey
No stronger then one's self can force away)
The kingdom of one's self, this he enjoy'd,
And his authority so well employ'd,
That never any could before become
So great a monarch, in so small a room;
He conquer'd rebel passions, rul'd them so,
As under-spheres by the first mover go,
Banish't so far their working, that we can
But know he had some, for we knew him man.
Then let his last excuse his first extremes,
His age saw visions, though his youth dream'd dreams.
~Sir Lucius Carie

ON DR. DONNE'S DEATH

Who shall presume to mourn thee, Donne, unless
He could his tears in thy expressions dress,
And teach his grief that reverence of thy hearse,
To weep lines, learned, as thy anniverse,
A poem of that worth, whose every tear
Deserves the title of a several year.
Indeed so far above its reader, good,
That wee are thought wits, when 'tis understood,
There that blest maid to die, who now should grieve?
After thy sorrow, 'twere her loss to live;

And her fair virtues in another's line,
Would faintly dawn, which are made saints in thine.
Hadst thou been shallower, and not writ so high,
Or left some new way for our pens, or eye,
To shed a funeral tear, perchance thy tomb
Had not been speechless, or our Muses dumb;
But now we dare not write, but must conceal
Thy epitaph, lest we be thought to steal,
For, who hath read thee, and discerns thy worth,
That will not say, thy careless hours brought forth
Fancies beyond our studies, and thy play
Was happier, then our serious time of day?
So learned was thy chance; thy haste had wit,
And matter from thy pen flow'd rashly fit,
What was thy recreation turns our brain,
Our rack and paleness, is thy weakest strain.
And when we most come near thee, 'tis our bliss
To imitate thee, where thou dost amiss,
Here light your muse, you that do only think,
And write, and are just poets, as you drink,
In whose weak fancy's wit doth ebb and flow,
Just as your reck'nings rise, that we may know
In your whole carriage of your work, that here
This flash you wrote in wine, and this in beer,
This is to tap your Muse, which running long
Writes flat, and takes our ear not half so strong;
Poor suburb wits, who, if you want your cup,
Or if a Lord recover, are blown up.
Could you but reach this height, you should not need
To make, each meal, a project ere you feed,
Nor walk in relics, clothes so old and bare,
As if left off to you from Ennius were,

Nor should your love, in verse, call mistress, those,
Who are mine hostess, or your whores in prose;
From this Muse learn to court, whose power could move
A cloistered coldness, or a vestal love,
And would convey such errands to their ear,
That ladies knew no odds to grant and hear;
But I do wrong thee, Donne, and this low praise
Is written only for thy younger days.
I am not grown up, for thy riper parts,
Then should I praise thee, through the tongues, and arts,
And have that deep divinity, to know,
What mysteries did from thy preaching flow,
Who with thy words could charm thy audience,
That at thy sermons, ear was all our sense;
Yet have I seen thee in the pulpit stand,
Where we might take notes, from thy look, and hand;
And from thy speaking action bear away
More sermon, then some teachers use to say.
Such was thy carriage, and thy gesture such,
As could divide the heart, and conscience touch.
Thy motion did confute, and we might see
An error vanquish'd by delivery.
Not like our sons of zeal, who to reform
Their hearers, fiercely at the pulpit storm,
And beat the cushion into worse estate,
Then if they did conclude it reprobate,
Who can out pray the glass, then lay about
Till all predestination be run out.
And from the point such tedious uses draw,
Their repetitions would make gospel, law.
No, in such temper would thy sermons flow,
So well did doctrine, and thy language show,

And had that holy fear, as, hearing thee,
The court would mend, and a good Christian be.
And ladies though unhandsome, out of grace,
Would hear thee, in their unbought looks, & face,
More I could write, but let this crown thine urn,
We cannot hope the like, till thou return.
~Mr. Mayne of Christ-Church in Oxford

UPON MR. J. DONNE, AND HIS POEMS

Who dares say thou art dead, when he doth see
    (Unburied yet) this living part of thee?
This part that to thy being gives fresh flame,
    And though th' art Donne, yet will preserve thy name.
Thy flesh (whose channels left their crimson hew,
    And whey-like ran at last in a pale blew)
May shew thee mortal, a dead palsy may
    Seize on't, and quickly turn it into clay;
Which like the Indian earth, shall rise refin'd:
    But this great spirit thou hast left behind,
This soul of verse (in its first pure estate)
    Shall live, for all the world to imitate
But not come near, for in thy fancy's flight
    Thou dost not stoop unto the vulgar sight,
But, hovering highly in the air of wit,
    Hold'st such a pitch, that few can follow it;
Admire they may. Each object that the spring
    (Or a more piercing influence) doth bring
T' adorn earth's face, thou sweetly did'st contrive
    To beauties elements, and thence derive

Unspotted lilies white; which thou did'st set
    Hand in hand, with the vein-like violet,
Making them soft, and warm, and by thy power,
    Could'st give both life, and sense, unto a flower.
The cherries thou hast made to speak, will be
    Sweeter unto the taste, then from the tree.
And (spite of winter storms) amidst the snow
    Thou oft hast made the blushing rose to grow.
The Sea-nymphs, that the watry caverns keep,
    Have sent their pearls and rubies from the deep
To deck thy love, and plac'd by thee, they drew
    More luster to them, then where first they grew.
All minerals (that earth's full womb doth hold
    Promiscuously) thou couldst convert to gold,
And with thy flaming raptures so refine,
    That it was much more pure then in the mine.
The lights that guild the night, if thou did'st say,
    They look like eyes, those did out-shine the day;
For there would be more virtue in such spells,
    Then in meridians, or crosse parallels:
Whatever was of worth in this great frame,
    That art could comprehend, or wit could name,
It was thy theme for beauty; thou didst see,
    Woman, was this faire world's epitome.
Thy nimble satires too, and every strain
    (With nervy strength) that issued from thy brain,
Will lose the glory of their own clear bays,
    If they admit of any others praise.
But thy diviner poems (whose clear fire
    Purges all dross away) shall by a choir
Of cherubims, with heavenly notes be set
    (Where flesh and blood could ne'r attain to yet)

There purest spirits sing such sacred lays,
In panegyric Alleluias.
~Arthur Wilson.

IN MEMORY OF DOCTOR DONNE BY MR. R. B.

Donne dead? 'Tis here reported true, though I
Ne'r yet so much desir'd to hear a lie,
'Tis too too true, for so we find it still,
Good news are often false, but seldom, ill:
But must poor fame tell us his fatal day,
And shall we know his death, the common way,
Me thinks some comet bright should have foretold
The death of such a man, for though of old
'Tis held, that comets princes's death foretell,
Why should not his, have needed one as well?
Who was the prince of wits, 'mongst whom he reign'd,
High as a prince, and as great state maintain'd?
Yet wants he not his sign, for we have seen
A dearth, the like to which hath never been,
Treading on harvest's heels, which doth presage
The death of wit and learning, which this age
Shall find, now he is gone; for though there be
Much graine in shew, none brought it forth as he,
Or men are misers; or if true want raises
The dearth, then more that dearth Donne's plenty praises.
Of learning, languages, of eloquence,
And poesy, (past ravishing of sense)
He had a magazine, wherein such store
Was laid up, as might hundreds serve of poor.

But he is gone, O how will his desire
Torture all those that warm'd them by his fire?
Methinks I see him in the pulpit standing,
Not ears, or eyes, but all men's hearts commanding,
Where we that heard him, to ourselves did feign
Golden Chrysostom was alive again;
And never were we wearied, till we saw
His hour (and but an hour) to end did draw.
How did he shame the doctrine-men, and use,
With helps to boot, for men to bear th' abuse
Of their tir'd patience, and endure th' expense
Of time, O spent in hearkening to nonsense,
With marks also, enough whereby to know,
The speaker is a zealous dunce, or so.
'Tis true, they quitted him, to their poor power,
They humm'd against him; And with face most sour:
Call'd him a strong lin'd man, a Macaroon,
And no way fit to speak to clouted shoon,
As fine words [truly] as you would desire,
But [verily,] but a bad edifier.
Thus did these beetles slight in him that good,
They could not see, and much less understood.
But we may say, when we compare the stuff
Both brought; he was a candle, they the snuff.
Well, wisdom's of her children justifi'd,
Let therefore these poor fellows stand aside;
Nor, though of learning he deserv'd so highly,
Would I his book should save him; rather slily
I should advise his clergy not to pray,
Though of the learn'dst sort; methinks that they
Of the same trade, are judges not so fit,
There's no such emulation as of wit.

Of such, the envy might as much perchance
Wrong him, and more, then th' others ignorance.
It was his fate (I know't) to be envy'd
As much by clerks, as lay men magnifi'd;
And why? but 'cause he came late in the day,
And yet his penny earn'd, and had as they.
No more of this, least some should say, that I
Am stray'd to satire, meaning elegy.
No, no, had Donne need to be judg'd or tried,
A jury I would summon on his side,
That had no sides, nor factions, past the touch
Of all exceptions, freed from passion, such
As nor to fear nor fratter, e'r were bred,
These would I bring, though called from the dead:
Southampton, Hambleton, Pebrooke, Dorset's earls,
Huntingdon, Bedford's Countesses (the pearls
Once of each sex.) If these suffice not, I
Ten decem tales have of standers-by:
All which, for Donne, would such a verdict give,
As can belong to none, that now doth live.
But what do I? A diminution 'tis
To speak of him in verse, so short of his,
Whereof he was the master; all indeed
Compar'd with him, pip'd on an oaten reed.
O that you had but one 'mongst all your brothers
Could write for him, as he hath done for others:
(Poets I speak to) When I see't, I'll say,
My eye-sight betters, as my years decay,
Meantime a quarrel I shall ever have
Against these doughty keepers from the grave,
Who use, it seems their old authority,
When (verses men immortal make) they cry:

Which had it been a recipe true tried,
Probatum esset, Donne had never died.
For me, if ere I had least spark at all
Of that which they poetic fire do call,
Here I confess it fetched from his hearth,
Which is gone out, now he is gone to earth.
This only a poor flash, a lightning is
Before my Muse's death, as after his.
Farewell (fair soul) and deign receive from mee
This type of that devotion I owe thee,
From whom (while living) as by voice and pen
I learned more, then from a thousand men:
So by thy death, am of one doubt releas'd,
And now believe that miracles are ceas'd.

EPITAPH

Here lies Dean Donne; enough; those words
Shew him as fully, as if all the stone
His church of Paul's contains, were through inscribed alone
Or all the walkers there, to speak him, bribed.
None can mistake him, for one such as he
Donne, Deane, or man, more none shall ever see.
Not man? No, though unto a sun each eye
Were turn'd, the whole earth so to overspy,
A bold brave word; Yet such brave spirits as knew
His spirit, will say, it is less bold then true.

EPITAPH UPON DR. DONNE BY ENDYS PORTER

This decent urn a sad inscription wears,
Of Donne's departure from us, to the spheres;
And the dumb stone with silence seems to tell
The changes of this life, wherein is well
Expressed, a cause to make all joy to cease,
And never let our sorrows more take ease;
For now it is impossible to find
One fraught with virtues, to enrich a mind;
But why should death, with a promiscuous hand
At one rude stroke impoverish a land?
Thou strict attorney, unto stricter fate,
Didst thou confiscate his life out of hate
To his rare parts? Or didst thou throw thy dart,
With envious hand, at some plebian heart;
And he with pious virtue stepped between
To save that stroke, and so was kill'd unseen
By thee? O 'twas his goodness so to do,
Which humane kindness never reached unto.
Thus the hard laws of death were satisfied,
And he left us like orphan friends, and died.
Now from the pulpit to the people's ears,
Whose speech shall send repentant sighs, and tears?
Or tell mee, if a purer virgin die,
Who shall hereafter write her elegy?
Poets be silent, let your numbers sleep,
For he is gone that did all fancy keep;
Time hath no soul, but his exalted verse;
Which with amazements, we may now rehearse.
~Dr. Endys Porter

APPENDIX

A reader-made index to John Donne's *Poems* (1633). Folger STC 7045 copy 2, 406. Page numbers align with the original pagination of the first edition of the 1633 poems.

Spelling here not modernized, as in the rest of the volume.